Perspectives on Written Argument

WRITTEN LANGUAGE SERIES

Marcia Farr, senior editor
Robert L. Gundlach, consulting editor

Perspectives on Written Argument
Deborah Berrill (ed.)

Collaboration and Conflict: A Contextual Exploration of Group Writing and Positive Emphasis
Geoffrey Cross

Subject to Change: New Composition Instructors' Theory and Practice
Christine Farris

Literacy: Interdisciplinary Conversations
Deborah Keller-Cohen (ed.)

Twelve Readers Reading: Responding to College Student Writing
Richard Straub and Ronald Lunsford

Literacy Across Communities
Beverly Moss (ed.)

Artwork of the Mind: An Interdisciplinary Description of Insight and the Search for it in Student Writing
Mary Murray

Validating Holistic Scoring for Writing Assessment: Theoretical and Empirical Foundations
Michael Williamson and Brian Huot (eds.)

in preparation

From Millwrights to Shipwrights to the Twenty-first Century
John C. Brockmann

The Literacy Link: The Participation and Practices of Scribes and Their Clients in Mexico
Judy Kalman

Portfolios and College Writing
Liz Hamp-Lyons and William Condon

The Computer and the Non-native Writer
Martha C. Pennington

Self-Assessment and Development in Writing: A Collaborative Inquiry
Jane Bowman Smith and Kathleen Blake Yancey

Perspectives on Written Argument

edited by
Deborah P. Berrill
Queen's University, Canada

HAMPTON PRESS, INC.
CRESSKILL, NEW JERSEY

Copyright © 1996 by Hampton Press, Inc.

All rights reserved. No part of this publication may be reproduced, stored in a retrieval system, or transmitted in any form or by any means, electronic, mechanical, photocopying, microfilming, recording, or otherwise, without permission of the publisher.

Printed in the United States of America

Library of Congress Cataloging-in-Publication Data

Perspectives on written argument / edited by Deborah P. Berrill.
    p. cm. -- (Written language series)
  Includes bibliographical references and index.
  ISBN 1-57273-038-2 (cl). -- ISBN 1-57273-039-0 (ppb)
  1. English language--Rhetoric--Study and teaching. 2. Persuasion (Rhetoric)--Study and teaching. I. Berrill, Deborah. II. Series.
PE1404.P454 1996
428'.007--dc20   96-24443
                                                                 CIP

Hampton Press, Inc.
23 Broadway
Cresskill, NJ 07626

Contents

Series Preface		vii
Introduction		1
1.	Argument as a Primary Act of Mind *Andrew Wilkinson*	17
2.	Discovering the Ripening Functions of Argument: Using Concepts From the New Rhetoric for Analysis and Response to Student Argumentation *W. Mark Lynch*	35
3.	Teaching and Learning Argumentative Writing in the Middle School Years *Marion Crowhurst*	57
4.	Writers, Readers, and Arguments *Trudy Govier*	73
5.	Genres of Argument and Arguments as Genres *Aviva Freedman*	91
6.	Fullness and Sound Reasoning: Argument and Evaluation in a University Content Course *Pat Currie*	121
7.	The Nature of Argument in Peer Dialogue Journals *Chris M. Anson and Richard Beach*	139
8.	Reframing Argument from the Metaphor of War *Deborah P. Berrill*	171

9.	Argument as Transformation: A Pacific Framing of Conflict, Community, and Learning *Karen Ann Watson-Gegeo*	189
10.	The Background to Argument in the Far East *Robert E. Carter*	205
11.	Rescuing the Failed, Filed Away, and Forgotten: African Americans and Eurocentricity in Academic Argument *Dorothy Perry Thompson*	221
12.	Opening the Composition Classroom to Storytelling: Respecting Native American Students' Use of Rhetorical Strategies *Karen A. Redfield*	241
13.	Other Voices, Different Parties: Feminist Responses to Argument *Catherine E. Lamb*	257

Author Index
Subject Index

Series Preface

This series examines the characteristics of *writing* in the human world. Volumes in the series present scholarly work on written language in its various contexts. Across time and space, human beings use various forms of written language—or writing systems—to fulfill a range of social, cultural, and personal functions, and this diversity can be studies from a variety of perspectives within both the social sciences and the humanities, including those of linguistics, anthropology, psychology, education, rhetoric, literacy criticism, philosophy, and history. Although writing is not often used apart from oral language, or without aspects of reading, and thus many volumes in this series include other facets of language and communication, writing itself receives primary emphasis.

This volume explores current perspectives on argumentation. More specifically, the chapters collected here consider several important themes: how arguments expresses difference of opinion in a context of connectedness and community; how argument can involve processes of learning; how argument sometimes resists resolution of the tensions of difference; and how argument, in recognizing differences, can contribute to a deeper sense of solidarity within a community. As Berrill notes in the introduction to the volume, included here are traditional Western perceptions of argument, non-Western perspectives drawn from anthropological research, and feminist critiques of traditional modes of argument. Taken together these essays challenge us to rethink our assumptions about what it means to argue convincingly and effectively in a variety of circumstances.

While the study of writing is absorbing in its own right, it is an increasingly important social issue as well, as demographic movements occur around the world and as language and ethnicity accrue more intensely political meanings. Writing, and literacy more generally, is central to education, and education in turn is central to occupational and social mobility. Manuscripts that present either the results of empirical research, both qualitative and quantitative, or theoretical treatments of relevant issues are encouraged for submission.

Introduction

In its long history, argumentation has been seen as interdisciplinary. This volume explicitly pursues an interdisciplinary approach, seeking new ways of understanding argument from subject areas not traditionally associated with argument as well as looking for new understandings from within disciplines traditionally associated with argument. Many if not all of the topics addressed here can be found in Western philosophy, rhetoric, and composition theory: The difference lies in the (de)construction of those topics by these authors.

This collection does not include renewed exploration of Aristotelian constructions of argument, but an understanding of that tradition is assumed by the authors as well as familiarity with scholars who have written about argument and about discourse as social construction. It voices fresh concerns about argument that have become illuminated in light of recent ideas about the social nature of all discourse, about ways in which traditional language structures and assumptions may be exclusory to nondominant members of our communities, about the nature of ideological differences, and about the functions of argument in these contexts.

These explorations take place in historical context as well. We wrote these chapters with understandings of argument as having important everyday functions. Argument is used to explore alternate points of view, sometimes with an attempt to resolve those differences, to explore personal beliefs, to help individuals or groups make decisions, to voice the friction of differences, or to voice the respect of the recognition of differences.

This collection of voices speaking about argument is intended to provide additional and different perspectives on written argument and, by so doing, to prompt a reexamination of what is essential about written argument. Must narrative and argument be seen as necessarily exclusive? If not, what is different about them? Must arguments have theses and evidence, written in a particular form and presented in particular ways? If not, how do we recognize argument? Does it matter? If we are doubting traditional formats and structures, how do we teach our students to write better argument? Underlying all of these questions is the essential question, "What is argument?" At the moment, we do not seek a resolution to that question, but rather a formulation of what the question means. We begin by voicing different understandings of argument, and we hope for reception and further exploration of these differences. We look forward to continued dialogue and response.

TRADITIONAL WESTERN APPROACHES TO WRITTEN ARGUMENT

Traditionally, Western argument has been about persuasion—about convincing others with different points of view that one's own point of view is best. At its most conciliatory, this understanding of argument emphasizes Aristotelian dialectic, that is, a final truth is discovered through a mutual process in which a new understanding grows from consideration of two different initial points of view. Dialectic/dialogic argument, then, does not silence opposing voices, but it does seek to resolve initial differences.

This sort of argument has been valued for the soundness of reasoning it incorporates, which has meant the polish of the logic used and the persuasiveness of the appeals to reason, emotion, or authority. Emphasis has been on argumentative structure with a well-defined thesis or claim and supporting evidence, warrants, and qualifiers that carefully build the foundation and framework. The metaphor of architecture so often used in reference to argument reveals the objectification of argument in this traditional understanding, as if arguments were artifacts, capable of transportation across time and space, their joists holding together provided they initially were constructed soundly.

This approach to written argument is also hierarchical. It posits a single best form for argumentative reasoning, a form that demonstrates higher order thinking exemplified through the kind of logic used. Embedded in this approach is an epistemology that asserts that it is possible to have knowledge and description of absolute truths provided the author uses logic carefully enough. The written text thus carries considerable burden: The concern is with perfection in language, and the question becomes, "does this language perfectly convey this idea?"

REINTERPRETATION OF TRADITIONAL UNDERSTANDINGS

By the middle of this century new considerations of language led to new understandings of argument. Persuasion was still the central function of argument, but argument was increasingly an analytical tool that could be used to reveal hidden assumptions. This recognition of the need to make explicit the embedded, tacit beliefs of arguments was helpful in revealing ideological aspects of argument that hinted at the political considerations of which we are now aware in all language. These considerations focus on issues of power and authority, and in argument they necessarily demand a revision of what argument is.

In addition, by the late 1950s, there was a shift to include concerns of "practical" argumentation, which carried with it a testimony to the impractical nature of "pure" logic, which had been associated with argument. (The importance of this inclusion is more apparent when one considers that there was one viewpoint that wished to "purify" language so that it could be more precisely logical.) It became appropriate for written argument to delve into areas of greater uncertainty, including exploration of personal beliefs. The types of evidence brought to support an argument were understood to be different, depending not only on the audience (the traditional arbiter of legitimacy of evidence), but also on the subject area itself and its demands. Issues of legitimacy of argument or successfulness of argument began to become muddied as scholars began to appreciate the importance of psychological and sociological approaches and systems of knowledge to argument.

More recently, additional systems of thinking and knowledge have made strong contributions to our exploration of what argument is or what it ought to be. Anthropologists, sociologists, and sociolinguists have identified some of the essential cultural and social aspects of argument. Community is redefined and reunderstood in much smaller units than before and constitutes part of the social context for (re)(de)construction of meaning from text. In conjunction with feminist pedagogy we have become aware of the privilege and elitism that has been operating in our appraisal of what constitutes validity. "Whose validity?" we are now learning to ask, recognizing that in the past it was primarily systems of knowledge of Western, white, middle-class heterosexual males that determined the validity of claims, of assumptions, of evidence used to support those claims. Our new understandings necessarily call into question the objectification of argument and traditional ways of assessing argument.

Anthropological and sociocultural contributions to this discussion have also become increasingly important in raising issues of language constraint and resistance. In a particularly well-written synopsis, Hill (1998) summarized work of this century's cognitive anthropologists, identifying issues surrounding the concept of universal modes of thinking. Hill demonstrated correlations between cultural world views and language structures, noting how language structures constrain and/or enable different kinds of thinking. For instance, she wrote;

> The components of the Navajo world view are all connected in a complex network, which lacks linear relations such as causality. Another example of a proposal for a very high degree of integration of world view which encompassses discursive practice in language is found in A. Becker's (1984) work on Burmese. Becker identifies a root metaphor of 'integrity' which is highly productive in Burmese 'ways of speaking' about the organization of language and the organization of the world. . . . According to Becker, this metaphor contrasts with a root metaphor of 'linearity' in English-speaking usage. For Javanese, A. Becker (1979) and J. Becker (1979) have emphasized the principles of cyclicity and coincidence as pervasive in Javanese music and drama, contrasted with English linearity and causality. (p. 26)

The relevance of these ideas to constructs of argument become especially germane as we (re)view our Western white assumptions of what constitutes "logical" argument, which has traditionally been seen as hierarchical and linear. The work of cognitive anthropologists challenges us to revisit our understandings of reasoning and logic—understandings that are constrained by our own world view.

This challenge takes on more palpable dimensions in very recent work of Dorothy Perry Thompson (this volume), in which she contrasts an African-American world view with a European-American world view and suggests that the differences may account in large part for the difficulties African-American students have in examinations that require them to write Eurocentric argument. Thompson stresses that not only do African Americans have a different concept of the word Nommo, but that they also (re)shape the priorities of Eurocentric argumentative tasks to become compatible with their own world view, supporting their arguments with more generalized community details rather than particularized individual detail.

On the one hand, this raises strong educational issues regarding privileged forms of learning. On the other hand, it adds to Hill's list of types of reasoning that appear "illogical" in relation to traditional Western argument, but that operate within different systems of reasoning. The sociocultural approaches to mind of Bakhtin and Vygotsky add an extra dimension to these conversations. Discursive constraints of language are noted by Hymes (1966) and in particular by Bakhtin (1981), whose notion of heteroglossia, or speaking through the words of others, reminds us that we are constrained by the meanings and histories associated with words themselves. Wertsch (1994) said we "appropriate" words of others so that our utterances are only half ours. As well, Wertsch noted the resistance that can occur when the cultural language tools available to us are not the ones we wish to use. What reasoning options are available to those whose world view differs from the traditional Eurocentric view? What language forms, what kinds of words, are compatible with alternate world views? And, finally, are there different forms argument can take and still be called "argument?" Or do we need a different word for reasoning processes that are logical in nonhierarchical ways?

Feminist pedagogy, semiotics, and renewed interest in epistemology combine to question the relationships between language and meaning. For many, the question is no longer whether or not language perfectly describes an idea. Rather, knowledge is understood as created through discourse, through dialogue, with historical, sociological, cultural, and political considerations to be treated as essential aspects of language. Discourse is seen not as being neutral, but as being charged with significances. These approaches, then, propose that meaning does not reside in language itself, but in the (re)construction and (de)construction of text by the reader.

We are in the process of beginning to hear voices that have been silenced for centuries; voices that feel constrained by traditional assumptions and forms of argumentation: voices of women; of homosexuals; of Blacks, Hispanics, Aboriginal peoples; of Hindus, Muslims, Zen Buddhists; of children; mothers and sisters as well as fathers and brothers. We are still largely unaware of the voices of working class individuals, of out-of-work individuals, of those who live in poverty, of the physically or the mentally challenged, of the chronically or the terminally ill, of the elderly. These different voices necessarily carry different beliefs about what constitutes validity, about what sorts of evidence are acceptable or even must be included, about what difference is all about and, hence, what argument is all about.

ARGUMENT TODAY

And so we find ourselves at this time with some wonderful arguments about argument. Is argument about persuasion, or is it about exploration of differences, or is it about learning or maintenance of social relationship? What sorts of forms are acceptable, to whom? Is argument necessarily hierarchical? What is the relationship of argument and narrative, a constructed dichotomy that has accompanied discussions of argument for a very long time?

Along with these explorations of what argument is or ought to be, educators struggle to find ways of helping their students to engage in reasoned ways of exploring issues. Many educators find the social nature of argument especially compelling and explore collaborative writing as argument. Others recognize personal writing, which used to be dismissed as self-indulgent, as a legitimate means of constructing oneself and one's considered view of the world. Some educators believe personal response to be the primary way that individuals can validate their subjective, often different (deviant?), thinking in the face of institutional canons that exclude a majority of the world's people.

In a different vein, the notion that argument is the highest form of thinking and writing is being challenged. Increasingly, we are recognizing the ways in which young children use argument in their daily lives, and some educators are calling for increased engagement with written argument by younger children. These approaches view the development of argument differently than it has been in the past: It is not something that must wait until other forms of thinking are developed; but, rather, is a different way of thinking that develops along with other ways. Some contributors to this volume would argue that there is not a single different way of argumentative thinking, but there are multiple ways of thinking argumentatively.

The intention of this volume is to voice some of these nontraditional argumentative issues. My view as editor of the volume is that the essential aspect of argument is the voicing of differences. That voicing carries with it an assumption that the differences will first be received in a Bakhtinian sense of dialogue. However, some voices in this volume speak to the fact that the first initial step of reception often does not occur: rather, differences are often silenced by those in authority, knowingly or unknowingly, before they can be received.

This volume, then, seeks to present a variety of ways of understanding argument. It offers no single point of view: It attempts only to voice some of the different ways of understanding argument and to question traditional assumptions of what written argument must be. Although there is no single definition of what argument is, the authors all value what they perceive as argument.

OVERVIEW OF THIS VOLUME

The chapters in this volume were collected with a view to explore argument from a variety of perspectives. Thus, scholars in different disciplines who have written about argument in recent years were invited to submit chapters for possible inclusion. Most chapters therefore appear here for the first time.

The collection opens with Andrew Wilkinson's "Argument as a Primary Act of Mind." Wilkinson reestablishes what he considers to be the essential aspects of argument by contrasting the logical reasoning of argument with the chronological reasoning of narrative, expounded by Barbara Hardy (1977) as "a primary act of mind" (p. 12). Wilkinson argues that argument is a comparable "primary act of mind," giving examples from children's speaking and writing to support this position and demonstrating their abilities to use evidenced thinking.

The next two chapters elaborate on Wilkinson's identification of "natural" features of traditional argument in oral and written texts of young people. These chapters explore the development of written argument, closely examining texts of student argument (which have usually been seen as "nonargument") and identifying features of traditional mature argument that are found in texts of 12- to 14-year-olds. The call is for a reassessment of development of argumentative writing, with attention to context and helpful teacher response that recognizes embryonic forms of mature traditional argument.

In Chapter 2, Mark Lynch writes as a teacher in describing how Chaim Perelman and Lucie Olbrecht-Tyteca's (1969) techniques of argumentation can be used for the analysis of written argument of early adolescents, especially regarding possibilities for teacher response. Cognitive and developmental difficulties that 13-year-olds experience in writing argument are discussed along with the concomitant difficulties of teacher response. Lynch, then, takes a traditional tool, applies it to the texts of young writers and thinkers, and explores the teacher's role as a respondent in dialogue as well as an evaluator of argument.

Marion Crowhurst brings her expertise as a language development researcher to Chapter 3 and continues the exploration of the teaching and learning of argumentative writing in the middle school years. Crowhurst contends that persuasion or argument makes certain demands of writers, but that students aged 10 to 14 are capable of writing argument, and that it is particularly appropriate for people of this age to engage in argumentative writing. She gives examples of the types of writing that argumentative questions elicit at this age level and demonstrates both the aspects of mature argumentative writing that are found as well as the problems students of this age have in writing argument. These problems are delineated, and instructional strategies of teacher intervention are suggested, especially stressing the importance of writing contexts.

The next three chapters look at the variability of traditional argument in different contexts. These chapters extend work like that of Stephen Toulmin that identified the possibilities of different tacit assumptions in different fields, along with different belief systems and forms of persuasion.

In Chapter 4, Trudy Govier shows a philosopher's perspective regarding the inapplicability of formal logic to many natural language arguments. Her attention to themes such as the quest for rigor, scientism, and uneasiness with ambiguity and the lack of provably certain results provides a clear connection between traditional Western approaches to argument and attempts to change those approaches, even from those who work within that tradition. Her chapter gives a philosophical context for all of the following chapters, stressing the importance of argument in acknowledging the possibility of difference and in its emphasis on *explicit* delineation of differences.

In Chapter 5, Aviva Freedman characterizes what she terms the "necessarily idiosyncratic" nature of argument. Freedman compares her studies of the highly specialized argumentative writing elicited in different content areas with the kind of general discursive argument about subjects of broad public interest typically elicited in composition classes. Emphasis is on the shaping power of context in each case; and, in her emphasis on content as context, Freedman questions traditional assumptions about the universality of argument. Freedman especially features argumentative writing as social action, the purpose of which is epistemic in its (re)interpretation of reality. She (re)interprets academic argumentative writing as a rite of passage for students, an initiation of the novice into a discourse community.

Pat Currie takes Freedman's contextual concerns into the realm of evaluation of argument in Chapter 6. Currie uses argumentative writing of upper year university students who are nonnative speakers of English to illustrate the difference between writers' abilities to complete a given conceptual task and their abilities to construct a written argument that matches what the evaluator has in mind. Like Freedman, she uses Stephen Toulmin's work as a grounding for her interpretations, but also incorporates issues of reader-response theory and textual reconstruction, as they relate to the professor as reader/evaluator. Currie argues for the need to make explicit the acceptable rhetorical conventions and assumptions of argument of the different discourse communities of different subject disciplines.

Chapter 7 opens in ways that should immediately alert readers to perceptions of written argument that are quite different than traditional Western approaches. Chris Anson and Richard Beach look at argument in dialogue journals, stressing the social nature of opposition in collaborative writing. Anson and Beach provide a synthesis on current views on argument in written communication, especially focusing on the literature that considers argument in alternative instructional modes such as journals or informal writing. Through examination of dialogue journals of undergraduates, the authors question assumptions about development of written argument put forward by those who see "deviant" forms of argument as occurring prior to the acquisition of full fledged persuasive strategies. The authors highlight argumentative strategies used by writers in dialogue journals and raise issues about ways of promoting dialectical reasoning within a social context that encourages tentativeness rather than definitiveness. Hopefully the article will prompt readers to (re)view their own opinions regarding the degree to which they feel peer dialogue journal writing exemplifies argumentative writing. Certainly the dialogic nature of entries presented are quite different from Aristotelian dialectic.

Deborah Berrill explores issues of race and gender in relation to argument and the development of written argument in Chapter 8. As her starting point, Berrill uses Lakoff and Johnson's identification of war as a metaphor that underlies commonly held assumptions of what argument is in Western society. Berrill argues that dialectic/dialogic argument is characterized by exploration of legitimacies of alternate positions that a war metaphor does not recognize in its assumptions of destruction and silencing of alternate positions. Manuscripts of 16-year-old females of minority cultures are used to illustrate how developing writers articulate and honor alternate positions in their written argument. Although these scripts would often be judged as nonargumentative, Berrill argues that their exploration of differences indicates argumentative processes at work and suggests that it may be our present framing of argument as war that inhibits the very processes we seek to develop.

In Chapter 9, Karen Watson-Gegeo brings her anthropological and sociolinguistic research from a Pacific island society to demonstrate how a different culture uses well-articulated forms of argumentation to settle disputes. However, here argumentation becomes a symbolically important teaching event, the goal of which is to use and teach the use of argumentation forms to bring about personal and social transformations that strengthen and/or restore connections (social relations) between people. She stresses cultural differences in dealing with differences of opinion, challenging traditional Western assumptions that difference necessarily means conflict.

In Chapter 10, Robert Carter continues the exploration of argumentation from different cultural perspectives. As a Western moral philosopher with expertise in Eastern (specifically Japanese) philosophy, Carter contrasts the combativeness of refutation with the harmony that can result from becoming the other and appreciating the otherness of different points of view. His philosophical stance echoes Watson-Gegeo's sociolinguistic findings as well as Berrill's educational ones. Carter goes on to highlight the Zen position, in which the stability of a privileged single viewing is rejected and the encouragement to look again and again takes its place. This also continues earlier questioning of notions of the possibility a single truth and calls for openness to ambiguity.

Dorothy Perry Thompson continues the exploration of the Eurocentricity of academic argument. She contrasts the Eurocentric cultural world view with an African-American world view and then demonstrates how African-American student writers approach argumentation in a way that is consistent and logical with their world view, but that is not from a Eurocentric world view. Through her discussion, Thompson challenges us to (re)view deeply held Eurocentric assumptions about interpretation of argumentation prompts, the limited range of evidence that has validity in academic argument, the acceptability of different linguistic styles in argumentation, and a different recognition of the power of the word in shaping discourse and ideas. Thompson herself bridges two cultures, and her challenge is for more of us to attempt to do the same.

In Chapter 12, Karen Redfield brings writing from yet another culture into our exploration. Redfield applies anthropological and sociolinguistic research on different thought patterns in different cultures to the writing of Native American students. She shows how understanding the structure of writing of Native American students depends on our recognition of a very different sense of the individual in community; and she demonstrates how community stories feature as "evidence" in the writing of two Native American students. She also demonstrates how "reading backward" as well as forward is important for us in reading the work of Native Americans if we are to see the rhetorical competence that these writers exhibit. Looking for the traditional academic linearity does not show us the logic and reasoning used in these texts.

Catherine Lamb completes the collection with an exploration of how it can be feminist to both at times be confrontational and at other times to advocate approaches that minimize confrontation. She approaches conflict resolution in relation to the use of power in situations of differing points of view and defines alternatives to hierarchical power structures. The role of personal voice is linked to empowerment in conflict by proposing that those with alternate positions "respond" to each other rather than attempt to "refute" each other. Lamb argues that responding rather than refuting widens the context of each participant's initial perceptions, creating an "unending conversation" to which no one needs an invitation and in which there would be greater silence "because people would be listening more."

CONCLUSION

In summary, this collection begins with the understandings that argumentative writing is about difference of opinion and about evidenced thinking in relation to those differences. The first three chapters note the presence of argumentative reasoning in conversations of very young children and in the writing of children in middle school years. To use Wilkinson's phrase, there is something "primary" about argumentative thinking.

The following chapters identify ideas not usually associated with argumentative writing. These include the following suppositions:

1. Argument operates best in contexts of connectedness and community.

This idea builds from Trudy Govier's emphasis on the purpose of argument being the explicit identification of difference. Chris Anson and Rick Beach note the way in which difference of opinion is raised in peer dialogue journals, in which challenges are raised and questions are asked within a context of social connection. Writers note their "confusion" rather than becoming adversarial.

The importance of this reception of difference, often of opposites, is explicitly stated by young women who are first-generation offspring of a visible minority population in Deborah Berrill's work. Karen Watson-Gegeo stresses how integral argument is to community maintenance for the Kwara'ae people of the Solomon Islands, and how it serves to "disentangle" conflict. Differences of individuals within the culture provide the twists and tangles of the different points of view within the community. Respect for differences of individual views is great, yet the interdependency of individuals within the community means that differences must be sorted out if they threaten the stability of the community.

The idea of recognition of difference within community is underscored by Robert Carter's chapter on the background of argument in Japan, where complementarity carries both associations of difference and sameness; opposites are understood as extremes of a continuum. Although most of the chapters refer to connectedness in human terms, Carter's explication of Japanese thinking shows how this notion of connectedness applies equally to ideas themselves.

2. Argumentative processes are learning processes.

Aviva Freedman describes argument as social action, its purpose being epistemic—the interpretation of reality according to the modes of a given community. She refers to the learning of argumentative processes as a rite of passage, an initiation into a discourse community that has distinctive "habits of mind and stances toward experience," which the initiate is expected to master. For Freedman, different academic disciplines are different cultures, each with "communally sanctioned and socially constructed modes of selecting evidence as well as reasoning from that evidence."

Pat Currie extends Freedman's rite of initiation through her work with the argumentative writing of nonnative speakers of English. This work makes clear the extent to which the thinking processes of cultures of academic disciplines are implied, rather than explicit. She demonstrates that the real task of argumentative writing in university courses is often not a conceptual task, but rather the demonstration of knowledge of the academic discourse community—Freedman's "habits of mind." Students who do not have familiarity with the rituals of academic argumentation go to great lengths to identify these habits of mind, and Currie calls for disciplines to make explicit the assumptions and conventions of their cultures.

This call for explicitness comes at an historical time when many traditional conventions are being challenged particularly by feminist scholars. However, until evaluation criteria for argumentative writing are made public and explicit, all the disempowered (including students) remain at risk of being labeled inept or nonrigorous.

Karen Watson-Gegeo describes argument as a learning process in the Kwara'ae teaching event of fa'amanata'anga, a holistic event that "always closes conflict-handling meetings . . . as a way of reinforcing cultural values, recognizing the validity of personal feelings, repairing social relationships." The Kwara'ae argument becomes a way of teaching and reinforcing the cultural norms of their community—not so very different from Freedman's recognition of argument as a rite of passage into a discourse community.

3. In argumentation, it is important to maintain the tension of difference for as long as possible, rather than seeking closure or resolution too quickly.

In another sense, the best argumentative processes are learning processes in that individuals seek to come to an understanding of the landscape of the other through explicit recognition of difference. This tenet is grounded, again, in Govier's formulation of explicit identification of difference as part of what argumentative writing is all about. In Freedman's terms, individuals learn what it is that distinguishes cultures and communities; and in a Bakhtinian sense, individuals learn the landscape of the other.

Robert Carter and Catherine Lamb both address this idea of maintaining differences. Carter illustrates how the Japanese seek to preserve contradictory terms and moments, with not an "either/or" but a "both/and" logic. This Japanese dialectic is reflected in the language, in which difference between subject and object is less pronounced than in the West, and everything that is in opposition also shares a commonality. It is recognition of difference and sameness at the same time that provides tension and harmony. Difference, then, does not need to be adversarial.

Catherine Lamb is concerned that spaces of difference are explicitly acknowledged and maintained as long as possible to allow often-silenced voices to enter into conversation. She proposes that argumentative processes should seek out and attempt to understand perspectives other than one's own. In order for differences to be truly acknowledged in a Bakhtinian sense, it is the openness and ongoingness of the argumentative process that is the germane element.

4. The acknowledgment of difference is a way to maintain relationship and community.

Building on earlier notions that difference need not be confrontational, Karen Watson-Gegeo demonstrates that in the Kwara'ae culture in the Solomon Islands the primary metaphors underlying argumentative processes revolve around gardening, rather than war. These metaphors illustrate argumentative processes of reasoning through a tangle of possibilities in dealing with conflict, which for the Kwara'ae imply community divisiveness. In this culture, conflict is "entanglement," and argumentation is "straightening out" and restoring community harmony.

In this context, the purpose of argumentation is social transformation—the creation or restoration of social relationship. This position brings to mind Freedman's perception of argument as social action. The anthropological and rhetorical positions are perhaps surprisingly complementary.

In Carter's appraisal of Japanese culture, it is the recognition of the sameness of differences that is essential to a view of existence that posits the connectedness of all things. Similarly, the voices of disempowered women in Berrill's work call strongly for maintenance of relationship, but *through* acknowledgment of the validity of difference. Lamb calls for the broadening of contexts to enable communities to become more inclusive. For Lamb, acknowledgment of voices of difference is the way to rebuild community, with "unending conversation" as testimony of that community.

Dorothy Perry Thompson demonstrates how African-American writers *assume* community relevance and understanding in their responses to argumentative tasks. The degree of community relevance shapes the form of the argument itself. Similarly, Karen Redfield notes how Native American writers frame their responses in terms of community connection.

The end of the book takes us back to the beginning, for implicit in many of the chapters and explicit in some is the belief that argumentation processes are essential processes that can and should be taught. Wilkinson's opening chapter reminds us that as soon as young children gain fluency with language they have begun argumentation. Crowhurst and Lynch identify middle school years as a time when written fluency is great enough that children can be explicitly taught the "rites" of which Freedman and Currie speak. The second reading then places these major views about argumentative processes into a community context of teaching succeeding generations about ways to approach difference.

The perspectives presented in this volume are meant to provide a response to many conversations about argument that have preceded this one. Issues of truthfulness have not been intentionally avoided; rather, part of what is is implied in many of the chapters is that we have come to understand that "truth" may be perceived very differently in different contexts, different cultures. Until we are able to recognize differences for all that they carry, we will be unable to arrive at decisions either about truthfulness or about what is the best action to take at any particular time in a particular setting.

Furthermore, many of the chapters in this volume are congruent with anthropological research of the last two to three decades that has made evident the different kinds of logic operating in different cultures and different languages. Some of the challenges to traditional Western argument of this volume that question the necessity of linear and hierarchical logic in argumentation bring to mind Navaho logic, which is based on circularity or Javanese logic of cyclicity (see Hill, 1988). Many of the authors of this volume deeply value the logics they see operating in different cultures; alternative logics that are not "better than" Aristotelian hierarchical logic, but rather are "other" than or "different" from that familiar argument. The call is not for elimination of any type of argumentation, but rather for an exploration of different kinds of thinking and, possibly, for an expansion of our present repertoires of argument.

REFERENCES

Bakhtin, M.M. (1981). *The dialogic imagination* (M. Holquist, Ed., C. Emerson & M. Holquist, Trans.). Austin: University of Texas Press.

Becker, A.L. (1979). Text-building, epistemology, and aesthetics in Javanese shadow theatre. In A.L. Becker & A.A. Yengoyan (Eds.), *The imagination of reality.* Norwood, NJ: Ablex.

Becker, A.K. (1984). Biography of a sentence: A Burmese proverb. In S. Plattner & E.M. Bruner (Eds.), *Text, play and story.* Washington, DC: American Ethnological Society.

Becker, J., (1979). Time and tune in Java. In A.L. Becker & A.A. Yengoyan (Eds.), *The imagination of reality.* Norwood, NJ: Ablex.

Hardy, B. (1977). Narrative as a primary act of mind. In M. Meek, A. Waslow, & G. Barton (Eds.), *The cool web: The pattern of children's reading.* London: Bodley Heads.

Hill, J.H. (1988). Language, culture, and world view. In F.J. Newmeyer (Ed.), *Linguistics: The Cambridge Survey, IV, Language: The Sociocultural Context.* New York: Cambridge University Press.

Hymes, D.H. (1966). Two types of linguistic reliability. In W. Bright (Ed.), *Sociolinguistics.* The Hague: Mouton.

Perelman, C., & Olbrechts-Tyteca, L. (1969). *The new rhetoric* (J. Wilkinson & P. Weaver, Trans.). Notre Dame, IN: University of Notre Dame Press.

Wertsch, J.V. (1994, March). *A sociocultural approach to writing.* Paper presented at the College Composition and Communication Conference, Nashville, TN.

CHAPTER 1

*Argument as a Primary Act of Mind**

Andrew Wilkinson

ACTS OF MIND

The distinction pointed to recently between *narrative* and *argument* as "acts of mind" (Bruner, 1985; Wilkinson, 1986) and given powerful circulation by Bruner (1986) is in fact a traditional one. Shelley, for instance, in *A Defence of Poetry* (1821), spoke of those two classes of mental action that are called *imagination* and *reason:*

> The one is the . . . principle of synthesis, and has for its object those forms which are common to universal nature and existence itself; the other is the . . . principle of analysis, and its action regards the relation of things simply as relations; considering thoughts, not in their integral unity, but in the algebraical representations which conduct to certain general results. (quoted in Enright & Chickera, 1974, p. 225)

---

*I gratefully acknowledge permission to reprint this slightly rewritten version of an article that first appeared in *English in Education*, 24(1), 1990, pp. 10-22.

Equivalent terms to *synthesis* and *analysis* are used when historians and anthropologists consider the differences between what may be called ancient and modern modes of thought, the one marked by *fusion*, the other by *differentiation*:

> It is likely that the political, economic and social life of humans before "civilized" times was based on ease of fusion. For forty or fifty thousand years before the rise of civilizations, the ability both to make and dissolve distinctions probably coexisted in harmony. The first civilizations, about 6000 years ago, forcibly separated these ways of thinking for the first time. In this moment of sorting one was confirmed and rewarded and the other was disconfirmed and punished. The two kinds of thinking could be pushed further and further apart. . . . Finally the philosophers of Greece came to regard differentiation as thought itself. (Bram, 1986, pp. 19, 21)

The first formulation of "narrative as a primary act of mind" to have an influence on English teachers was Hardy's (1968) paper, which was made available in Meek, Wardlaw, and Barton (1977):

> My argument is that narrative . . . is not to be regarded as an aesthetic invention used by artists to control, manipulate, and order experience, but as a primary act of mind transferred to art from life. . . . For we dream in narrative, daydream in narrative, remember, anticipate, hope, despair, believe, doubt, plan, revise, criticize, construct, gossip, learn, hate and love by narrative. In order really to live, we make up stories about ourselves and others, about the personal as well as the social past and future. (pp. 12-13)

This is heady stuff and one important source for much of our present enthusiasm for narrative. But it seems to predicate a kaleidoscopic fantasy life to the exclusion of anything else. Can the reader of the present sentences be said to be "learning" their content through narrative? Does the builder who "constructs" a house imagine he or she is the Third Little Pig, or does the builder do so on rational principles? In order "really to live" do we "make up stories about ourselves and others," or do we count our cash and negotiate our mortgages? The questions are of course rhetorical. If narrative is a primary act of mind, it is not, therefore, the only primary act of mind.

The other primary act of mind is, of course, constituted by a variety of differentiating analytical activities—recording of evidence, evaluating, persuading, classifying, deducing, arguing, and so on—which is related together under the heading of *argument*.

Regarding developmentally, neither of these acts is primary. The first thinking seems to be *associative:* the first language acts of naming connect the object being signified with the (arbitrary) signifier. Then thinking is seen to become *classificatory:* Children use plurals, concepts, or subordinates. When children have quite considerable command of language, arrangements take place in *chronological* terms. It is only after this that we can begin to talk about narrative—when there is some connection between events as well as sequence. Chronology must be important for a coherent ordering of experience because we live in a temporal world.

Classification is of a different order from association and chronology. It is an arrangement on rational grounds: Pigs, dogs, elephants are all animals because there is a similarity between them capable of demonstration. It is in fact the earliest example of logical thinking, and one of the chief elements in it. The basic characteristic of logical thinking is cause and effect. Modern civilization is organized by means of a vast number of causes and effects.

What differentiates narrative from argument? Obviously there are formal differences that can be described in genre terms. But the ultimate distinction lies in the nature of their validation. It is assumed that speakers/writers use language to tell the truth (that is why lying is often effective). People are concerned to support what they say. For example, a group of 5-year-olds are talking to a visitor sitting at their table:

> Kelley: I'm making an Easter basket.
> Gemma: I'm painting mine green and pink.
> William: James has spoilt his. He's cut this off (shows detached tab).
> James (ruefully): Yes, I have, I'm poor with scissors.

Four statements were made. The evidence for the first two is immediately visual. James gives a small demonstration for the third. The fourth is about the nature of James, who explains why it has happened. We feel the need to be believed, to feel justified.

Validation in narrative and similar imaginative forms is different: It requires a willing suspension of disbelief. Amanda, who has just celebrated her fourth birthday, is very conscious of this:

> Amanda: Once upon a time a little mouse lived. And he couldn't have a hole because he was so fat, and he didn't have time to spare because he was so happy. And I didn't know what to do, so I had an idea "I'm giving him a new home." So I did. That was in my mummy and daddy's room—there was a little mousehole.

Adult: Was there?
Amanda: And there really is.

Amanda has a real sense of story beginning with the traditional opening, then presenting a problem—that of a home for an overweight mouse—and then finding a solution to it, neither of which are traditional. The validation takes several forms. One is explanation—the mouse did not have a home "because he was so fat"; he did not have time to look for one "because he was so happy" (enjoying himself). Another is the exact details—the little girl quoted her own thoughts, "I'm giving him a new home"; and she specified the mousehole—"in my mummy and daddy's room." A very interesting feature of this piece is Amanda's evaluation—"There really is"—that is, this was a real mousehole she was talking about, not one made up.

The distinction between narrative and argument as acts of mind is a fundamental one, each with its own validities. Unfortunately the two are commonly confused. This is understandable in early cultures with no recording system and no means of verification. The rain dance is danced and the rain falls—what could be more logical? If it does not, it is because the Spirits are displeased—what more reasonable explanation could you want? It is much less understandable when people in modern civilizations are unable to distinguish fantasy from fact—institutionalized religions, for instance, constantly offer myth as literal truth. There are few signs that magical thinking is diminishing. Father Christmas, lotteries, and horoscopes may be fairly harmless manifestations of this. But we cannot say the same of those occasions in which TV evangelists in the US have people with organic diseases throw away their crutches and dance in a frenzy only to collapse off camera with doctors desperately attempting to revive them.

THE POSITION OF NARRATIVE

It may be that narrative is "primary" with argument. Nevertheless, theory and practice in English teaching over many years have given narrative place of pride. It is interesting to consider why this is.

Hourd's early classic, *The Education of the Poetic Spirit* (1949), ushered in a program of "creative writing," with a large investment in narrative. Other forms of writing were dismissed as "recording" (Thompson, 1964, p. viii). Associated with this was the assumption that poetic and narrative writing occurred first developmentally: "Whereas adults differentiate their thought with specialized kinds of discourse such as narrative, generalization and theory, children must, for a long time, make narrative do for all" (Moffett, 1968). Recent fashions in the teaching of writing, with concepts such as *ownership*, have tended to emphasize narrative. Process writing as described by Graves (1983) is particularly concerned with "children's right to choose their own topic," even if it means writing on the same topic repeatedly. Given such free choice children usually choose narrative, and indeed Graves's examples are nearly always narrative. Ideally they need not do so, but it is the tendency of a model that is important in the classroom, not the fine print that qualifies it. Children choose narrative; they do not choose argument. (Whether *ownership* ought to be equated with *choice of topic* is another question.)

Of course our culture reinforces narrative: Early literary experiences are nursery rhymes (usually stories), fairy tales, and legends. At school reading is taught using narrative material, whether the approach is with basal readers or "real books." There are indications that teachers prefer to prompt and to receive stories from their classes. Parents share bedtime stories with their children, not bedtime arguments. The press is full of "stories"; the media offer drama, sitcoms, soaps—all stories.

It seems, therefore, that there are all kinds of cultural, social, motivational factors pressing us toward narrative. It is certainly important in our lives. One significant reason for this is that it is so deeply entrenched in the home. Home, we might say, is a place where stories are told. This is a fundamental definition of home that is not found in the dictionary. A family lives by its stories. Without them it is without past and future, without imagination, vision, or aspiration. It is here, and it is now—but no more.

The stories are of many kinds. There are those that retrieve and construct the history of the family, and those that go beyond it; there are those that envisage the future—what we will do when. There are stories of humorous, scurrilous, pathetic incidents, polished by constant retelling. There are garrulous, reiterant, obsessive stories. There are stories that originally belonged to other people that subtly pass into one's own family history. There are stories that are retellings from books, and stories read from books. There are stories made up to amuse children on a wet day, which—once started—continue week after week, until their originators are heartily sick of them, although the children never tire. They are stories children themselves create, sometimes in imaginative play, often the most inventive of all.

Children are far from being minor partners in the stories of the home world. They release the imagination, both their own and that of the adults. Adults enter imaginative worlds through reading, television and drama, fantasy, planning for the future, or dreaming about the past. A few write or act themselves. But otherwise there are strict limits to what is overtly permissible. The poet William Blake said that spirits and angels dictated his poems to him. He used to make remarks such as, "The prophets Isaiah and Ezekiel dined with me, and I asked them . . ." (quoted in Keynes, 1956, p. 185). Many people thought him mad. But the worlds of children are not suspect in that way. In their stories and in their play they give free rein to their imaginations, and adults may slip into these worlds with them without suspicion of insanity.

Let us look at one example, an imaginative story by a 5-year-old. This, told at home, seems to have its germ in a story told at school, which was reported as: "I knew a man, his name was Egg. One day he swallowed seeds. Next week he was all covered with daffodils." The story at home started with the idea of a daisy chain:

> When I was walking along that time thinking about that man I thought, "Why don't I make a necklace and tie it all round myself?" I picked up some daisies and began to make a necklace, and I began to knit some clothes. And first I said a jumper and a vest of daisies, of crocuses. I began to knit an underskirt, and out of again crocuses. I began to knit a shirt, and out of daffodils I began to knit a jumper. And I said trousers, put daisies all round my trousers, and then I covered my feet with leaves. And for ears I got some long leaves long sticks and tied them onto my hair. Then I looked like a rabbit, and I started to go all round the town dressed up as a rabbit (said with evident enjoyment). (Adult: Did you meet anybody?)
> Yes, and they said Who's that then?
> Then a child said, Mr Rabbit, Mrs Rabbit, walking along.
> (Adult: And did you greet people? Did you say hello?)
> Yes. I said, would you like to dress up as a rabbit like me. And they said Yes, well . . . (doubtfully).
> I said, Just knit a uniform of crocuses, and for your ears sticks and tie them onto your hair when you get some. And then you can go round the town with me. Should I knit them for you? They'll be ready next day. Where I live is 8 Clarendon Road. You can collect them at one o'clock.
> (Adult: So what did they say?)
> The end.

The child's imagination builds rapidly from a daisy chain to a full outfit of clothes, from flowers, from herself to a rabbit, from a thoughtful walk to a parade in town to display her finery, from solitariness to a leadership of other children in instructing them what to make, and eventually doing it for them because they are uncertain. The story helps aspiration to wider roles with greater freedoms and initiatives—walking unsupervised, receiving public admiration, doing things for others rather than having them done for you. Sometimes such stories by children become part of the family legends.

HOMEMADE ARGUMENT

The agreement of educationalists that narrative is *primary* in the sense that it occurs first developmentally, is not borne out by a careful study of the language of preschool children. Their language abilities in general have been underestimated, partly because they have been judged by their performance when they come to school, in which conditions are different (Tizzard & Hughes, 1984; Wells, 1987).

Within preschool children, there is commonly found an ability to argue and to narrate at a surprisingly early age. Let us take argument first. Andrew at 2.4 is trying to persuade his mother to get up.

> It's time to get up Mommy.
> Time to have cornflakes.
> Laura's Mommy is up.
> Lynda's Mommy is up.
> (He goes and looks out of the curtains.)
> You can see the window if you like.

The validation of his first statement is impressive. First, an incentive is offered (the cornflakes), then validation of its being time to rise is given by citing two parallel instances. Last, verifiable evidence of these is put forward (that the curtains in the other houses are drawn back).

In another example, Janet (3.6 years old) is disputing possession of a doll with Cory (2.6 years old). She offered her one in return: "Cory do you want this pretty one, cause she has this hat? Want this pretty one? Look, she has these flowers in her hat. Look that one, OK?" Cory supported her offer with two reasons: The doll had a hat, and the hat had flowers. This did not work so she offered a rabbit, but when this was refused she tried a different strategy—if you are not sensible enough to accept this then it follows that you must do without: "Oh, where's the bunny? Where's the bunny? OK. If you won't have one, none." But the threat was quickly withdrawn and the principle of fairness substituted: "There, cause you have the soft one, so I have to have soft one." Later the objects of contention were the dolls' hairbrushes. For her right of possession of the two brushes, Janet appealed to an eternal law: "Little babies aren't supposed to have two, but I am." But Cory, at

2.6 years old was not to be outdone and could also appeal to the same law: "I am [supposed to]." Both children are beginning to recognize that assertions have to be supported.

This fact is even clearer in a discussion between two 4-year-olds. Edmund and Lois. When Lois said, "I'm going to clear this zoo up, I am." Edmund not only forbid her, but gave a reason: "Oh, don't, you'll have a mess." When he realized she was not convinced, he offered a further explanation, linked with the authority of the researcher's name: "You'll have a mess. Dr. Wilkinson's got to do that."

Lois's counterstrategy was to constantly challenge Edmund for his reasons:

> Edmund: Don't touch the microphone.
> Lois: Why?
> Edmund: Cause you can't.
> Lois: Why can't you?
> Edmund: Cause it's Uncle Tom's
> Lois: Why is it Uncle Tom's?
> Edmund: Because it stays here. He'll take it back to Uncle Tom's.

Lois would not accept the circular reasoning of "Cause you can't," and Edmund had to offer a further reason ('It's Uncle Tom's'). But both knew this was not true, that the microphone belonged to the researcher. So Edmund had to try to square this with what he had said, by implying that the researcher had borrowed it from Uncle Tom (imaginative but untrue).

Both pairs of children used validations common in adult discourse—in terms of consequences, ownership, fairness, authority, explanation, or "laws" or absolutes. (Full texts and discussions of the two conversations can be found in Wilkinson, Davies, & Berrill, 1990, ch. 4)

I now turn to narrative. It is really profitless to debate minutely whether narrative or argument occurs first. It partly depends on how the terms are defined. It could be argued that the more extended stretches of language (long turns), less supported by the immediate interactions of short turns, require greater maturity. Certainly the stories of 3-year-olds showing features of narrative grammar are well documented. Take Helen's story at 3.6 years old:

> Right, one day I said to a little pony who was in the field over a fence, "I'm not going to bang you, I'm only going to ride on you." I said, "Shut the door, and I'll ride on you." "I haven't got a door," said the horse. (This is only a tease game.) So off they went down the

lane to Banbury Horse Cross. They brought a white horse home. They didn't know where their home was. (A wasp interrupts). Oh dear, what's this? Bizbiz. Go on. Stoop (Stup-id)! And there was little girl who says, "Hallo flower. There you are." And that's the end of the story, Daddy. (Wilkinson, 1975, p. 107)

The conventional introduction, the orientation, the interactive conversation, and the development and rising action are all there. The entry of the wasp causes the storyteller to lose her train of thought, but she still offered a denouement by recognizing a familiar flower, implying presumably a return home as well as the storybook conclusion, "The End."

THE ARGUMENT OF ARGUMENT

If features of argument, as well as narrative, develop so early, why is it that we place such emphasis on narrative, particularly in the early years of schooling? It is, of course, undeniable that narrative is very useful. Pox (1989) interestingly demonstrated some of the kinds of thinking present in the stories children themselves create. But is narrative all they have? Must it, to quote again Moffett, "make do for all"? If it does, then what is Catherine, at 5.2, doing orally presenting a piece of straight exposition and explanation that owes nothing to narrative structure? (For the purposes of identification this has been given a title):

Tying shoelaces
Well I said to these kids—you know the loops they have to do, she did those but not the first part which they have to pull up. She just did that and I said that's wrong, you've got to learn—I can't spend all my life doing that and this knot and this knot and all the others as well. So I never can do that all by myself. and if there was another child could help with the shoelaces to do them in my classroom they could come to both of us but there isn't so I'm the only person and I get busy doing shoelaces and now I'm worned out and all these years that I've been at school I've been doing shoelaces all these days that I've been at school before I've been doing shoelaces every day.
A. What did you say about children who are five?
That they should know that—I know that children about 5 year old can do shoelaces. Anyway Kelly's taller than me, though we're both 5, and I said that if she's taller than me she should know how to do it. And I'm sick of doing them everyday, everyday, everyday. I don't what any more days but I mean every day because the problem is if there any PE the

> children should just slip out of their knots and they come to me in a little queue, in a little group, and they never learn how to do it and instead I fasten them and I have a little group to do shoelaces and it would be much better. But from now on I hope I'm not going to do it any more. And I know that's what you hope because if . . . if I do I will be disappointed and sad because I know when they're an adult they'll have to to them by theirselves.

The argument is clear: "The children can start tying their laces but do not know the final processes. If there were someone else in the class to help I would be less worn out, but there isn't. Children of 5 should know how to tie their shoelaces. Kelly, particularly since she's taller than me, should know how to do them. One solution would be for children to wear slip-on shoes for PE. But if they don't I really need a team to help me. As it is I despair, thinking of my classmates arriving at adulthood without being able to tie their laces."

Catherine lays out the problem, speaks of the effects it is having, and proposes several solutions, predicting dire consequences if they are not adopted. But she should not be approaching the matter so directly. She should be wrapping it up in a story. Obviously she has not read her Moffett.

The argument for argument lies in its importance of the development of evidenced thinking and in the demonstrable ability of children to carry it out under appropriate conditions. It may be that we have not provided those conditions and have made a virtue of not doing so. The conditions we have been examining have occurred in spoken language, and clearly we need to develop argumentative skills in this mode (see, for instance, Berrill, 1988; Wilkinson, Davies, & Berrill, 1990). Such work will often take place in short-turn situations such as discussion. But long turns (such as Catherine's earlier discussion) are also important. Wells, Chang, and Wells (1986, p. 130) pointed to the value of "sustained oral production":

> The advantage of oral monologue that we particularly wish to emphasize is that it provides an opportunity to develop some of the skills of composing—planning, selecting, marshalling and organizing ideas that are so necessary for writing, and that it does so in a medium in which pupils feel more at ease and in which they are more likely to be successful.

Conditions in the written language are different from those in group discussion in that the writer has to organize a long stretch of language without supportive or evaluative responses. It is the problem of written argument that Freedman and Pringle (1984) had focused attention on in their notable paper, "Why Students Can't Write Arguments." They pointed out that (in marked contrast to narrative) there is no genre scheme for argument in the written mode. The tennis match of oral discussion offers no pattern. There is some folk wisdom—"Stick to the point", "There are two sides to every question," "Don't jump to conclusions"—but beyond such homely advice there is no model.

Some work carried out at the University of East Anglia has relevance to this. Kell gave written tasks to 8-year-old children, followed by instruction, after which the tasks were repeated (Kell, 1984). Two of the tasks were argument and an aspect of argument—Explanation.

In argument, the topic was "Is playtime a good or a bad thing?" The response was one that we observed in the Crediton Project with children of this age (Wilkinson, Barnsely, Hanna, & Swan, 1980, p. 11), in which they failed to notice there were two aspects to the topic and just argued for one. Thus five out of the six compositions concentrated on the "bad" side, with only one stating both. The "bad" things were such items as the effects of cold and wet (on the children's legs), accidents (to heads), pushing and shoving, fighting, and lack of positive supervision.

Part of the discussion lesson was firmly led by Peter, and several points emerged. The frame offered was: Give a personal view on playtime, then one paragraph for the "good side" and one paragraph for the "bad side," and finally a summary, restatement. Cognitive gains appeared everywhere, such as Michael's first version. Although he called it "For and Against," it was nearly all against. The only virtue he could see in playtime was the negative one that if you refrain from sliding you "don't hole your trousers."

> *For and against*
> Play time is a good thing in one way and bad in another way because if you hit someone on the head and hit him back and Mrs. Case is near by its you who gets caught and not the person who hit you in the first place the good thing about play time is if one person is slideing and your not you don't get holes in your trousers because Paul Steed was with me and Danny. Johny pushed Paul off the tyre Paul started fighting then Johnny, got off then Stuart Lomax started fighting with him then luckaly mrs. seaman came alogne and stopped it.

Michael's piece, after listing some of the disadvantages of playtime, goes off into an anecdote about a fight which was mercifully stopped by the teacher. There is one explanation, about how one may be reprimanded for someone else's misdemeanor.

Michael's second piece, written after the class discussion, read:

> Is playtime a good or a bad thing?
> This writing is about playtime.
> The good side of playtime is you get fresh air and meet some of your friends if they are in anouther class and to have nice games and not to fight with each of you.
> Some bad things about play is do not thump each uther unless you want to get told off by the teacher who is on duty. anouter bad thing is that some people just be beserk and have a game of cross cars and some gets heurt by acendent and then that person goes and tells when he did not mean it. then that gets stopped and then some one starts a game of piggy backs then the bell goes then it's all over
> I hope you agree with one of these things, I mean the god are the bad.

Michael started with a general description of his piece. Then he listed three advantages of playtime—fresh air, meeting friends from other classes, and having friendly games. The disadvantages were: that you cannot "thump each other" with impunity; that you might get hurt in a vigorous game by accident. There is a hint of an anecdote, finishing with the bell, but it is by no means as prominent as in the first version. Michael is learning to control his material.

In explanation, the task chosen was "How to prepare, make, and fire a clay pot," written for someone who did not know the process but wished to carry it out. The process was familiar to all the writers from their craft lessons.

The first writings on the whole did not grasp what the reader would need to know. Michael's was typical:

> First you have to get some clay and some water and then you put it on the table ant then you start. first you will have to make it soft then you will have to get the correct shape next you will have to put your thumb in it and then arrange it to make the bottom nice and smooth then take your thumb out. then it need to be put in the clim and after a few days you have pot.

The ambiguities of "get some clay and water" (without mixing), "correct shape," and "put your thumb in it" are not realized by the writer. The narrative sequence is, of course, usable here, but Michael did not know what to assume and what to state ("put it on the table and then you start" should obviously be assumed).

The best first piece was Wanda's, using a chronological sequence classified into stages:

Telling how to make something

Clay making.

(1) First you have to prepare the clay. For this you will have to need it. When you need clay you push the palms of your hand into the clay over and over again. If you find the clay is getting drie then dab a little water on it.

(2) Next roll the clay in the to a ball. When you have got a nice neat ball then press the bottom of it on to your clay board so the bottom is nice and flat.

(3) When this is done then push your thumb into the ball until you have a hollow in it.

(4) Next smooth down the sides and tops of the pot with a spatualer. If you think you need some more water then dab a bit on. (You probally will need it).

(5) Once you've done that then pick your pot up and put it in the kiln. (If there is anything else in the kilm then put it away from them).

(6) When it comes out of the kiln then glaze it by dipping your pot into the glaze it by dipping your pot into the glaze but be careful not to get any on the bottom. Then put it back into the kiln.

(7) When it comes out again then if you like you can paint it. After you've painted it then glaze it again. Eaven if you hav'nt painted it you will still have to glaze your pot.

The discussion lesson concentrated on the children getting the process clear to themselves, for example, by drawing the stages, and helping them to envisage the reader, for example, a child who does not know how to carry it out. The writers were given models—instructions for making a toy and a simple cookery recipe. Again a frame was suggested: listing materials for the reader—"you will need:" explaining the process, and conclusion (end product).

Wanda's second version was as follows:

Telling How To Do Something

A Clay pot.

You will need:

A lump of clay.

A clay bord.

Some water.

Spatualer.

How to make:

(1) Take your clay and roll it into a neat ball.

(2) Then push your thumb into the clay ball and turn your thumb round until you have a nice hollow in the clay. (don't go threw the bottom of the clay ball.)

(3) Smooth down the tops and sides of the pot.

(4) Your pot will now be fired in the kiln. (before this it will be glazed).

(5) When it comes out of the kiln your pot will be glazed again.

(6) After this you may paint your pot, and then you will have the finished product.

The listing of materials at the beginning was an asset. In the listing of stages, what Wanda learned to do was to go for the central points. Unnecessary linkages ("Once you've done that you pick your pot up and put it back in the kiln") were excluded. The assumption under item one was that the reader would know the clay had to be kneaded, and what this meant. In the second version the word *glaze* was used; in the first we were also told how this was carried out ("by dipping your pot in the glaze"). Both versions warned the reader what could go wrong, but did it with different details (damping the clay on the one hand, going through the bottom of the pot on the other).

Here we have something of a paradox. Wanda seems to have made cognitive gains in that she was developing the ability to summarize and to separate more essential from less essential information: to produce a more succinct description. On the other hand, she lost the explanation of kneading and the reassurances about the moisture content, which were very good teaching points, made in a friendly informal tone: "If you think you need some more water then dab a bit on. (You probably will need it.)" She (temporarily) lost the cognitive virtues of some of her explanations in the first piece. This need not surprise us, nor lead us to think the exercise was not worthwhile. This is one of the features of development, to push forward on one front as opposed to another.

The Crediton Project (Wilkinson, Barnsely, Hanna, & Swan, 1980), devised an instrument—the cognitive model—for describing levels of thinking in children's writing. Not surprisingly, at the age of 7 on cognitive tasks this thinking was predominantly on the recording (information giving) and low explanatory levels. If we examine the data another way, as manifesting acts of mind, we find these to be predominantly chronological, not only in narrative situations, but also in autobiographical ones. Moreover, in situations in which the associative or the logical is required, they nevertheless tend to move back to the chronological. Nevertheless, the research suggests that at least some children of 7 are capable of handling the logical act without the associative and the narrative. The following, for example, is a piece by a 7-year-old from the Crediton Project in response to the task, "If children could come to school when they wanted to, and could do what they wanted there, would it be a good thing?":

> I think school should stay like it is. Because if we did not come to school we would not have anufe education to get a job then we would get no money and we would become tramps then we would diey but if we went to school we would get some education and we could go to college then we could get a very good job and get lots of money. So I think school is very good.

The girl was aware of the need to validate her statements, and the reasoning seems clearly helped by the logical structure she adopted.

The undue dominance of narrative as seen by some has been one of the factors leading toward an advocacy of genre teaching:

> In learning to write, children have to learn genre—and their formal characteristics—which are characteristic of specific social occasions. The occasions in which speech and writing occur differ, along the lines of larger cultural and social structures. Hence written genres have to be learned as new forms, distinct from spoken genres. (Kress, 1986, p. 199)

CONCLUSION

This chapter, following in many footsteps, described argument as a primary act of mind. It expressed surprise that, in view of the manifest abilities of very young children in argument, we have not done more to develop this talent in them in our schools. Instead we have seized on narrative as a primary act of mind and wallowed in our much-loved stories, as though they could do everything for our children. But they cannot. Daniel Defoe, traditionally the first great novelist in English, dedicated his *Jure Divino* (1706) to The Most Serene, Most Invincible, and Most Illustrious Lady REASON, First Monarch of the World.

REFERENCES

Berrill, D.P. (1988). Anecdote and the development of oral argument in sixteen-year-olds. In M. MacLure, T. Phillips, & A.M. Wilkinson (Eds.), *Oracy matters*. Milton Keynes, UK: Open University Press.

Bram, M. (1986). In the course of human affairs. In *Funk and Wagnall's New Encyclopedia* (N.A. Dickey, Ed., Ch. 1). New York: Funk and Wagnall.

Bruner, J. (1985). Narrative and paradigmatic modes of thought. In *Learning and teaching: The ways of knowing* (1985 Yearbook of the National Society for the Study of Education).

Bruner, J. (1986). *Actual minds, possible worlds*. Cambridge, MA: Harvard University Press.

DeFoe, D. (1706). *Jure divino*. National Library Co.

Enright, D.J., & Chickera, E. de (1974). *English critical texts*. Oxford: Oxford University Press.

Fox, C. (1989). Children thinking through story. *English in Education, 23*(2), 25-36.

Freedman, A., & Pringle, I. (1984). Why students can't write arguments. *English in Education, 18*(2), 73-84.

Graves, D. (1983). Writing: *Teachers and children at work*. Portsmouth, NH: Heinemann.

Hourd, M. (1949). *The education of the poetic spirit*. London: Heinemann.

Kell, J. (1984). *The early development of discursive writing.* Unpublished MA dissertation, University of East Anglia School of Education, Norwich, UK.

Keynes, G. (Ed.). (1956). *Poetry and prose of William Blake*. London: The Nonesuch Press.

Kress, G. (1986). Interrelations in reading ant writing. In A.M. Wilkinson (Ed.), *The writing of writing* (pp. 198-214). Milton Keynes, UK: Open University Press.

Meek, M., Wardlow, A.,& Barton, G. (Eds.). (1977). *The cool web*. London: Bodley Head.

Moffett, J. (1968). *Teaching the universe of discourse*. Boston: Houghton Mifflin.

Thompson, D. (1984). Foreword. In A.B. Clegg (Ed.), *The excitement of writing*. London: Chatto and Winders.

Tizzard, B., & Hughes, M. (1984). *Young children learning*. London: Fontana.

Wells, G., Chang, G.L., & Wells, J. (1986). From speech to writing: Some evidence of the relationships between oracy and literacy from the British study "Language at Home and at School". In A.M. Wilkinson (Ed.), *The writing of writing*. Milton Keynes, UK: Open University Press.

Wilkinson, A.M. (1975). *Language and education*. Oxford: Oxford University Press.
Wilkinson, A.M. (1986). Argument as a primary act of mind. In A.M. Wilkinson (Ed.), *Aspects of English composition* [Special issue]. *Educational Review, 38*(2), 127-138.
Wilkinson, A M., Barnsely, G., Hanna, P., & Swan, M. (198()). *Assessing language development*. Oxford: Oxford University Press.
Wilkinson, A.M., Davies, A., & Berrill, D. (1990). *Spoken English illuminated*. Milton Keynes, UK: Open University Press.

CHAPTER 2

Discovering the Ripening Functions of Argument: Using Concepts from The New Rhetoric for Analysis and Response to Student Argumentation

W. Mark Lynch

> The only good kind of instruction is that which marches ahead of development and leads; it must be aimed not so much at the ripe as at the ripening functions.—(Vygotsky, 1962, p. 104).

THE PROBLEM OF TEACHING ARGUMENTATION

Teachers often dread asking their students to write persuasively. One reason is simply the reading of the papers. Even though students are highly motivated to argue enthusiastically about their own beliefs and opinions, they rarely argue well or even adequately. Each paper seems only one more failed attempt to persuade, and teachers wince at the yearly return of the same faults: poor arrangement of arguments, contradictory arguments, and little elaboration by explanation or illustration. Recent national assessment tests likewise reveal the inability of students at elementary and secondary levels to write adequate argumentation

(Nelms, 1990). It is, then, not surprising that teachers might have little enthusiasm for facing stacks of faulty attempts at argument and persuasion, feeling that they have failed in their instruction and possessing little confidence in the effectiveness of any method for responding to student writers.

DEVELOPMENTAL AND COGNITIVE PROCESSES

As teachers learn about students' developmental processes, however, they will realize that many of their students' papers' shortcomings result not from inadequate teaching, but from the natural processes of maturation and cognition. Only after a careful consideration of these two factors might teachers then consider possible instructional inadequacies.

To begin with, cognitive psychologists believe intellectual tasks such as argumentation are *developmentally* difficult for students moving from concrete and less abstract thought to a more complex thinking in which they can "subordinate reality to possibility" (Jacob, 1984, p. 37). The fact that most students are inexperienced at thinking abstractly accounts for much of the struggle evident in student argumentation.

Another limiting developmental aspect is *egocentricity*—the inability to comprehend the perspective of others (Bjorklund, 1989). Educators see a strong link between egocentrism and lack of audience awareness (Barritt & Kroll, 1978; Lunsford, 1979). Writing that is not directed toward an audience but to the writer—for example, Flower's (1979) writer-based prose—shares many features of the egocentric speech discussed by cognitive psychologists such as Piaget and Vygotsky (cited in Lunsford, 1979). Novice writers do not communicate to an audience so much as they simply express their own cognitions in language that is full of meaning for them but often vague or incomprehensible to readers. Even though students' papers may be addressed to a specific audience in outward form, those papers often remain simply a record of a kind of inner dialogue on paper, an exploration of ideas and rhetorical possibilities with which the writers themselves are still unfamiliar. Students are, in effect, talking to themselves on paper. At this stage, they produce discourse that is highly associative, in which careful reading can reveal the path of the student's thoughts, but which fails to make a presentation of ideas and facts that is clear, well organized, or strongly reasoned.

Finally, the limitations of cognition itself constrain the act of writing. Many developmental psychologists compare cognition with the information processing of computers and suggest the idea of limited capacity (Bjorklund, 1979). Writers have many tasks to deal with when writing and only so many "megabytes" of cognitive resources at any one moment. Using another analogy, Flower and Hayes (1980) refer to the writer's "juggling of constraints" (p. 33), in which a writer's struggle with the constraints of composition resembles a juggler's attempts to manipulate three balls at once. In other words, the writer must manipulate the constraints of content, written speech, and the rhetorical problem itself. The computer and juggling analogies explain why, when students struggle with the demands or constraints of abstract argumentation, they have fewer mental resources to expend on the problems of written discourse; therefore, it is natural that student writing errors— at both surface and content levels—may multiply when the creation of discourse involves strong emotions or unfamiliar concepts, conditions often present in persuasive writing.

The following student's letter effectively illustrates this combination of limitations and high enthusiasm. The enthusiasm occurred when the local state board of education announced its intentions to increase the school year by 20 days. My eighth-grade students were hopping mad and anxious to let others—especially the governor—know how they felt. But even with all their passion (and possibly in part because of it), students' letters to the governor exemplify the young writer's struggles with persuasive discourse because of difficulties with abstract thought, lack of audience awareness, and cognitive juggling. Although this letter writer (I call her Darlene) is an eighth grader, teachers of older students will recognize weaknesses common to many novice writers:

Dear Governor,

(1) I really think the idea of 20 more days of school is truly unfair. (2) Kids don't want to go, plus they need a break. (3) Why don't you ask the kids what they feel about this? (4) It's them who are going to school, not you, and it's their vacation that will be cut short by this, not yours. (5) Anyway, the heat will make them so tired by the end of the day that they can't learn.

(6) This idea of yours will also put a strain on the school. (7) They will have to come up with enough money to pay for many different people's salaries for these extra 20 days and since it will be so hot outside we will need much more air-conditioners in the school. (8) Why don't you just spend that money on better textbooks, other than 20 extra days of school, which will cost a lot more?

(9) There are many solutions to this problem. (10) You can hire better teachers, keep kids with bad grades in school longer, or like I said before, buy new and better textbooks for the students to use. (11) Another thing you can do is cut back on the days we have off

and only let us off in an emergency, because a half an inch of snow is really no big deal. (12) So please take my ideas into consideration and you will see that 20 extra days of school is really not necessary.

Sincerely,

Darlene

Darlene's letter, with its haphazardly arranged and scantily developed arguments (not to mention surface errors of syntax and punctuation) is typical. But if teachers read papers like hers with an awareness of developmental and cognitive factors and understand the real problems that students experience when they attempt to write effective argument, they should feel less disheartened. Most importantly though, it should indicate to writing teachers the need for a response to student persuasive discourse that is developmentally and cognitively realistic— a response that respects and utilizes what is known about how students develop, think, and write.

RESPONDING TO STUDENT ARGUMENTATION

What type of response would that be? Ironically, even though teachers may lack methods of effective response, they do not lack information on how *not* to respond. Many educators concerned with improving writing instruction have identified ineffective and even harmful teacher responses. These include making highly diffused, unfocused comments (Hillocks, 1986); overwhelming students with both editing and content concerns at the same time (Freedman, 1987; Sommers, 1982); making comments that befuddle students with problems that they are unable to solve or sometimes even to understand (Freedman, 1984; Sommers,1982; Sperling, 1984; Zamel, 1985); overemphasizing surface-level errors (Griffin, 1982; Sperling, 1984; Zamel, 1985); and commandeering the paper away from the student (Freedman, 1987; Sommers, 1982; Zamel, 1985). Additionally, Lindemann (1987), in her guide for writing instruction in higher education, *A Rhetoric for Writing Teachers*, lists others: damning a paper with faint praise or snide remarks, intensive mistake marking to prove the teacher to be a superior error hunter, and condemning the writer's ideas. Obviously, these responses not only ignore maturational and cognitive factors, but they are traps into which over burdened teachers desperate to offer some kind of response can quite easily fall, especially when faced with scores of weakly argued, error-ridden papers.

Certainly, teachers want to avoid the pitfalls listed here. They want to respond to developing writers in a way that offers "feedback and guided learning" (Lindemann, 1987, p. 208), and they want to respond in a way that respects what educators know about how students grow, think, and write. But again, what type of response might that be?

One possibility lies in using concepts from Perelman and Olbrechts-Tyteca's *The New Rhetoric* (1971) to analyze student discourse. *The New Rhetoric* is, in large part, a compilation of what the authors call "techniques of argumentation" (pp. 185-349). These techniques are the basic elements of all rhetorical discourse, even those of the novice; these are rhetorical strategies as old and as new as argument itself—strategies that appear whenever people attempt to convince or persuade one another. If teachers reexamine student argumentation, looking for evidence of Perelman and Olbrechts-Tyteca's techniques of argumentation, they will find themselves looking through a different set of lenses and seeing something very new in student discourse. More importantly, this kind of analysis suggests ideas for effective teacher response.

What follows is an example of this kind of analysis, looking again at Darlene's letter, but this time trying to discover what strategies the writer might have used.

ANALYZING STUDENT DISCOURSE FOR TECHNIQUES OF ARGUMENTATION

One technique of argumentation reveals itself in the first four sentences of Darlene's letter:

> I really think the idea of 20 more days of school is truly unfair. Kids don't want to go, plus they need a break. Why don't you ask the kids what they feel about this? It's them who are going to school, not you, and it's their vacation that will be cut short by this, not yours.

In this segment, Darlene asks the governor to look at things from a different point of view: the students' perspective. Perelman and Olbrechts-Tyteca's *The New Rhetoric* (heretofore cited as TNR) identifies this type of argument as the "technique of reciprocity" (1987, pp. 221-227). This technique involves the "concept of symmetry" (p. 221) and "can result from the transposition of points of view" (p. 222). In other words, one should treat others as one would wish to be treated. Perelman and Olbrechts-Tyteca consider this technique to be one of the main precepts of Judeo-Christian and humanistic ethics (p. 222). A label more apt for the writing classroom might be "How Would You Feel?" Students often argue for fairness, as if to say, *We are all equal; there is no privileged position.* Asking "How Would You Feel?" is one of their main strategies.

Another technique appears in sentence 5: "Anyway the heat will make them so tired by the end of the day that they can't learn." Here is an example of what Perelman and Olbrechts-Tyteca call the "dissociation of appearance and reality" (pp. 415-420). Darlene suggests that what seems true is only the *appearance* of reality. She argues that, although it appears logical to believe that 20 more days of school would produce more learning, this is only the appearance of reality. The real truth is that the heat—a likely accompaniment of those extra days in June and August—will create conditions so uncomfortable that the students will be unable to learn. In this way, Darlene tries to dissociate what her audience has associated with reality from what is, to her, only the appearance of reality. Students find this age-old dissociation of A (what looks real) from B (what is, in actuality, the truth) quite useful in many persuasive situations. A good practical label for this strategy is "The Real Truth."

TNR's "technique of act/consequence" (pp. 263-273) is also one that students frequently use. This technique—which can be called "Consequences"—dominates most of Darlene's second paragraph (sentences 6 and 7):

> This idea of yours will also put a strain on the schools. They will have to come up with enough money to pay for many different people's salaries for these extra 20 days and since it will be so hot outside we will need much more air-conditioners in the school.

When rhetors make a causal link between an act and its (real or possible) results, they use the "technique of act/consequence." This pragmatic argument demands that any act be judged good or bad by its consequences. Simply stated: If good comes of an act, the act is a worthy one; if evil ensues, the act that caused it is undesirable. Darlene uses the "Consequences" of higher costs to label the act of adding 20 days to the school year unwise.

Darlene's next four sentences (8-11) display the technique of "means/end dissociation" (TNR, pp. 273-278) or "A Better Way":

> Why don't you just spend that money on better textbooks, other than 20 extra days of school, which will cost a lot more.
>
> There are many solutions to this problem. You can hire better teachers, keep kids with bad grades in school longer, or like I said before, buy new and better textbooks for the students to use. Another thing you can do is cut back on the days we have off and only let us off in an emergency.

This is a strategy of dissociation similar to the "dissociation of appearance and reality technique" explained earlier. First, the rhetor dissociates the act that is undesirable to her (in this case, 20 extra days of school) from its purpose, which we can assume to be better education for students. Then the writer elaborates other solutions that might be more effective or less costly. Darlene suggests that the governor could buy better textbooks, keep only the "kids with bad grades" in school longer, hire better teachers, and not let students have snow days when road conditions are not serious. Using this "A Better Way" technique, rhetors claim that other solutions to a problem are available, and that these alternatives are better than the one they oppose.

The last technique uncovered by this analysis of Darlene's letter is "speech and speaker interaction" (TNR, pp. 316-321) in the closing sentence: "So please take my ideas into consideration and you will see that 20 extra days of school is really not necessary." Like many of these patterns of argument found earlier, "speech and speaker interaction" is described in the teachings of classical rhetoricians who cautioned that "a speaker should inspire confidence" (p. 318). When Darlene politely asks the governor to "please take my ideas into consideration," she uses courtesy to give a good impression of herself, which might lead her audience to a kinder consideration of her case. Writers try to indicate through their words that they are good and reasonable people; they hope that this goodwill reflects back on their writing, making their words even more credible and valuable. This technique, which can be called "You Are What You Write," is a powerful way to explain the need for proper form and courtesy in writing.

Looking at Darlene's paper through the lenses of *The New Rhetoric* has revealed new things. Darlene, in less that 250 words, has intuitively utilized five techniques of argumentation. Where before many teachers might have seen only failure, this analysis reveals a genuine richness of argument. Moreover, her paper is typical in its richness. Other students used these same techniques and others as well. (See Table 2.1 for a summary of this analysis.)

The following is a list of other strategies found often in my students' letters to the governor, and they will be recognized by anyone familiar with student argumentation. For each technique there is a short explanation as well as an example from my students' discourse. Also, the TNR label is given as well as a term that is more student-oriented. (These are the techniques from *The New Rhetoric* that students used most often, but there are many more. I hope interested teachers will consult this work or the more concise The Realm of Rhetoric (1982) by Perelman.)

Table 2.1. TNR Analysis.

Student Discourse	TNR Analysis
(1) I really think the idea of 20 more days of school is truly unfair. (2) Kids don't want to go, plus they need a break. (3) Why don't you ask the kids what they feel about this? (4) It's them who are going to school, not you, and it's their vacation that will be cut short by this, not yours.	How Would You Feel? (TNR's Technique of Reciprocity)
(5) Anyway, the heat will make them so tired by the end of the day that they can't learn.	The Real Truth (Dissociation of Appearance and Reality)
(6) This idea of yours will also put a strain on the schools. (7) They will have to come up with enough money to pay for many different people's salaries for these extra 20 days and since it will be so hot outside we will need much more air-conditioners in the school.	Consequences (Act/Consequence)
(8) Why don't you just spend that money on better textbooks, other than 20 extra days which will cost a lot more?	A Better Way (Means/End Dissociation)
(9) There are many solutions to this problem. (10) You can hire better teachers, keep kids with bad grades in school longer, or like I said before, buy new and better textbooks for the students to use. (11) Another thing you can do is cut back on the days we have off and only let us off in an emergency, because half an inch of snow is really no big deal.	
(12) So please take my ideas into consideration and you will see that 20 extra days of school is really not necessary.	You Are What You Write (Speech/Speaker Interaction)

"Who Said So?" ("Argument From Authority," TNR, pp. 305-310)

The rhetor uses the prestige of a person who holds an opinion to raise the status of that opinion: "My mother who teaches in public school also doesn't want the school year extended." The rhetor advances the argument or opinion by advancing the status of the person who holds it. (This technique includes the high status of a unanimous opinion: "My whole school is signing a petition against the 20 days.")

"Equal Treatment" (Rule of Justice," TNR, pp 218-220)

The rhetor requests the same treatment for two beings or situations of the same type. This is very similar to "How Would You Feel?", but instead of asking the audience to "Do unto others . . . ," rhetors ask for all similar beings or situations to be treated uniformly. The arguer's job is to show similarity between the two cases: When a student argues, "I think this is unfair because look at you, you are the governor, and you did just fine with only 180 days of school," that student must elaborate correspondences between the situation of the governor when he was in school and the situation of present-day students. (Note also that this sentence can also include the "Consequences" argument as it implies that the old system can produce successful people such as the governor. Teachers can reveal these two possibilities to students and then let the students decide which direction to take as they elaborate.)

"Can You Pay the Price?" ("Argumentation by Sacrifice," TNR, pp. 248-255)

This is a technique of comparing two things by what one is willing to give up or sacrifice for them. The audience is asked to decide how much it is willing to pay to achieve a certain result: The rhetor asks, *In order to get A, are you willing to sacrifice B?* Many of my students tried to convince the audience that other uses of educational money should not be sacrificed to the cost of 20 more school days, for example, "the *money squandered on this plan* could be *better spent on more helpful programs.*" (See Table 2.2 for a summary of all the TNR techniques discussed.)

USING TECHNIQUES OF ARGUMENTATION IN THE CLASSROOM

One valuable benefit from analyzing student persuasive discourse for the techniques of argumentation is that it leads to a new appreciation for students' argumentation and away from an emphasis on faults and

Table 2.2. TNR Response Terms.

TNR Techniques	Examples from Student Prose
How Would You Feel? (TNR's technique of reciprocity)	Why don't you ask the kids *how they feel* about this? It's *them* who are going to school, not you and it's *their* vacation that will be cut short, not *yours*." "Most adults think it will improve our education and that we will thank them when we are older. Students have very different opinions."[a]
The Real Truth (dissociation of appearance and reality)	"(*You think they will learn but . . .*) The heat will make them so tired by the end of the day that they can't learn." "Most *adults think* it will improve our education and that we will thank them when we are older. *Students* have very *different opinions*."[a]
Consequences (act/consequence)	"This idea of yours *will put a strain on the schools* They will have to come up with enough money to pay for . . . salaries . . . air conditioning." "The cost alone is *overwhelming*."
A Better Way (means/end dissociation)	"Why don't you just spend that money on better textbooks. . . . *There are many [other] solutions* to this problem . . . hire better teachers, keep kids with bad grades in school longer, or . . . buy new and better textbooks. . . . cut back on days we have off . . ." "The money squandered on this plan *could be better spent on other programs*.[b]
You Are What You Write (speech/speaker interaction)	"So *please* take my ideas into *consideration*. (Proper form, politeness, courtesy)
Who Said So? (argument from authority)	"My *mother who teaches in public school* also doesn't want the school year ended. My *whole school* is signing a petition . . ."

Table 2.2. TNR Response Terms (cont.).

TNR Techniques	Examples from Student Prose
Equal Treatment (rule of justice)	I think this is *unfair* because look at *you*, you are the governor, and *you did just fine* with only 180 days of school."
Can You Pay the Price? (argumentation by sacrifice)	"The money *squandered* on this plan could be better spent on more helpful programs."

[a]Arguments can cover two or more techniques simultaneously. In this case, Darlene is asking the reader to see things from her perspective *and thereby* see the real truth.

[b]Again, the same statement uses two techniques: The writer first points out that other solutions exist, and then claims they will be sacrificed if the initial plan is implemented.

inadequacies. Writing teachers can see the rich potential of students' efforts; for, whether from conversation, from the media, from books, or possibly even from instruction, young writers do internalize at least the germinal aspects of many of the major methods of argumentation. Furthermore, finding these beginning points of mature, effective argument suggests an answer to the most crucial question of response: How can teachers best help young writers improve their persuasive writing?

Teachers can first use the "techniques of argumentation" to respond to student writing in perhaps the most important way: They can communicate the sense of discovery of rich potential they find in student discourse to the students themselves.

Certainly teachers must let students know how much work they have yet to do to convince their readers, but first they can reveal to young writers the possibilities for elaborating strategies already begun. Shaugnessy, in *Errors and Expectations* (1977), asked writing teachers to search students' writing for "clues to their reasoning" as well as for gaps and misjudgments (p. 292). She believed that teachers could point out to students certain patterns of thought already in their writing that could be expanded further (pp. 257-258, 274). Revealing "techniques of argument" to the students is a method of response that can enable teachers to do just that; moreover, their response will be grounded in the venerable tradition of rhetoric.

Beginning writers often become confused and discouraged when they try to evaluate their early drafts for improvement. The teacher's new perceptions gained from searching student writing for potential rather than error can help students precisely at that crucial evaluation and revision stage. Instead of centering students' attention on their papers' shortcomings, teachers can use TNR analysis and response to reveal the techniques and directions that students have already begun. "Look at this argument you have used," the teacher says. "This is a technique used by great speakers and writers for centuries. How might you expand what you have started?" Rather than failed attempts, first drafts become rough maps of techniques begun and paths to follow.

Most teachers, of course, would find it impossible to do this kind of analysis of every student's paper, but a realistic alternative would be to pass out to the class copies of one or two students' papers, identifying and explaining important techniques of argumentation, similar to the previous analysis of Darlene's paper. Students will see that they too use "Consequences" or "A Better Way." They will appreciate the appeal of "How Would You Feel?" that a classmate uses and see opportunities to apply it themselves. Students can return to their own first drafts (and respond to their peers' drafts) armed with a sense of the possibilities they find and of the directions in which to take those techniques they now can see. A good follow-up activity to this, of course, would be discussions on how to elaborate some techniques.

There are other possibilities as well. During a prewriting discussion on a topic, the teacher can list techniques as they surface in students' comments. Then, after the discussion, the teacher can explain the techniques and ask students for ways to expand and elaborate on them. Not only does this exercise give structure to a favorite class activity, it also provides review of the idea of techniques of argument and practice in expanding arguments. The papers written after this preliminary activity should be fuller and more controlled because much of the preliminary idea thrashing has been done en masse. Other related assignments that can be made to individuals, pairs, or groups are: (a) after introducing a technique, the teacher asks students to list other topics for which this technique would be effective; (b) students argue for or against a given topic using specified techniques; or (c) after identifying techniques used by one writer, students construct an opposing argument by weakening one of the writer's techniques and finding other techniques that make opposite points. Students can search many sources for evidence of techniques of argument, such as editorials, editorial cartoons and letters to the editor, political speeches, ads (video and print), and class discussions. A more dramatic assignment is for writers to create a dialog in which fictional characters argue about a topic. When the dialog is enacted, classmates in the audience can list the techniques they hear the characters using, commenting on the effectiveness of each.

When teachers guide students to elaborate the techniques they have begun, they set the stage for something more than simply a judgmental or evaluative act. The teacher and students collaborate. This collaborative student-teacher venture provides learners with understandings of rhetorical problems and then, most importantly, offers strategies for their solutions. Moreover, this understanding of, practice in, and gradual internalization of rhetorical techniques resembles the instructional scaffolding (Knudson, 1990) and substantive facilitation (Scardamalia & Bereiter, 1986) that has been shown in recent research to be effective in writing instruction.

Furthermore, opportunities for collaboration can be widened to collaboration among students. This becomes apparent when the potential for TNR response is investigated in relation to two educators' recent work on collaborative groups and writing workshop classrooms. Examining the ideas of Gere (1987) and Brooke (1991) discloses how well TNR techniques would suit collaborative learning and writers' roles in workshops.

Gere (1987), in her work on writing groups, lists three imperatives for successful collaborative learning: (a) groups must be sufficiently prepared and committed, (b) appropriate tasks are clear, and (c) evaluation or debriefing is built into the life of the group.

First, in order to prepare students for semi-autonomous collaborative tasks, Gere (1987) encourages teachers to reinforce needed skills with activities built into classroom routine. Opportunities for TNR skill reinforcement activities can be built around everyday classroom procedures. For example, teachers can present discourse (either published or written by students) to the class at the beginning of the period and as attendance is taken ask for short individual responses about the argumentation. Teachers can ask questions such as: What technique or argument is used first? . . . second? How does the writer elaborate that technique? Why do you think the writer presented this technique first? . . . this one last? What technique seems to you to be weakest? . . . strongest? What technique could be used to argue in another or the opposite direction? What type of audience does each technique appeal to? Are there any other techniques not used that could advance this writer's cause? Would you rearrange the order? What would happen if the last argument were used at the beginning? In this way, students learn the basics of identifying and then expanding arguments on an everyday basis.

When Gere stated in her first criteria that students must be committed, she meant that collaborative groups must have a purpose. Rather than merely evaluating final drafts, they must be involved with reading and working with unfinished work. This "indeterminate" situation is what empowers them, and without this empowerment there is no commitment. Obviously, TNR analysis and response is a technique of revision response that can "invest [students'] work with the authority of shaping future drafts" (Gere, 1987, p.106).

TNR response can advance Gere's second and third criteria as well. It is a response that is, as mentioned earlier, appropriate to revision, and it is also *developmentally* appropriate to the students because they will be working with ideas mat they have generated themselves. Working on improving arguments that they have begun, students are operating in what Vygotsky calls the "zone of proximal development" (cited in Gere, 1987, p. 109). (I return to this aspect of TNR analysis later.) For that same reason, it is a procedure that can be made clear to students with frequent practice (as discussed earlier) and modeling. (See the following section on Brooke (1991) and Ritchie (1991) for more on practice and modeling.) Therefore, when students have made it a part of their writer-response repertoire, it will facilitate end-of-the-session evaluation reports, for example, "Our group found three techniques in Jim's paper: 'Consequences,' 'How Would You Feel?', and 'You Are What You Write,' and we started expanding the first by thinking up more of the long-term costs of the change." Asking students to identify and suggest ways to enlarge techniques of argument they find in peers' rough drafts would be a great improvement over vague or overly broad task assignments Gere (1987) mentioned such as "critique your partner's paper" (p. 108).

Gere also mentioned the importance of trust in the atmosphere of the collaborative writing class: "All writers find sharing their work risky because their language is vulnerable to attack by others" (p. 103). TNR analysis could help build an environment of trust because it is nonevaluative. The task is to find beginnings and to elaborate, not to correct or delete. Because the goal of reader and audience is to assess and to amplify, students collaborate as Gere would recommend, and "both writer and audience become members of the same language community" (p. 84) rather than fashion an uncomfortable imitation of teacher-critic versus student-writer.

While Gere's work explores collaborative settings and writers' groups in general, Brooke (1991) examines the more autonomous writing workshop setting and how it leads novice writers to take on broader and deeper roles, allowing them to connect writing with real uses in their lives. Here, too, TNR analysis fits well as can be seen in an examination of Brooke's list of criteria for successful writing workshop classrooms. (He used criteria from Atwell's [1987] *In the Middle* and then incorporated two criteria of his own that referred to his ideas on writers' roles.)

He stated that for a writing workshop environment to be successful, student writers should experience: (a) ownership (their own topics, their own decisions about their drafts); (b) predictable times for predictable writing activities; (c) response in many modes (writers can choose different ways for readers to respond, e.g., as evaluators, editors, critics, or collaborators); (d) writing as a process; (e) cues to students that signal different roles for the student beyond student-as-examinee; and (f) a variety of writers' roles.

First, Brooke (1991) believes that "to teach writing effectively, we teachers need to create environments where writers' roles can connect directly to situations our students care about" (p. 27), and their writing experiences must fit students' own agendas and purposes (p. 84). When students begin to write about things they care about, they usually find themselves in the argumentational-persuasive mode, and TNR response clearly applies. Because this procedure helps students expand their own topics, ownership is a given. Second, as explained in the section on Gere earlier, TNR response is clear enough to be routinized by student writers, so it can become one of the "predictable" writing activities that writing workshop participants call into use. There should be many ways for responders to collaborate with writers—as stated earlier—and TNR response would be used when the writer wanted the responder to be in a collaborative mode.

Once again, this type of response reinforces the idea of writing as process and can be presented to students with the types of teacher and group demonstration sessions done by Ritchie (1991) in Brooke's work, similar to Atwell's (1987) writers' workshop minilessons, familiar to many writing teachers. For example, Ritchie gradually familiarizes her students with what she calls "writerly behavior" when she brings in a piece of her own writing in draft stage and reads it to the class, asking for suggestions. Then she rewrites the paper and asks for input. Eventually, she expands this into modeling peer-response group behavior as she and a few other students help her revise her paper in a fishbowl demonstration to the rest of the class. Little by little students use the behaviors she models with their own papers in writers' groups. This could be done in a similar fashion with argumentation. The teacher brings in a letter-to-the editor- style piece; reads it to the class; and asks for help from the class in identifying techniques, suggesting other techniques, finding the weakest and strongest techniques, finding ways to elaborate, and suggesting the best arrangement. Finally, the collaborative-response mode for groups can be demonstrated in a fishbowl presentation with the teacher and an improvised response group in front of the class.

Brooke's (1991) last two criteria deal with writers' roles. The first of these has to do with what he calls "cues." When students have been seated facing front and are told to be attentive and take notes, these are cues for the student-as-examinee role. New cues are needed to signal students to "explore other roles as reflective thinkers, as contributors to social debate, as persuaders" (p. 3). When students are given opportunities to create knowledge rather than simply to receive it, to choose topics and make decisions about what and how to write, this points them toward new roles (Brooke, 1991). The realm of argumentation and persuasive discourse is *the* medium for many of these new roles of reflecting, exploring, and persuading. Therefore, clear, demonstrable tools for discourse revision such as TNR will be a great help in these new roles.

THREE OTHER CONCEPTS FROM THE NEW RHETORIC

Beyond the techniques noted earlier, three other rhetorical concepts from TNR offer a great deal to the teaching of persuasive writing: presence, convergence, and adherence.

The first, *presence* (TNR, pp.115-119), refers to the "verbal magic" (p. 117) that a writer or speaker uses to influence the audience. This is not the ability to appear logical or reason clearly, but the "evoking [of] realities that are distant in time and space" (Perelman, 1982, p. 35). The rhetor makes others feel the presence of things they would otherwise ignore or discount. Concrete description, illustrations, and vivid word choice are all ways for the writer/speaker to project his or her beliefs into the audience's consciousness. For example, Darlene might bring presence to the discomfort of those extra days of school by vividly describing a sticky, humid classroom during the boiling heat of summer.

The second term, *convergence* (TNR, pp. 471-473), has to do with the arrangement of information or arguments to lead the audience to a single conclusion. Perelman discounts the idea of a single, most effective order for all arguments and believes that rhetorical arrangement must fit the demands of each particular argument. If he were teaching adolescents to arrange their argumentation, he most likely would suggest trial and experiment to find the arrangement that produces the best effect. Teachers should assign students or collaborative groups to construct different arrangements of the same arguments, and then have students report on their choices of arrangement, describing the results and justifying their final choices. Additionally, the class can analyze, explain, and even rearrange the persuasive discourse of other writers. Such exercises in experimentation with convergence or arrangement of argument would not lead to a general formula of argument organization, but would instead produce writers experienced in building effective discourse organization.

Finally, the third term, *adherence* (TNR, pp. 1-4), gives the teacher and student of written argument a fruitful context or environment in which to work. The authors of TNR write that people argue to change me ideas of others not totally, but in *some degree* (Perelman & Olbrechts-Tyteca, 1971). Arnold (1982), in the introduction to Perelman's *The Realm of Rhetoric*, wrote, "Perelman makes a happy choice of terms. Instead of writing of 'acceptance' and 'rejection' of claims, he speaks of the writer or speaker as seeking 'to elicit or increase the *adherence* of an audience'" (p. xii). Because it lessens the potential for student failure in an extreme win or lose situation, the idea of adherence produces an environment more conducive to trial and error in arguing. Teachers and students can think in terms of *degrees* of persuasion rather than total success or total failure. This change in the sometimes warlike atmosphere of classroom argumentative discourse may make it easier for students to consider alternative points of view.

A further word on the potential of the concept of adherence needs to be said because it seems so relevant to much of the current thought on the type of student-owned writing mentioned earlier in the ideas of Gere and Brooke; and it seems doubly valuable because of the unformed positions of young thinker-writers.

Any writing teachers who have opened their classrooms to include student-generated topics such as abortion, censorship, school board policies, dress codes, community problems, and political elections have probably seen students go through a rich, but painful odyssey, from certainty about a subject to confusion and then, the teacher hopes, to a deeper understanding. Often the task of writing about a particular topic forces students to closely examine what may be strongly held but perhaps little examined beliefs. This confusion is amplified when they encounter the sometimes powerful reactions of their classmates, often blinking in wonderment that others could believe so differently from themselves and that there could be such good objections to their own arguments. These students experience—as do others whose beliefs are not so strongly held initially—what Perelman and Olbrechts-Tyteca (1971) might call a shift in their "degrees of adherence."

Brooke wrote, "I suggest that we see writing as part of a much larger and more basic activity: the development of negotiation of individual identity in a complex social environment" (p. 5). He called this "development of self within a complex arena of competing social forces," identity negotiation (p. 12). He believes that our individual selves, as seen by ourselves and others, are composed of a "conglomerate of stances we take towards the role expectations that surround us" (p. 17). In other words, as these students become engaged with topics they care about, and as they explore those ideas and the responses of others, they not only learn about writing but about the rhetoric of the self. For example, in Brooke's book on writers' roles, Ritchie (1991) chronicles the experiences of one of her college composition students, Brad, who moves from what she called an "authoritarian" to a "dialogic" stance (pp. 125-135). In the writing workshop environment Ritchie provided, Brad moved from writing in which he merely made imperious pronouncements about the goodness of his own beliefs and the illogic and immorality of those who hold beliefs other than his own to writing that took into account "multiple perspectives, and recognize[s] the complexity of the issues he was writing about" (p. 133). The writing classroom that allows students to change their ideas and their attitudes toward the ideas of others not only leads to better argumentation, but may help students gain deeper understandings of their own beliefs and those of others. As students become aware of the range of opinions diverse from their own, writing becomes an "aid for tolerance" (p. 150). If, however, teachers, set up a battlelike or pseudo-debate context for argumentation, then they freeze students' positions in their initial stances. Defining argument in terms of degrees of adherence allows students to modify, deepen, and enlarge their newly forming beliefs.

Another phenomenon teachers with students engaged with self-determined subjects note is that at first the writing can often be much worse than the writing students perform when working on lighter, less consuming topics. As mentioned earlier in the section on juggling constraints, when students' mental resources are struggling with what they really believe and how their audiences might respond, they have less attention and cognitive resources for the actual task of writing. Teachers will need to find simple and flexible procedures for students to use to deal with life-changing, emotionally stormy topics. Here, again, TNR analysis and response fit well. To learn the TNR response routine, teachers and students can look at the discourse of published and classroom writers and simply ask, "What are the techniques (or arguments) and how are they expanded?" Then, once it is a familiar procedure, students will have TNR analysis and response as a form of structure to hold onto as they examine, reexamine, and reform their ideas and stances.

RESPONSE AND COGNITIVE DEVELOPMENT

Beyond the aptness of these three concepts is *the central* value of TNR response: It allows teachers and students to see potential rather than error. The reason it is able to reveal the potentialities in writers' papers is because it respects developmental realities. Students naturally utilize only those argumentation structures of which they already have at least an intuitive grasp, and with TNR response, rhetorical understanding identifies and advances what has occurred developmentally. Building from students' own beginnings ensures that the terms of progress will be realistic: not so far distanced from students' real abilities as to leave them behind in confusion, and not lagging so far behind as to leave them bored and uninterested. Teachers would not be focusing on strategies that the students either already have mastered or were not yet even approaching, but rather on what Vygotsky (1962) refers to as *ripening functions*. Student rhetors would feel linked to the vast historical background of argument and debate, but only gradually, as they understand and begin to use it. It is this developmental aspect that should allow TNR response to apply to all levels of writers. If such richness exists in the writing of eighth graders, then how much more readily might older students grasp and utilize the techniques of argumentation identified in their writing?

Because developmental and cognitive limitations determine much of students' abilities to argue and persuade, teachers cannot suddenly transform students into expert persuasive writers. But with these new lenses from *The New Rhetoric*, teachers can begin to make inexperienced writers aware of what they have begun and clarify the rhetorical directions they can follow. Using Perelman and Olbrechts-Tyteca's (1971) techniques of argumentation as a basis for analysis of and response to student persuasive discourse offers an effective way to discover and strengthen students' "ripening functions" of argument.

REFERENCES

Arnold, C.C. (1982). Introduction. In C. Perelman (Ed.), *The realm of rhetoric* (pp. vii-xx). Notre Dame IN: Notre Dame Press.

Atwell, N. (1987). *In the middle: Writing, reading, and learning with adolescents.* Upper Montclair, NJ: Boynton Cook.

Barritt, L.S., & Kroll, B.M. (1978). Some implications of cognitive developmental psychology for research in composing. In C. Cooper & L. Odell (Eds.), *Research on composing: Points of departure* (pp. 49-58). Urbana, IL: National Council of Teachers of English.

Bjorklund, D.F. (1989). *Children's thinking: Developmental function and individual differences.* Pacific Grove, CA: Brooks/Cole.

Brooke, R.E. (1991). *Writing and sense of self Identity negotiation in writing workshops.* Urbana, IL: National Council of Teachers of English.

Flower, L. (1979). Writer-based prose: A cognitive basis for problems in writing. *College English, 41*(1), 19-33.

Flower, L., & Hayes, J.R. (1980). The dynamics of composing: Making plans and juggling constraints. In L.W. Gregg & E.R. Sternberg (Eds.), *Cognitive processes in writing* (pp. 31-50). Hillsdale, NJ: Erlbaum.

Freedman, S.W. (1984). *The evaluation of, and response to student writing.* Paper presented at the 68th Annual Meeting of the American Educational Research Association, New Orleans. (ERIC Document Reproduction Service No. ED 247 605)

Freedman, S.W. (1987). *Response to student writing.* Urbana, IL: National Council of Teachers of English.

Gere, A.R. (1987). *Writing groups: History, theory, and implications.* Carbondale: Southern Illinois University Press.

Griffin, C.W. (1982). Theory of responding to student writing: The state of the art. *College Composition and Communication, 33,* 296-301.

Hillocks, G., Jr. (1986). *Research on written composition.* Urbana, IL: ERIC.

Jacob, S.G. (1984). *Foundations for Piagetian education.* Lanham, MD: University Press of America.

Knudson, R. (1989). Effects of instructional strategies on children's informational writing. *Journal of Educational Research, 83*(2), 91-96.

Lindemann, E. (1987). *A rhetoric for writing teachers.* New York: Oxford University Press.

Lunsford, A. (1979). Cognitive development and the basic writer. *College English, 41*(1), 38 46.

Nelms, B. (1990). Writing—A decade of progress? *English Journal, 79*(7), 92-93.

Perelman, C. (1982). *The realm of rhetoric* (W. Kluback, Trans). Notre Dame, IN: University of Notre Dame Press.

Perelman, C., & Olbrechts-Tyteca, L. (1971). *The new rhetoric: A treatise on argumentation* (J. Wilkinson & P. Weaver, Trans). Notre Dame, IN: University of Notre Dame Press. (Originally published as La Nouvelle Rhetorique: Traité de l'Argumentation. Presses Universitaires de France, 1958)

Ritchie, J. (1991). Connecting writers' roles to social roles. In R.E. Brooke (Ed.), *Writing and sense of self: Identity negotiations in writing workshops* (pp. 113-139). Urbana, IL: National Council of Teachers of English.

Scardamalia, M., & Bereiter, C. (1986). Research on written composition. In M.C. Wittrock (Ed.), *Handbook of research on teaching* (pp. 778-803). New York: Macmillan.

Shaugnessy, M. (1977). *Errors and expectations: A guide for teachers of basic writing.* New York: Oxford University Press.

Sommers, N. (1982). Responding to student writing. *College Composition and Communication, 33,* 148-156.

Sperling, M. (1984). *A look at response and the teaching of writing.* Paper presented at the 74th Annual Meeting of NCTE, Detroit, MI. (ERIC Document Reproduction Service No. ED 260 437)

Vygotsky, L.S. (1962). *Thought and language* (E. Hanfmann & G. Vakar, Trans). Cambridge, MA: MIT Press.

Zamel V. (1985). Responding to student writing. *TESOL Quarterly, 19*(1), 79-97.

CHAPTER 3

Teaching and Learning Argumentative Writing in the Middle School Years

Marion Crowhurst

The argument implicit in the title of this chapter—that persuasive/argumentative writing should be taught in the middle school—will seem surprising to some. This kind of writing is often considered too difficult for young students. It is best left, the argument goes, until the high school years.

In recent years, however, influential voices have been recommending that argumentative writing be included in the elementary school curriculum (Kress, 1982, Martin & Rothery, 1981, White, 1989). Indeed, White (1989) suggests that, in view of the importance of argument, to exclude elementary students from practice in writing argument "amounts to a form of linguistic disenfranchisement" (p. 9).

The argument of this chapter is threefold: (a) persuasive/argumentative writing is, in some ways, more difficult than some other kinds of writing; (b) it is not so difficult that is beyond students in the middle school years; and (c) it is a particularly appropriate kind of writing for students in the middle school because it is easy for alert teachers to help students find real purposes for writing in this mode.

In the first section of the chapter, selected typical student responses to argument assignments are discussed. In the second section, the question of difficulty is addressed with particular reference to student responses. The last section of the chapter suggests ways for teachers to help students develop skill in this important kind of writing.

STUDENT RESPONSES TO ARGUMENT ASSIGNMENTS

Most young writers in the 10 to 14 age range produce recognizably argumentative pieces when asked to persuade. Some of them write well. However, there are characteristic ways in which their compositions deviate from arguments written by more able, more mature students. Three characteristic problem areas are: structure, content and its organization, and style. Each of these problem areas is considered in turn in the discussion that follows. The discussion is based on approximately 1,200 arguments written on a variety of topics by students in grades 5, 6, and 7 for several different studies by the author (Crowhurst, 1977; 1986; 1987; 1991). In most cases, students were given approximately 40 minutes to write on an assigned topic.

Structure

Poor organization, often associated with lack of knowledge of argument structure, has often been commented on, not only for young students, but also for those in higher grades (Conry & Rodgers, 1978; Gorman, White, Brooks, MacLure, & Kispal, 1988; Pringle & Freedman, 1985). Common problems are beginnings and endings and, sometimes, responses that deviate in major ways from expected forms.

Beginnings and Endings.

Beginnings and endings are problematic for young students in writing argument—and, it may be noted, in other kinds of writing as well.[1] Arguments written by young writers commonly begin with opening position-taking statements of the "I think . . ." or the "No, I don't think . . ." variety. Usually, there is no further elaboration of the topic under discussion. Two examples of this kind of beginning follow:

---

[1]Langer (1986) described how typical ways of beginning and ending changed from age 8 through age 14 for both narratives and reports; and Crowhurst (1991b) described how sixth graders developed appropriate ways of beginning and ending letters in the course of long-term correspondence with older pen friends.

Example 1

I think that a fifty dollar clothes allowance is not a good idea because the six grader might spend it on cigarettes or other bad things. Also they might buy unacceptable clothing or use it for weird hairstyles. Also there is a good chance of it being stolen or lost and that is a lot of money to be missing. They also could keep it in the bank and have a fortune soon, and be using you. I think you could if you as a parent went with you. Also they would have nothing to get as clothes for Christmas and birthdays. I think it is a terrible idea. (Grade 6)

Example 2

I think the gym should be bigger because when you play basketball and stuff in there the gym is too small. I think the gym should be bigger because when you play basketball and your running down the court there's not enough room and the ball hits the stage or when you're taking a shot at the rafters also in vollyball it hits the rafters. The most important reason is that the gym is packed when there's an assembly and it's stuffy and when there's dances like the carnaval dance its crowded and everyone is pushing. That's why I think the gym should be bigger. (Grade 6)

Conclusions—if there are any—are commonly a repetition of the opinion with which the composition began, as seen in Examples 1 and 2. Other common ways of ending arguments include: hopes ("So I hope you will be able to change your mind"; "I sincerely hope that you consider on us using lockers"), appeals ("So please stop homework!" "So please don't let that rule go into effect"; "So please let us have pools. DECIDE QUICK."), thanks ("Thank you"), or some remark that clearly terminates the composition, most likely in an inappropriate way ("That's about it"; "I guess that's all I can think of"). A considerable number of arguments by young writers have no ending at all. That is, the last point in the argument is the last sentence of the composition; there is no concluding statement of any kind[2] as in Examples 3 and 4.

Example 3

Yes I think our parents could give us a clothing allowance of fifty dollars because I'm tired of my mom buying clothes I don't like. But I doubt I could persuade them to give me fifty dollars because they would probably think I would spend it on something else. (Grade 6)

---

[2]Langer (1986) and Crowhurst (1991b) found that letters and reports by young writers often ended without any kind of concluding statement.

Example 4

(ASSIGNMENT: The student was shown a picture of a performing whale and asked: Do you think the manager should be forced to close down this kind of entertainment? Persuade your teacher.)

No, it shouldn't be closed down because men keep them protected with medicine, drugs and bandages if they get sick or hurt. It allows them to play in a safe area without getting shot with a whale gun. Also when they have babies they're protected from enemies.

It provides entertainment (for) people, and some money they raise will go toward the food and the expansion of the property.

It allows scientists to study the animals more closely, find out about them, their speaking abilities, their ancestors, their habits, and the difference between each whale.

It teaches the whales to do tricks and to learn which colours are black, blue, red, and so on, and to trust people.

It could increase the population of whales since the whale population is low.

It creates jobs for people to train the animals and to teach them, and jobs of cleaning the pools and their cages. (Grade 6)

Compositions with a well-developed introduction, like that in Example 5, and a conclusion that attempts to make some kind of summary of the argument, as in Example 6, are uncommon at this age (see also British Columbia Ministry of Education, 1989):

Example 5

The manager has a hard decision ahead of him. Should or shouldn't he close down on this kind of entertainment? This kind of entertainment deals with sea creatures such as whales, seals, fish and others. This picture has a killer whale in it. Some people object to treating the whales this way. My opinion is that they should allow the whales to go free and not treat them this way. People should not take a wild creature, put him in a confined area, and train it to do tricks. The people in the picture seem to be enjoying the show, but they don't stop to think about what it does to the animal. The whale sometimes dies because of the cramped area, overfeeding or underfeeding, lack of proper foods, and even loneliness for a companion. I think whales or any other type of animal should not be subjected to this kind of treatment. Some people agree with me and others don't, but if you stop and think about it you may be able to see it my way and understand. How would you like it if you were used to the wild and (they) took you away from it, put you in a small area and taught you tricks? Would you like it? I don't think you would. So try to see it my way. The whale likely feels the same as you would if it happened to you. He doesn't like it any more than you would. Please think about it and try to understand. The manager should close down this entertainment, but then it is his hard decision. What do you think he should do? I hope he does close down and let all the sea animals free to go back to the wilds. (Grade 6)

Example 6

(ASSIGNMENT: The student was asked to persuade a young Australian, about to emigrate to Canada, that Vancouver would be a good place to live.)

Vancouver is a beautiful place to live with all its new smells and interesting places to visit. One main attraction is the Stanley Park Aquarium, and the Stanley Park Zoo, with all its new and exotic animals, reptiles and so much more.

One reason for living in Vancouver is that there are so many interesting places, such as the Pacific Science Centre, Chinatown, Granville Market and Stanley Park. Granville Market is always bustling with excitement and mouth-watering aromas, little shops tucked away in corners, and the big market with every vegetable and fruit imaginable. Smoked salmon is one favourite treat sold at Granville.

Downtown Vancouver is full of cars zooming up and down the roads and people talking gaily about their business trips, family, etc. Vancouver, with all its sights and sounds, new smells, and interesting places to visit, is surely a beautiful and exciting city to live in. (Grade 6)

Nonarguments.

Sometimes students, when asked to persuade, produce writing that does not resemble the expected form of an argument. The two most common forms of nonarguments are narratives and dialogues.

Narratives.

Sometimes a composition is produced that is entirely narrative, as in Examples 7 and 8:

Example 7

(ASSIGNMENT: The student was asked to persuade the teacher that a certain kind of punishment was appropriate for a misbehaving classmate.)

One day while our teacher was showing us how to do our math a boy shot an elastic band at me and I happen to be in a committee that decides what kind of punishments the children should get for breaking the rules of the class. I thought that he should get garbadge duty for two weeks because that would teach him not to shoot elastic bands any more and besides, it hurts. The teacher is in the committee too except we had a substitute that day. So I tried to convince her that my punishment would work, but she wouldn't hear of it. Finally I convinced her and the boy didn't shoot any more elastics. (At least not in school.) (Grade 5)

Example 8

I didn't like that, and I knew it. It just wasn't fair. Why, the poor whale didn't know any better, and the trainer made the whale jump up to touch the post, by bribing it. That is, just so some people could have some entertainment. On the other hand, though, I was in for a real problem now. The teacher had been to a whale show before, and she liked it alot. Now it was my job to convince the teacher I was right. So I went to the teacher one bright afternoon, and I told her my opinion. Now, when I told her this she said I had no right at all to say the whale didn't enjoy jumping up to the pole. There was fish on the end of the pole. Thats the whole point. I continued to explain that the whole deal was just a bribe, and the only reason Poirpy, the whale she saw in California, jumped up to the pole was because of the fish. Now that really got the teacher thinking. A tear trickled down her cheek, but she tried to controll herself and not look soft-hearted, rather firm. She said she never really knew what it was really like. What could you feel like if you spent the rest of your life entertaining people, but not on your own free will? Think about it. (Grade 6)

In both cases, the composition records the story of a disagreement and an attempt to persuade—what might be considered an argument in embryo. Narratives written in response to argument assignments were invariably of this kind.

In some narratives, the attempt to persuade is more fully developed, as in Example 9:

Example 9

The boy in the class started the whole thing. He was going to shoot an elastic at somebody with something in the elastic and wouldn't you know it, it was when they had a substitute teacher. It was also when a girl was writing something on the board, and naturally he figured the teacher wasn't watching him but was watching the girl up at the blackboard. But fortunately the teacher was watching him instead. But than comes the hard part trying to decide what to do with the boy. I think he should have a detention after school cleaning the floor or else sitting on his hands. If he would have hit somebody with it, it could do a lot of damage for instants it could hit him in the eye or other parts of his face. I think he should have detentions for the rest of the week. I think he should because he did something he wasn't supposed to so if I were the teacher I would give him the detention. (Grade 7)

Perhaps the explanation for this kind of response is that the student starts in the more familiar narrative mode as a way of easing into an unfamiliar kind of writing. If so, this kind of response may be viewed as yet another manifestation of problems students have with the beginnings of compositions, especially compositions in unfamiliar kinds of writing.

Dialogues. A small proportion of students respond with a dialogue recording a disagreement between two people,[3] as in Examples 10 and 11:

Example 10

I think it's okay for whales to be treated this way, because it's good entertainment for the people.

I don't think it's okay. Why? Because ever since whales started their own species they were free in their own waters, and able to live for themselves.

What do you mean, live for themselves?

I mean, for instance, they could catch their own food and be reliant on themselves.

Yes but their caretakers can feed them and they can be reliant on them.

Oh, of course, but they have to do a trick or stunt before they can get their food (just like a reward).

Yes, there's that too! But still, the people enjoy it, but the whales maybe don't.

Do you really think it's fair for a whale to be held in captivity for it's whole life until it's useless, just for the enjoyment of crowds? If the crowds ever thought of what it would be like working almost every day of their life just to be fed they wouldn't think it was so fair.

Well, I guess you're right. It isn't really fair for a free-born beast to be held captive. He should be free! (Grade 6)

Example 11

"You mean to say you don't like camping," I said.
"No I don't. I hate being outside."
"You must be crazy. The fresh air and sunshine is good for you."
"What I really hate is the bugs," she said.
"They aren't that bad if you put on repellant."
"Well what if you tip over the canoe."
"You'll live. You can swim."
"I guess it's okay. I'll give in. I'll go camping." (Grade 6)

In both compositions, the influence of the students' spoken language is clear. A persuasive composition is like a written version of an oral persuasive exchange.

---

[3]Dialogue responses to argument assignments have been reported also by Gorman et al., 1988; Gunderson, 1981; and by L. M. Fowler (personal communication) after the presentation of her paper, "Descriptive and Persuasive Writing Skills of Children" at the Annual Meeting of the American Educational Research Association, Montreal, April 1983.

Content and its Organization

Content in arguments is often very thin. Compositions are commonly shorter than narratives written by the same students (Bereiter & Scardamalia, 1982; Crowhurst, "1977, 1980, 1986; Pringle & Freedman, 1985). Compositions are sometimes very short as in Example 12.

Example 12
No I don't because children wouldn't get a good education. Children shouldn't be able to rule the school and thats what your doing. If everybody takes over the school there wouldn't be a school. (Grade 6)

Such compositions have been likened to a single conversational turn (Bereiter & Scardamalia, 1982) consisting of an opinion and a single reason.

Reasons are usually baldly and briefly stated without elaboration. Indeed many compositions consist of an opinion and a list of reasons. Reasons are commonly strung together in one paragraph as in Example 1 and Example 2 above. Sometimes the list structure is emphasized by numbering as in Example 13:

Example 13
I think kids should not have homework because:
1. It would cut out their social life.
2. They would be complaining of too much homework.
3. It would cut out any sports they want to do.
4. They can't go anywhere.
5. They would get detentions because their grumpy.
6. no games to play outside.
7. no friends in the house.
8. They wouldn't be aloud to watch T.V. (Grade 6)

Comparatively few students organize their work into logical paragraphs. Note that even the rather able argument in Example 5 earlier is written as a single paragraph. Students often fail to gather together related information. In Example 13, for example, reasons numbered 4 and 7 ("They can't go anywhere" and "no friends in the house") are related to number 1 ("It would cut out their social life"). In Example 4, the second to last sentence ("It could increase the population of whales since the whale population is low") is logically related to the point made near the beginning of the composition—that babies born in captivity are protected. Unrelated material sometimes appears unexpectedly, as in Example 1, in which—"I think you could if you as a parent went with you"—is unrelated to the reasons that precede and follow it. Longer compositions often repeat information rather than adding new information. Content, then, is often inadequate, repetitive, and/or poorly organized.

Style

The language of young writers in their written arguments is often marked by inappropriately informal and immature language. Crowhurst (1987) found, for example, that 6th graders were less likely than 12th graders to use the kinds of conjunctives that appropriately signal the development of an argument (*first of all, next, for one thing, all in all, finally*), that they made excessive use of the immature causal conjunctive *so*, and that they made little use of any adversative conjunctive except *but*, whereas 12th graders used a range of adversatives (*for example, however, rather, yet, on the other hand*). Young writers use less diverse, less precise vocabulary. Expressions and structures reminiscent of spoken language are common, like the appeals used to end compositions.

Summary

Arguments written by students in the middle school years often exhibit weaknesses in structure, content, and style. As to structure, compositions begin and end abruptly, reasons are usually not elaborated, and some students respond with unexpected kinds of writing such as narratives and dialogues. As to content, many students have little to say, and those with more content often fail to organize their material coherently. As to style, the language of young students echoes spoken language, they use a small number of connectives and lack the specialized connectives that mark the development of an argument, and they often lack specialized vocabulary.

Two points need to be made. The first is that the kinds of problems evident in the work of students in the middle school are different in degree but not in kind from those of students in the upper grades, except for the fact that it is very rare for an older student to respond with a nonargument (a narrative or a dialogue). The report of large-scale assessments in the United Kingdom, for example, noted that there was considerable overlap when the writing of 11-year-olds was compared with the writing of 15-year-olds (Gorman et al., 1988). The second point is that all compositions by young students show that the writers had some understanding of what an argument is; even narrative responses related the story of a difference of opinion, and most included at least an argument in embryo.

DIFFICULTY

A number of studies have found that young students perform less well in persuasive/argumentative writing than, for example, in narrative (Conry & Rodgers, 1978; Gorman et al., 1988; Pringle & Freedman, 1985; Purves, Degenhart, & Lehmann, forthcoming). Various reasons are suggested for students' poor performance in argument. One is that it is cognitively more difficult than narrative and some other kinds of writing (Moffett, 1968; Scardamalia, 1981; Wilkinson, Barnsley, Hanna, & Swan, 1980). Others point to the fact that students have little experience either reading or writing argument and so have no opportunity to learn the linguistic forms and structural patterns of argument (Gorman et al., 1988; Purves et al., forthcoming). Others criticize assignments that involve sterile topics far removed from the interests of young writers (Dixon & Stratta, 1986). All three of these factors undoubtedly play a part.

Writing a formal argument is a demanding cognitive task. Written argument characteristically employs linguistic forms that are not mastered early. The organization of argument depends on the logical development and arrangement of points. This is a more difficult task than the chronological ordering of narrative. Finding appropriate content is also more difficult in writing argument than in writing narrative. Story writers can take their narratives in any direction they wish and may draw on their whole world of experience in doing so. Relevant material is considerably more restricted when composing an argument; it is likely to be stored in scattered nodes in memory and not easily accessible.

However, not all argument topics are equally demanding. In the 1983 National Assessment of Educational Progress in the United States, more fourth graders were successful in persuading "Aunt May" on an issue of personal concern than in persuading the principal to change a school rule (Applebee, Langer, & Mullis, 1986). The second topic required more general arguments than the personal opinions that were appropriate for Aunt May. Universal topics and issues of public policy are especially difficult; they require information—and often vocabulary—outside students' usual experience.

Given the fact that argument topics are variably difficult and evidence that even young writers clearly have a concept of argument, even if limited, there seems no good reason to exclude argument from the elementary school. Persuasion and argument develop early in oral language, as any parent knows. Wilkinson claims that argument is one of two "natural or universal genres rooted in the human psyche"—the other being narrative (see chapter 1, this volume). Recent evidence suggests that precursors of exposition and argument appear in the writing of children in the primary grades (Martin & Rothery, 1981; Newkirk,

1985, 1987). Newkirk (1985) cited, as an example, the complex argument made by 6-year-old Sarah on a sign for a booth where children could make their own pin-on buttons:

> Desin-a-button
> only 75 cents the desins
> cuck.E.Cheese
> Unicorns rainbows
> and much much
> more
> it's better pric
> than last year
> 75 cents

The argument, Newkirk pointed out, was as follows:

> Major Assertion: Buy a design-a-button (implied).
> Major Reason: Low cost.
> Evidence: The cost is 75 cents.
> Evidence: The cost is lower than last year.
> Major Reason: The many designs (implied).
> Evidence: Chucky Cheese, Rainbows, Unicorns and more. (pp. 297-298).

A further reason for including persuasive/argumentative writing in the middle school curriculum is that it is easy to find contextually relevant topics for students in this mode of writing. There are always issues in a school or classroom about which students have firm opinions. In one set of compositions written by sixth graders, the following proved to be hot topics on school matters: the need for better facilities and equipment (lockers, a larger gym, a cafeteria, more computers, a swimming pool!!), requests for changes to the time table (more time for gym; longer recesses), unpopular colors for school T-shirts ("brown and yellow are dull and boring colors"), and the color of the newly painted inside walls ("pink is a girlie color and other kids will think we're sissy"). In addition to topics within the school, issues constantly arise within the community that are hotly debated in the media, such as on radio and televisions talk shows, in news broadcasts, or in editorials and letters to the editor. Such topics can often be productive for classroom discussion and debate and can provide rich opportunities for persuasive writing to real audiences, such as to newspapers; to local, state, and national politicians; or to public figures and organizations. Writing argument need not be a sterile exercise on topics far removed from students' interests. Relevant writing is likely to be motivated writing, and motivated students can more easily be helped to persevere until they have produced a strong case and a good piece of writing.

TEACHING ARGUMENT

"Teaching" argument does not mean only or mainly instructing students in the structure and linguistic forms of argument. Indeed, some believe that direct instruction is not useful because the acquisition of written language is a natural process akin to the acquisition of oral language (Emig, 1981; Newkirk, 1985; Teale, 1982). Martin pointed out that "since text and context are in a deterministic relation, various techniques can be used to improve a student's writing without him ever knowing what schematic structure [is]" (p. 28). For good writing to be produced, good writing contexts are necessary. Good writing contexts exist when students know clearly what they are writing about, who they are writing to, and why they are writing. As noted earlier, alert teachers will find abundant opportunity both within the school and in the larger community to promote such contextually relevant writing. A major component in a successful teaching program, then, is to help students find issues of real concern about which they can write for real purposes and real audiences.

A second useful component in an instructional program is to give instruction to students, individually or in groups, when they are ready to profit from it. In an intervention study (Crowhurst, 1991a), students in four sixth-grade classes were randomly assigned to one of four instructional groups for 10 lessons of differentiated instruction. One group received instruction in a simple model for persuasive/argumentative writing and practiced writing arguments for nine classes. A second group received instruction in the model and read and discussed pieces that exemplified the model, but did no writing. The other two groups read novels and wrote book reports. Both groups that were instructed in the model improved in the quality of their written arguments and in the organization of their compositions. Some students seemed particularly ready to benefit from the instruction. Compare, for example, the two compositions in Example 14 and Example 15, which are, respectively, a pretest and a posttest composition written by a boy in the writing group:

Example 14 (Pretest)

You have a very good idea about the fifty dollars for clothing each month. Sixth graders start running out of clothes fast because of them growing so fast. Parents, you usually get clothes that we don't like and won't wear. We want to get the things that are in, before the teenagers do. It would be a lot more fun than just sitting at home waiting for our parents to get home with our new clothes. We know what size we take and parents usually get too small of a size or too big. Parents and grandparents always get cute or really nice outfits for Christmas and special occasions, which we don't like but still have to wear, to please our parents and grandparents.

Example 15 (Posttest)

I believe that recess should be longer because we only have childhood once in a lifetime. Childhood is also supposed to be fun and it's not fun if we don't have much time to play.

Firstly, recess should be longer because we need more time to finish games and see friends from other classes. Take the soccer games grade 6's have at recess and lunch. We sometimes (most of the time) stay after the bell rang to finish the game. Recess is the only way we can see friends from other classes.

Secondly we don't get enough fresh air if the recess is too short. When it's nice and sunny it's nice to stay outside for a while longer. It gets hot inside and it's nice to go outside because sometimes cool breezes go by and cool us off.

Thirdly we don't wear off very much energy inside school or else we'll get in trouble, but outside we can wear off as much as we want. But the recess has to be long enough to be able to wear off at least 10 minutes of it.

We need more times to see other friends, we need fresh air and we need to wear off energy. So that's why I believe that there should be a longer recess.

The boy who wrote these pieces had no difficulty thinking up relevant things to say. His pretest composition was longer than many; he presented several persuasive reasons to support his point of view. However, organization was poor; related reasons (for example, problems associated with parents' choices) were not presented together. And he had no conclusion. His posttest was better organized and had a conclusion that summed up his argument and repeated his position. Instruction in form was not much help to students who could think of little to say. But it proved very helpful to those who, like this boy, could easily think of relevant content.

A third desirable component in an instructional program is the provision of opportunities for students to read persuasive/argumentative writing. Students will not learn the forms and structures of written argument if they never see these forms. One of the more interesting findings in the intervention study mentioned earlier (Crowhurst, 1991a) was that students who read and discussed arguments made significant gains in writing quality and organization, even though their instruction involved no writing practice at all. If topics of current public interest are brought into the classroom for discussion, editorials and letters to the editor can often provide relevant reading. Discussion of the relative effectiveness of different letters can facilitate discrimination between strong or weak arguments, between effective or less effective expression. Not all students will agree, of course, as to what is strong and what is weak, as to what is effective and what is not. But the discussion provoked by their disagreement is likely to lead to productive learning.

CONCLUSION

Young students do less well writing argument than writing, for example, narrative. There are several reasons for this. One is that argument is more cognitively demanding—in the location of relevant content, for example, and in the organization and logical use of that content. A second reason is their lack of experience; young students often lack the kind of experience that would give them information and vocabulary to discuss issues, and they also lack experience writing and reading argument—experience that would help them to acquire the organizational and linguistic structures that typify argument. The fact that they perform less well in argument is not reason enough to exclude argument from the middle school curriculum.

Indeed, there are several arguments for including argumentative writing in the curriculum of the middle school years: (a) persuasive uses of language occur early in spoken language, (b) precursors of argument appear in the writing of primary school children, (c) even poor persuasive writing in the preteen years reveals embryonic forms of argument, and (d) there are abundant opportunities for contextually relevant writing. It is important for teachers to be able to recognize the beginnings of argument in writing that does not yet conform to conventional expectations and to be able to recognize what children can do and not merely the deficiencies in their writing.

Argument comes naturally to children. There is every reason to encourage them to argue on paper as they so readily do in speech.

REFERENCES

Applebee, A.N., Langer, J.A., & Mullis, I.V.S. (1986). *The writing report card: Writing achievement in American schools.* Princeton, NJ: The National Assessment of Educational Progress.

Bereiter, C., & Scardamalia, M. (1982). From conversation to composition: The role of instruction in a developmental process. In R. Glaser (Ed.), *Advances in instructional psychology* (Vol. 2, pp. 1-64). Hillsdale, NJ: Erlbaum.

British Columbia Ministry of Education, Student Assessment Branch. (1989). *1988 B.C. Reading and Written Assessment Provincial Report.* Victoria: British Columbia Ministry of Education.

Conry, R., & Rodgers, D. (1978). *The British Columbia assessment of written expression: Summary report.* Vancouver: The University of British Columbia.

Crowhurst, M. (1977). *The effect of audience and mode of discourse on the syntactic complexity of the writing of sixth and tenth graders.* Unpublished doctoral dissertation, University of Minnesota.

Crowhurst, M. (1980). Syntactic complexity in narration and argument at three grade levels. *Canadian Journal of Education, 5*(1), 6-13.

Crowhurst, M. (1986). Revision strategies of students at three grade levels. *English Quarterly, 19*(3), 217-226.

Crowhurst, M. (1987). Cohesion in argument and narration at three grade levels. *Research in the Teaching of English, 21*(2), 185-201.

Crowhurst, M. (1991a). Interrelationships between reading and writing persuasive discourse. *Research in the Teaching of English, 25*(3), 314-338.

Crowhurst, M. (1991b). Two-way learning in correspondence between pen-friend pairs. *English Education, 23*(4), 212-224.

Dixon, J., & Stratta, L. (1986). Argument and the teaching of English. In A. Wilkinson (Ed.), *The writing of writing* (pp. 8-21). Milton Keynes: Open University Press.

Emig, J. (1981). Non-magical thinking: Presenting writing developmentally in schools. In C.H. Frederiksen & J.F. Dominic (Eds.), *Writing: The nature, development and teaching of written communication* (Vol 2, pp. 21-30). Hillsdale, NJ: Erlbaum.

Gorman, T.P., White, J., Brooks, C., MacLure, M., & Kispal, A. (1988). *A review of language monitoring 1979-83.* London: Assessment of Performance Unit, HMSO.

Gunderson, L. (1981, November). *Developmental characteristics of the writing of urban students at grades 2, 5, and 11.* Paper presented at the Annual Meeting of the National Council of Teachers of English, Boston.

Kress, G. (1982). *Learning to write.* London: Routledge and Kegan Paul.

Langer, J.A. (1986). *Children reading and writing: Structures and strategies.* Norwood, NJ: Ablex.

Martin, J.R. (1980). Exposition: Literary criticism. In J.R. Martin & J. Rothery (Eds.), *Working papers in linguistics* (No. 1. Paper 2). Sydney: Linguistics Department, University of Sydney.

Martin, J.R., & Rothery, J. (1981). The ontogenesis of written genre. In J.R. Martin & J. Rothery (Eds.), *Working papers in linguistics* (No. 2, pp. 1-59). Sydney: Linguistics Department, University of Sydney.

Moffett, J. (1968). *Teaching the universe of discourse.* Boston: Houghton Mifflin.

Newkirk, T. (1985). The hedgehog or the fox: The dilemma of writing development. *Language Arts, 62*(6), 593-603.

Newkirk, T. (1987). The non-narrative writing of young children. *Research in the Teaching of English, 21*(2), 121-144.

Newkirk, T. (1989). *More than stories: The range of children's writing.* Portsmouth, NH: Heinemann.

Pringle, I., & Freedman, A. (1985). *A comparative study of writing abilities in two modes at the grade 5, 8, and 12 levels.* Toronto: Ministry of Education.

Purves, A.C., Degenhart, R.E., & Lehmann, R. (forthcoming). *The IEA study of written composition II: International patterns of instruction and performance in writing.*

Scardamalia, M. (1981). How children cope with the cognitive demands of writing. In C.H. Frederiksen & J.F. Dominic (Eds.), *Writing: The nature, development and teaching of written communication* (Vol 2, pp. 81-103). Hillsdale, NJ: Erlbaum.

Teale, W.H. (1982). Toward a theory of how children learn to read and write. *Language Arts, 59*(6), 555-570.

White, J. (1989). Children's argumentative writing: A reappraisal of difficulties. In F. Christie (Ed.), *Writing in schools: Reader* (ECT 418 Language Studies Course, pp. 9-23). Geelong, Victoria: Deakin University Press.

Wilkinson, A., Barnsley, G., Hanna, P., & Swan, S. (1980). *Assessing language development.* Oxford: Oxford University Press.

CHAPTER 4

Writers, Readers, and Arguments

Trudy Govier

Written arguments appear in written texts—be these personal letters, newspaper columns, editorials, letters to the editor, magazine articles, legal opinions, scholarly works, or nonfiction books.[1] A writer who uses an argument provides, or tries to provide, a rational justification for a claim stated or implied in the text. Arguments offer evidence, or provide reasons, for claims made. By definition, an argument is minimally composed of premises (one or more) and a conclusion. The premises are put forward by a writer in the expectation that they will be deemed accept-

---

[1] Arguments may also appear in works of fiction. For instance, one character may be depicted as arguing with another. In such a case the argument is not necessarily one that the author puts forward on his or her own. Or the author may ruminate on the meaning of events he or she is depicting and in the course of doing so offer arguments. (This style in a novel is usually regarded as overly didactic, but it is nevertheless used sometimes.) Also, a fictional work may be seen as implying an argument for some broad conclusion (e.g., Steinbeck on poverty in *The Grapes of Wrath*). In such a case critics attribute to the author arguments they take to be implied by his or her work. The topic of argument in fiction seems to be an interesting one. Here, however, I treat written arguments as they appear in nonfictional contexts.

able by readers and in the hope that they will support the conclusion so as to render it acceptable too. Premises support the conclusion by logically entailing it, supplying empirical evidence on its behalf, or supplying good reasons for it. The roles of premises and conclusion differ. The premises are to support, the conclusion to be supported.

Argument is given when the conclusion is in some way at issue: The writer takes it to require rational support—either because she is writing in a context or for readers who she thinks will contest the conclusion, or because she herself believes that it requires justification or "back up."[2] Argument is directional: The premises are to lead readers to the conclusion. The rational acceptability of the premises is taken as given, for the purposes of that argument, and is supposed to render the conclusion acceptable. Pragmatically, the function of written argument is to rationally persuade readers that the conclusion is true or rationally acceptable—to make the conclusion believable on the grounds stated in the premises. Of course, not all arguments succeed in doing this. Sometimes readers fail to identify an-argument at all, do not accept the premises, can make no logical connection between the premises and conclusion, are unable to follow the argument, or persist in disputing the conclusion despite evidence supplied in the premises. And some times written arguments are weak or fallacious, so that even those readers who do accept the premises and are thereby persuaded of the conclusion are not thereby *rationally* persuaded of it. To refer to a written argument is to say that a written text contains a conclusion claim related to premise claims; conclusion and premises are put forward so as to imply that the premises support the conclusion.[3] It is not to say that the argument is cogent or convincing: Written arguments may be weak or fallacious or, even when strong, may fail to persuade the reader.

Of course, there is typically much more to written argument than the mere statement of premises and conclusions. Written arguments occur in a context, usually surrounded by nonargumentative discourse—variable background or stage-setting material such as definition of terms, explanation, description, narrative, and so on. For writers, expressing an argument is rarely only a matter of stating: "Premise, Premise, therefore Conclusion." (That won't get you into print, even if you're a logician or philosopher!) Background and context have to be supplied. In many cases premises themselves often need defense, so sub-arguments appear. A premise in the main argument may need support,

---

[2]One can offer arguments for conclusions already believed—to show they are capable of being rationally justified. Arguments in this sense may be regarded as tools of inquiry.

[3]Written arguments may have unstated or "missing" premises and conclusions. But to be properly "read in," these must have a tight relations to the stated text. For my approach to these topics, see Govier (1992).

therefore a subargument may be offered: "Premise a, premise b, therefore Premise 1." That structure can be iterated: A premise in a subargument may itself need support. From a main conclusion, the writer may seek to derive a supplementary conclusion or conclusions. Or, from the same set of premises, the writer may try to infer two quite independent conclusions. Here it is dearest to speak of two different arguments based on the same premises. The premise-conclusion structure can become quite complicated when subarguments are given and when a premise in one argument is, in effect, a conclusion in another. So the premise-conclusion (PPC) structure can represent only the core of an argument; and extended argument can include subarguments and further conclusions.[4]

And these are not the only ways in which the premise- conclusion structure can be filled out. Writers may complete their case on behalf of a claim by considering views differing from that expressed in their conclusion and addressing them. Consider, for example, a writer who wants to argue that "discovery" learning strategies in education are inefficient and inadequate for mathematics education, and that teachers should return to traditional methods of teaching. He or she might develop the argument by trying to rebut critics of traditional learning strategies in mathematics. The writer might try to show, for instance, that drill—a feature of traditional technique—need not be boring for students. Or he or she might supplement support for the conclusion by describing, and then trying to rebut, particular criticisms of his or her own arguments.

These structural adumbrations are not going to be a major theme of the present chapter, but nevertheless it may be convenient to have pertinent terminology. By *main argument*, I refer to the basic premise-conclusion (PPC) structure, where C is the main conclusion. By extended argument, I refer to the main argument with any attached subarguments wherein the premises or conclusion of the main argument function, in turn, as conclusions or premises of further arguments. By *full argumentation*, I refer to the main argument, extended argument, and any pro-and-con considerations of the positions of objectors to premises, conclusions, or inferences in the main argument. Full argumentation in this sense, can be—and often is—lengthy and complex and can include many distinct, main, and extended arguments.

So described, written argument probably seems dreadfully dull—a little like that prose you have been speaking all your life without knowing it. But even as described here, written argument has several noteworthy features that turn out to be of some importance for contemporary theory and debate.

---

[4]For diagramming techniques intended to represent subarguments and further conclusions, see Govier (1992) and Thomas (1986).

First, argument is open and direct in its statement of, and support for, a conclusion or position. The writer who uses argument does not merely suggest a point of view; he or she does not hint at themes and ideas and does not suggest statements through rhetorical questions, irony, paradox, or satire of a theory or opinion.[5] The arguer tells his or her readers outright what is claimed and sets forth reasons for it: Argument is characteristically explicit. Now this style may strike some people as pedestrian, unmodern, or downright misleading, but that is basically the way argument is. The writer who offers arguments for conclusions is likely to make it pretty clear to the reader just what those conclusions are and why he or she takes them to be true.

Second, argument acknowledges the possibility of disagreement about what the truth is or what the best decision is. To argue in writing for a conclusion is to recognize that it is disputed by some readers or to anticipate that it might come to be disputed by some of them. It is to recognize that other persons, reasonable persons with whom the writer stands in a relationship by virtue of the fact that they become readers of one's work, can differ from the writer in their beliefs, judgments, values, and opinions. That written argument acknowledges the possibility of difference or dissent between writer and the readers is more significant than might be supposed. This acknowledgment of, and response to, such difference sets argumentative writing apart from some other styles of writing, which ignore, gloss over, or seek to disguise differences in outlook, beliefs, and values.

Writers may disguise or avoid recognition of difference or disagreement by simply announcing that they are making assumptions or writing for a particular audience—overtly preaching only to the converted. More common, however, is a covert avoidance of differences in belief and opinion. A writer may ignore the reality or possibility of disagreement, blurring over differences, pretending they do not exist, or deliberately keeping them out of view. In contexts when there is real and reasonable disagreement on issues, writers may nevertheless use terminology and prose strategies that presume agreement between them and their readers. For instance, one might use words such as *reform* to refer to changes in policy that some believe to be negative without providing any reason to think the change would be for the better and merits the label *reform*. One might use use *we* tendentiously to presume an inclusiveness ("we in the union movement"; "we who share family values") that is inaccurate for the context in which one writes. One might offer explanations for "facts" ("the fact that traditional educational methods did not work") that are not recognized by all of one's readers to be facts, and so on and so forth.[6]

---

[5]These aspects can appear in material immediately preceding of following an argument, and conclusions or premises can be "stated" in rhetorical questions.

[6]Such techniques are discussed in Govier (1988).

There are, then, many strategies writers can use to ignore, avoid, or disguise differences in belief and opinion. Argument is not one of them. To offer an argument for a claim is to acknowledge the existence, or possibility, of differing beliefs about it and to respond to that difference of belief by trying to persuade or convince the envisaged reader on the basis of evidence or reasons purporting to support one's position. The writer seeks to persuade or convince the reader by stating plausible premises from which he or she hopes will move, via clear and correct reasoning, to the conclusion. The arguments are intended to set out a cogent case for his or her beliefs, to bring readers around to those beliefs, and thereby—by virtue of cogent argumentation—to eliminate the disagreement. In arguing, the writer responds to disagreement by setting forth reasons and evidence and *invites* in readers what he or she regards as reasonable change of mind. The writer tends to persist in his or her commitment to the conclusion: It is not amended in deference to beliefs he or she anticipates in readers.[7] Neither, on the other hand, does the writer attempt to *force* or *coerce* readers into taking his or her position. The writer offering arguments or argumentation does not have the readers up against a literal or figurative wall: He or she is merely setting out support, in a line of thought that he or she hopes they will come to accept.[8]

WHAT IS THE PURPOSE OF WRITTEN ARGUMENT?

Part of the answer to this question is already obvious. Written arguments are intended to support (some of) the writer's claims. The writer is making a case for some of his or her beliefs, judgments, and opinions. The central claims have not been pulled out of the air; they are not purely expressions of personal whim, emotion, or wishful thinking. They arise from other grounded beliefs regarded by the writer as shared with readers and as leading to his or her conclusions. Arguments are intended to show that the writer has a nonarbitrary, well-grounded, solid case to support the conclusions.

We can link two further themes with this one. The writer seeks to persuade readers, on the basis of reason and evidence, of the truth or

---

[7] The expression *tends to* is used to allow for cases in which the writer qualifies or amends his or her position in the course of extended argumentation in which he or she evaluates other people's objections to it. Such a strategy for refining one's position is fairly common in written academic philosophy.

[8] Argument has been deemed implicitly coercive by some. But what seems to me coercive—apart from outright violence, threats, and blackmail—is the manipulation of opinion by such devices as euphemism, loaded language, selective presentation of facts and evidence, and hiding the existence of responsible disagreement.

rational acceptability of his or her claims. The writer attempts to show that he or she is epistemically responsible—that he or she has a point of view, position, and style that respects logic, reason, and evidence. The use of argument in one's writing is intended to show that one is not just "talking off the top of one's head" or "spouting off." (Of course, if one's arguments are bad enough, one will not succeed in conveying this impression of credibility!)

Writers who argue for claims, who rely on argumentation to build a case of a position, typically have some further purpose in doing so. Consider, for instance, the example of the man who writes a newspaper column defending the use of traditional teaching techniques in mathematics.[9] Yes, he wants to persuade his readers, by using good arguments, that traditional methods are best here. In doing so, he wants to put forward a good case and show himself to be a credible, epistemically responsible thinker and writer. But the matter does not stop there. The columnist has some motive for being concerned with what his readers think about mathematics teaching: He does not think more fashionable methods work well, regards them as trendy and ill conceived, thinks the results are baneful, and seeks a return to old-style teaching. By putting forward arguments in print, he is trying to affect his readers' beliefs in the hope of influencing public opinion and bringing about change. (Note that seeking to influence is not seeking to dominate.) He is arguing his case in a quest for a broader social goal.

This account applies naturally to written argument on social issues: Writers do not argue points about environmental policy, medical ethics, animal rights, U.N. peacekeeping missions, arms control, and so on, merely to show themselves to have a credible case and persuade others to agree with them. By arguing in writing, they are responding to a social situation and hoping to change (or preserve) some of its aspects by affecting what other people—their readers, in the first instance—think.

The same can be said—although perhaps more controversially—about other sorts of written arguments. Consider a scientific research paper about a fairly technical topic—for example, the difference in chemical activity between mountain snow fields and mountain glaciers. The author of the paper will state some technical point which is, in effect, his main conclusion (call it C') and offer evidence for it. In doing so, he is clearly trying to make a good case for C', persuade his readers of the truth or acceptability of C', and show himself to be an epistemically responsible thinker and writer. We might think of this writer as being interested in snow fields, glaciers, and his particular conclusion C' purely for themselves or—as it is sometimes put—"just as an academic mat-

[9]I have in mind Andrew Nikiforuk's weekly education column in the Toronto *Globe and Mail*, in the winter and spring of 1992.

ter." But this conception is both unrealistic and simplistic. It is unrealistic, because if C' were of interest only in itself, there would be little point in deliberating about it and—in all likelihood—no opportunity to publish one's results about it. (C' must have implications for other claims about snow fields, mountains, glaciers, avalanches, or the chemistry of water and rocks; that is why it is of interest to the writer, his readers, the scientific community, and others.) It is simplistic because it presumes the feasibility of a kind of science in which people take an interest in the truth or acceptability of statements purely for their own sakes. Ever since Kuhn, we know that kind of science does not exist (for a pertinent discussion, see Midgley, 1990, chapters 1-3).

WHO IS WRITTEN ARGUMENT FOR?

It is obvious is it not? Written arguments are for those who will read them; writers write for their readers. But there are interesting distinctions and qualifications to be made.

Consider the personal letter. Who the reader is seems basically clear. Suppose Margaret Thatcher writes a letter to Ronald Reagan in which she argues that the Gulf War was a failure because at its end Saddam Hussein remained in power in Iraq, terrorizing Kurds and Shiites and hindering the work of humanitarian agencies and U.N. arms inspectors. Suppose that in her letter Thatcher set forth an argument to this effect, trying to bring Reagan around to share her appraisal of the effectiveness of the war. Such a letter would be written to and for Ronald Reagan. Of course, even this apparently simple case allows for qualifications: Reagan may have aides who read his mail for him, helping him to sort through and understand it. Perhaps Nancy reads his mail—or perhaps he reads choice bits to her. Perhaps someday Thatcher's letters will be collected and published, and future historians will study them, noting carefully her *post bellum* assessment of the war. Still, if Thatcher writes to Reagan, it is he who is her intended reader. If she is arguing a point in her correspondence, her premises and style of reasoning should be directed to him and adapted to his beliefs and abilities. And so it will be for any case of personal correspondence: The writer-reader relationship is personal, particular, and—at least in its primary focus—known to the writer. The writer can, if he or she chooses, use particular knowledge of the reader's beliefs, abilities, and interests so as to construct an argument likely to be understood and accepted by the reader.[10]

---

[10]Such a strategy is to be recommended. It does not imply relativism and is open to criticism only insofar as the arguer might use premises or argumentative techniques he or she knows or believes to be erroneous. I do not recommend that.

rtually all cases of writing for publication, there is no
[ind]ual reader the writer has in mind. The reader may be
[, bu]t he or she is likely to be an anonymous construct stand-
[ing for] readers who are somewhere "out there" and who, the
writer hopes and assumes, will someday read his or her work.[11]

The writer should, I think, form a general idea as to who his or her potential readers are: It is impossible to write so as to suit just anyone. As a writer, one needs some conception of what sorts of people are likely to read one's work. How would they come upon one's writing? In what context and under what circumstances would they be likely to read it? Why would they be interested in the topic? How much would they already know or believe about it? Would they have relevant biases, prejudices, or misinformation? What would they be likely to know or believe about closely related topics? What sort of vocabulary would they have—would they know technical or scholarly words in the subject area or oft-used foreign terms? Without some conception of who the readers might be, the writer cannot define a stance with regard to them, risks arbitrariness or inconsistency in assumptions about their interests and knowledge, and is unlikely to present to them clear, reasonable, and persuasive arguments.

It is desirable, then, to have a good sense of one's intended readership. One may understand oneself to be writing for a particular subgroup: peace activists, teachers of high school mathematics, undergraduates in a first philosophy course, high altitude hikers, adolescent girls, prospective tourists to Central Asia, young parents, or whatever. Some intended audiences are broader and to a large degree defined by topic, for example, "those interested in education" or "those interested in environment." One may aim for a very large and diverse audience defined in one's mind, such as "the lay public." To write for this audience is ambitious and, for some purposes, admirable. But in my experience it is difficult to find a suitable style, tone, vocabulary, and knowledge base for this purpose. The prudent writer envisages potential readers as comprising a subgroup or fitting into a category. Accordingly, the writer makes assumptions about the audience for his or her writing and, in particular, his or her arguments.

The writer may operationalize these assumptions by envisaging a particular individual as a stand-in. One author of a nonfiction book

---

[11]Some writers say they are writing for themselves. If this is literally true, then one's intended reader is one's (future) self. I suspect, however, that when people say this they do not mean it quite literally. They mean that they have set their own standards that they are trying to measure up to, that they are not writing for a specific audience or with a prospective publisher in mind, or that they are not writing in an attempt to make money or in the interests of some broader social cause.

about the history of partition as a solution to ethnic conflict in such countries as Palestine, Ireland, China, and Korea wrote with his mother in mind as the intended reader. She is interested in the topics he chooses and has a good general education, but is neither a political activist nor a scholar in these areas. His book sold well and received reasonably good reviews, so the technique seems to have worked for him. Neighbors, friends, colleagues, or students may also serve as the envisaged reader. Some writers use themselves as stand-ins. This a risky technique if one is trying to recognize and respond to disagreement.

For writers, references to a category specifying one's likely readers as students, activists, scholars, or the larger public, or subjective constructions of "my Reader," are necessary and useful. Still, they cannot disguise the fact that the actual readers, those to whom written arguments must be directed, are not known to the writer. Prospective readers have interests, background beliefs, values, and expertise the writer can only guess at. They are many in number, indefinitely and unpredictably diverse. They may be members of other cultures who will eventually read the work in translation or even—for some especially successful writers—people living decades or centuries after the writer's own death. Trying to write for, and argue to, such readers may seem futile. Do such factors show that writers should not even try to predict their readership, should not construct a hypothetical reader at all?

Some people think so. One man I knew was trying to write a book on moral expertise. I asked him for whom it was intended. Students? Academic philosophers? Scholars outside philosophy? The lay public? He said, "I try not to ask myself that question." He meant, I think, that he was trying to do justice to his topic and make a case for his views without relativizing his problem, vocabulary, assumptions, and arguments to any particular subgroup. It seems an admirable Platonic vision, but one with practical hazards. Seven years after our conversation, the book has not been successfully completed.

What this writer presumed, I think, was a universal audience: One's readers could be anyone. This conception may seem attractive when we consider the possibility of readers in other cultures and future epochs. But try to imagine a study of moral expertise written for no one in particular and everyone in general. The "thinking human being" is to come to understand why there is a problem about the notion of moral expertise. To this "person-in-general" one seeks to communicate the structure of the problem and one's own response to it. One seeks to make a case for a particular approach (the writer's own, although developed in the latter 20th century in an Anglo-Saxon culture) that is supposed to be meaningful and interesting to any thinking human being anywhere. The writer seeks to understand and grasp a central issue in philosophy—a (supposedly) timeless problem about moral knowledge, who has it, what they should do with it, how others they have it—and he seeks to make a case for his own account of moral expertise.

The idea of the universal audience was developed by C. Perelman and M. Olbrechts-Tyteca in *The New Rhetoric* (1971). It seems to fit some writing, especially in abstract areas such as philosophy, science, and mathematics. A contemporary philosopher, considering the possibility of readers in the 22nd century, might try to write only for the human condition in its most general sense, shedding what he or she took to be particular preoccupations of the present era, omitting reference to all but the best-known current thinkers, and avoiding vocabulary and jargon linked to current trends and problems. (How are such expressions as "the New World Order" and "postmodernism" understood in China or in central Africa? How will they be understood 30 or 100 years from now? Five hundred years from now?) The writer can try to distill an historical situation and topic to reach its most broadly human elements, and for some topics such efforts are creative and useful. But however seriously and for whatever purpose it may be construed, the universal audience cannot literally be addressed. One's readers are human beings of various types, in various situations and with various beliefs, values, and preoccupations (Govier, 1987, chapter 13).

The question—"just whom are you writing for?"—should provoke some uneasiness in writers. Readers are nearly always unknown to writers; they are indefinite in number, unpredictably variable in their characteristics. And yet their knowledge, values, and needs are something to which writers must be sensitive. Thus, writers are in a peculiar position with regard to readers: They have to attend to readers' beliefs, interests, values, and capabilities, but they are in no position to know whose attitudes and capabilities they are trying to take into account. Assumptions and predictions as to which categories of people might read one's work and constructed stand-ins for the reader are useful, but limited, heuristic devices.

For written argument, these points are significant. Argument acknowledges or anticipates disagreement: The writer needs some idea of who might or might not agree, as well as in what respects and for what reasons. Using arguments, the writers seeks to respond to disagreement by offering evidence or reasons in premises. For written argument to succeed in its goal of rationally persuading the reader of the writer's point of view, the premises of the arguments must be accepted by readers, and the inferential links involved must be comprehensible to them. But the writer, not knowing who the readers will be, can only estimate what they will need and will accept. Supposing someone disagrees with the writer's view on X; the writer must then ask what other claims—R, P, Z, and so on—could serve as suitable premises to make a case for X. The writer plants points of agreement from which to proceed to try to achieve further agreement on disputed points. And for all of this, the writer needs a style, tone, and vocabulary suited to that reader whose interests he or she knows not. It is a dilemma bordering on antinomy or paradox, but one all writers face.

Can readers talk back? Can they tell writers when they got it wrong? ("I'm not interested"; "you're juvenile"; "you're boring"; "you presume too much"; "you can't pull the wool over my eyes with that point"; "what a fallacy!") Well, *sometimes*: Readers may know writers, or come to know them, and may literally be able to talk to them. But usually if readers "talk back" at all, they do so in writing. Readers may write to writers, care of newspapers, magazines, or publishers, and tell writers what they think of their work in general and their arguments in particular. If they are skilled and suitably situated, readers may be lucky enough to have their responses published in a review, letter to the editor, or scholarly journal, and they may achieve a kind of public exchange with the writers. In such an exchange readers can, in some respects, function as interlocutors, and writers may be moved to respond to their queries and criticisms. Thus, some readers occasionally achieve a kind of limited dialogue with the writers. Consequently, the possibility of correspondence with the writer is there, in principle, for any reader. So the writer and a reader can come to have a kind of exchange.

But realistically, most readers, most of the time, do not and cannot engage in dialogue with the writer. If readers talk back at all, they mutter to themselves or exclaim or complain to friends. Many readers are entirely passive and do not do even this. Written arguments are constructed for and addressed to others, but those others are silent partners in a one-sided "exchange" that is not a real exchange.

These facts are noteworthy in light of the popularity of dialogical models of argument such as the pragma-dialectical theory put forward by Van Emeren and Grootendorst (1992). Van Emeren and Grootendorst apply speech-act theory to argument, understanding argument as a kind of conversation in which two parties seek to resolve a conflict or difference in opinion. Most of their examples depict conversational situations in which both parties are present. Van Emeren and Grootendorst are, of course, aware of the many contextual differences between argument in actual conversation between two people and the writing of arguments for indefinitely many absent and silent readers. But they do not take these differences seriously for the purposes of understanding written argument.

In their most recent book, Van Emeren and Grootendorst (1992) alluded to the *discursive text*, which may be written or spoken, allowing in a footnote that:

> In argumentative discourse there are, in principle, always two parties involved, but in a discursive text the contributions of one of the parties are, as a rule, only implicitly represented: the argumentative text, which is basically dialogical then manifests itself monologically. (p. 13)

The argumentative text (written text, here) manifests itself as a monologue. But it is *implicitly* dialogical.

This is quite an idealization. A situation of indefinitely many readers and one writer is modeled as one in which there are one reader and one writer. A situation that, on its face, is a monologue is understood as dialogue. A situation in which readers rarely talk back and, when they do so, can do so only in limited ways is modeled on rules for a cooperative interchange between parties who can talk equally. A situation of anticipated but barely understood disagreement is modeled as one of face-to-face disagreement in which parties have an active conversation in which they converse together (using rules) to resolve their "conflict" of opinion. I suspect that the idealization is too far from the reality of written texts to be helpful.

SOME FEMINIST DOUBTS ABOUT ARGUMENT

Several prominent feminist theorists have claimed that arguing is implicitly oppositional, adversarial, and domineering. In this view, one who argues is trying to "win," trying to defend and protect his or her cherished views and force them on others. Argument is too confrontational; arguers are intolerant of differences in opinion and bent on dominating those whom they seek to persuade.[12]

Consider, for example, the matter of militaristic terms in the language of arguing and argument, noted by Deborah Berrill in her chapter in this volume. People have opponents, seek to win an argument, engage in a battle of wits, employ tactics and strategy to defend positions, make points, secure their positions. Difference in belief or judgment is modeled as a conflict in which there are two sides, each out to win by besting the other. Argument is modeled as conflict; one has an opponent over which one seeks victory. Like many other metaphors in our culture, these go deep and are hard to avoid. Some years back a widely circulated book was called *How to Win an Argument*. A popular critical thinking text is called *Logical Self-Defense*. One of Van Emeren and Grootendorst's texts has a title page showing two men fencing,

---

[12]See, for example, Moulton (1983); Ayim (1990). Reflections on various metaphorical terms used for argument, including some of the militaristic ones, may be found in Chapter 15 of Lakoff and Johnson (1980).

pointing swords at each other to illustrate the battle of proponent and opponent.

When argument is understood in an oppositional way, difference is disagreement, and disagreement is regarded as conflict; conflict leads to contest between opponents, and contest to battle—real or metaphoric (see Pinxten and Balagangadhura, 1989). Those who disagree about a claim are cast as opponents, enemies, each seeking victory over the other. Although the sliding of categories from difference to disagreement, to conflict and opposition, is natural, it is undesirable and conceptually unnecessary and could be stopped at any point along the way. Difference need not amount to disagreement; disagreement can be understood as something other than conflict; conflict need not be a contest, but can be an opportunity for constructive change. And contests need not amount to battles. There are decisively important logical gaps between a difference of belief and a battle of the wits—even though the language of strategy and opposition, as applied to argument, encourages us to jump over these gaps to land at the hasty conclusion that argument is some kind of war of the wits. With the dead metaphors of defense and victory a key part of our conceptual apparatus, we all too easily leap the gaps, interpreting disagreement as conflict and conflict as something calling for winners and losers. In fact, as much current practice in mediation and negotiation clearly indicates, even nonmetaphoric conflict does not require winners and losers for its resolution. Win-win resolutions of conflict are a reality for those determined to achieve them—even in many apparently intractable situations.

Feminist thinkers have rightly pointed out the depth and dangers of the militaristic win-lose construal of argument. These construals make arguing an adversarial matter and can unnecessarily polarize people and their positions.

Contrary to some popular current opinion, the pervasiveness of "argument is war" metaphors in our culture does not show that argument must be understood in confrontational and militaristic terms. The depiction of written argument given earlier illustrates the possibility of avoiding them. I described arguments, subarguments, and the purpose of argument without using any militaristic words and without implying that a person who writes arguments is trying to vanquish, conquer, or dominate the intended readers. The writer is, to be sure, trying to put forward evidence or reasons for claims made and trying to persuade others, by reason, that these claims are true or acceptable. But such persuasion need not amount to victory or conquest. One who argues recognizes that the reader, although a perfectly reasonable individual, may have different beliefs from the writer and will agree only after being given evidence and reasons in the form of argument. A reader persuaded by reason is not coerced; still less has she had her mind pierced, battered, or dominated by the writer, as some feminist critics of logic have suggested. To offer reasons and evidence in an attempt to persuade does not imply or require a winner-take-all attitude or attempt at some kind of cognitive victory. On the contrary, the writer who offers reasons thereby shows a recognition of differences in belief and a respect for the autonomous thinking of the reader.

There is no realistic substitute in our culture for argument in the general sense in which it has been defined earlier in this chapter. There are differences in belief, judgment, and opinion. We are presented with diverse claims and must select among them; we do so, some of the time at least, by considering relevant evidence and reasons and seeing which claims are supported by the most accurate and cogent arguments. Those who have criticized argument as unduly adversarial have not, on the whole, recommended an alternative to this sort of procedure in thinking and writing. Some speak of cooperation and consensus as though they could replace argument, but that is a loose and misleading way of talk. Argument, properly understood, is compatible with cooperation; back and-forth argument is in many circumstances a necessary prelude to, or concomitant of, cooperation. In many contexts, consensus is also more a consequence of argument than an alternative to it; consensus is often reached only after many different arguments have been presented, debated, and considered. Logical critique and back-and- forth, pro-and-con argument are essential in what Western culture regards as responsible deliberation and consultation.

Unfortunately, when people argue back and forth, they can come to see each other as opponents, become angry and dogmatic, even yell. They may approach argument defensively, militaristically, and there is much in Western culture and in English metaphors for arguing that would encourage them to do so. Clearly these things are generally not desirable, and feminist critics are entirely right to point this out. There really are dangers latent in our militaristic metaphors for argument. Confrontation, animosity, and opposition can be avoided while argument is maintained. Oppositionality, which features anger, yelling, and hostility, is neither ubiquitous among arguers nor intrinsic to argument as such. In effect, this fact is implicitly acknowledged by critics who offer evidence and arguments while criticizing adversariality in traditional logic and argument. Feminist critics of argument themselves offer arguments—many of which are convincing, politely expressed, nonantagonistic, and respectful of persons.

We need to—and can—understand difference and disagreement nonadversarially. To facilitate such understanding, there are alternative conceptual frameworks for thinking of argument, frameworks that are constructive and nonadversarial. One can think of argument as building. One is building a case, trying to get good evidential foundations, that will support one's position. Or one can think of argument as inquiry or exploration: In arguing one explores what reasons and evidence there are for various positions and, by comparative critical evaluation, comes to better understand the content of these positions and their comparative merits. These two alternatives to the "argument as war" metaphor already have a strong basis in our vocabulary for argument. No doubt other metaphorical frameworks exist; still others could be developed.

Feminist and other criticisms of the "argument as war" metaphors show that we need to think in a more sophisticated and careful way about such concepts as difference, disagreement, conflict, contest, and opposition. They show that we need nonmilitaristic metaphors to describe arguing and argument. But they do not show that alternative conceptual frameworks are impossible or that those who offer arguments necessarily seek to dominate the minds of others. Still less they show that we can or should eliminate arguments and arguing from writing, conversation, or general intellectual practice.

ALLEGATIONS OF ETHNOCENTRISM

Some have criticized Western models of argument as unwittingly ethnocentric and as misleadingly assuming that strategies and paradigms appropriate to Western postindustrial cultures are norms for all human thought. An example is a recent essay by Pinxten and Balanjangadhara who contend that current argumentation theory, as pursued in Canada, the United States, and the Netherlands, is culturally biased, reflecting "a set of highly culture-specific assumptions" and carrying with it "a mantle of universality which is rather illusory" (cited in Maier, 1989). They make their case for pragma-dialectical theory, a theory held by Van Eemeren and Grootendorst that seems especially vulnerable because it is based on implicit norms of *conversation*. Conversation is conducted in every human culture. But its style, norms, and goals vary from one culture to another.

Argument theorists sometimes claim that argument in the sense of back-and-forth exchanges featuring premises, conclusions, criticism, qualification, pro-and-con, and so on, is the *only* nonviolent way of responding to conflicts in opinion and belief. That claim is surely false. To ignore a difference in belief may be undesirable, but it is, after all, nonviolent. Alternately, differences may be cherished, not even seen as something to be overcome. Even in a case in which differences of belief are regarded as disagreements amounting to conflict that calls for resolution, arguing is not the only way to achieve that resolution. There are other methods: consulting an authority, searching tradition for a precedent, drawing lots, or continuing to talk until somehow (perhaps only from exhaustion) a consensus is reached. To say that argument in the pragma-dialectical sense is the only nonviolent way people can respond to differences of belief is just not credible. It strikes me, then, that Pinxten and Balajangadhara are correct in criticizing this assumption in Van Emeren and Grootendorst's account. And to the extent that other theorists of argument share the assumption, they are open to the same criticism. It is clearly hasty to view argument as the only nonviolent way of resolving differences in opinion and belief.

But to admit this is to admit only that one particular theory of argument has been guilty of a false presumption. It is not to say that theory or practice of argument as such is inevitably ethnocentric. Although it is not the only nonviolent approach to conflicts of belief and opinion, argument remains an important social and intellectual tool. Giving and testing evidence and reasons for claims is such a basic intellectual activity, required to test the soundness of beliefs that may be of central practical importance, that it is hard to believe that a working human culture could persist without it. The practice is essential in reflecting on and discussing the reliability of beliefs. To be sure, there are nonargumentative approaches to differences in opinion or belief. But some of these (for example, depending on traditions, ritual, or authority) are likely to be less reliable than the weighing of evidence and pros and cons that occurs when arguments are given and considered. It is in fact very difficult to imagine a culture that makes no use of evidence or argument—although, of course, the circumstances, frequency, and favored patterns of argument will vary among cultures.

Some apparently nonargumentative approaches to resolving doxastic differences are not in practice alternatives to argument. Although they appear superficially to be alternatives, in practice, they require some recourse to argument. We have seen that this is the case for consensus, and there is every reason to think that the point holds as well for the consultation of an authority. Suppose, for instance, that a particular group or tribe has a practice of consulting an authority to pronounce a judgment whenever members face a significant difference of opinion. Such a culture would have to handle cases when there was a dispute as to who the authority was, what a sentence written or uttered by an authority meant, or how a conflict in the sayings of an authority or several authorities was to be resolved.

Argument, both spoken and written, openly acknowledges difference in belief and responds to those differences in one particular way. That style has been characteristic of the Western intellectual tradition since at least Socrates. It gives benefits and poses risks, including, as we have seen, an unhealthy emphasis on confrontation and victory in a battle of wits. And its presence in various cultures will surely be variable. But it is scarcely plausible to think that there is a human culture in which people never support claims with reason and evidence. One can describe what argument is and recommend it as serving interests of clarity, openness, system, accuracy, and truth without assuming either that it is a tool to be used to dominate others or that it is in every context in every culture the most desirable response to differences of belief. With all respect to the readers who may differ on these matters, that is what I have tried to do here.

REFERENCES

Ayim, M. (1988). Violence and domination as metaphors in academic discourse. In T. Govier (Ed.), *Selected issues in logic and communication* (Chapter 16). New York: Routledge.

Govier, T. (1987). *Problems in argument analysis and evaluation.* Dordrecht, The Netherlands: Foris.

Govier, T. (1988). Are there two sides to every question? In T. Govier (Ed.), *Selected issues in logic and communication* (Chapter 4). Belmont, CA: Wadsworth.

Govier, T. (1992). *A practical study of argument* (3rd ed.). Belmont, CA: Wadsworth.

Lakoff, G., & Johnson, M. (1980). *Metaphors we live by.* Chicago: University of Chicago Press.

Midgley, M. (1990). *Wisdom, information, and wonder.* New York: Routledge.

Moulton, J. (1983). A paradigm of philosophy: The adversary method. In S. Harding & M. Hintikka (Eds.), *Discovering reality.* Dordrecht, The Netherlands: Reidel.

Perelman, C., & Olbrechts-Tyteca, M. (1971). *The new rhetoric: A treatise on argumentation* (J. Wilkinson & P. Weaver, Trans.). Notre Dame, IN: University of Notre Dame Press.

Pinxten, R., & Balagangadhura, S.N. (1971). Comparative anthropology and rhetorics in cultures. In R. Maier (Ed.), *Norms in argument.* Dordrecht, The Netherlands: Foris.

Thomas, S.N. (1986). *Practical reasoning in natural language* (3rd ed.). Englewood Cliffs, NJ: Prentice-Hall.

Van Emeren, F.H., & Grootendorst, R. (1992). *Argumentation, communication and fallacies.* Hillsdale, NJ: Erlbaum.

CHAPTER 5

Genres of Argument and Arguments as Genres

Aviva Freedman

INTRODUCTION

As Andrew Wilkinson demonstrated in this volume (Chapter 1), and as Bruner's discussion in *Actual Minds, Possible Worlds* (1986) confirms, to consider argument as a primary act of mind can be immensely revealing. This chapter, however, takes a different perspective, viewing argument—by focusing on the written arguments produced by students as part of their disciplinary studies through the lens provided by recent reconceptualizations of genre. Genre studies in the past 15 years have emphasized the social and cultural dimensions of textual regularities, as well as the notion of texts as forms of action: Genres have come to be seen as typified rhetorical responses to recurring situations or contexts. To see argument in this light is to offer a complementary perspective to that suggested by Wilkinson and Bruner. It is beyond the scope of this discussion to make a case for the priority of the social over the cognitive, along the lines suggested by Vygotsky (and extended in recent work emanating out of the social constructivist paradigm and Russian activity theory).[1] In this chapter, I make a more modest claim that viewing argument as social action can enhance our understanding of what happens when students engage in the process of written argumentation.

Drawing on a familiar convention of the genre, I begin by describing the staging of my own argument in the pages that follow. The analysis of written argument as genre that forms the core of this chapter is prefaced by a theoretic overview of current reconceptualizations of genre. This theoretic discussion provides the context for a more focused discussion and analysis of a specific genre or subgenre of written argument, specifically the writing produced in an undergraduate law course (for a particular instructor, in a particular institution, over one academic year). The idiosyncratic textual features of this subgenre of written argument is specified first, and then these textual regularities are probed using the prism of genre studies in order to clarify what it meant for the students to have written such pieces. Ultimately, I argue that the social action undertaken in this writing is typical of that undertaken in much school writing, in that its purpose is *epistemic*—not in the sense of producing knowledge new to the reader, but rather in the specialized sense of enabling its writer to see and interpret reality in new ways; in that these ways are the ways of currently constituted communities of scholars, the purpose of, and the action undertaken in, such writing is social and cultural as well.

In the final section, I draw on another generic convention to consider implications and applications. Respect is encouraged for the ecological complexity involved in the creation of discipline-specific genres of written argument, and a warning is sounded against reifying genres. Educationally, we must recognize as well that, although typical of much school writing, the social action evinced in the genre examined differs from that of most workplace argument as well as the argument of public discourse. Finally, questions are raised concerning the commonalities that underlie written argument in general, as seen through the prism of genre studies, questions that raise from another perspective some of the same issues concerning the values and methods of Western knowledge and rationality that are addressed elsewhere in this volume, as well as more generally in postmodern and poststructuralist literature.

REDEFINITIONS OF GENRE

Earlier definitions of genre, in both composition and literary studies, focused primarily on recurrences and regularities in texts. (For examples, see Wellek and Warren, 1977, on literature or Brooks & Warren, 1970, on

---

[1]For example, work by Lave and Wenger (1991) located learning in the social processes within communities of practices—rather than with the minds of the learners.

rhetoric.) In the past 10 to 15 years, however, some very different conceptions of genre have been presented. Characteristic of the interdisciplinary nature of the new tradition of rhetoric, these new notions of genre can be traced to very different and quite independent intellectual sources: modern rhetorical theory; speech-act theory and general semiotics; literary theory, especially the work of Bakhtin, his circle, and his followers; philosophy, in particular the new empirical study of logic by Steven Toulmin and his colleagues; and linguistics, especially the social theory of language developed by M.A.K. Halliday, and the recent work in applied linguistics by John Swales. These different discussions are remarkably convergent, yet each illuminates different facets of a newly evolving conception of genre. For this reason, I recapitulate briefly several different, and somewhat independent, theoretic discussions of genre.

Typified Rhetorical Action

In a seminal article entitled, "Genre as Social Action," Miller reconceptualized genre as typified rhetorical action. Drawing largely on the tradition of modern rhetorical theory, Miller picked up notions suggested in the work of Bitzer (1968) and Burke (1969), while elaborating on and sharpening the approach taken to genre by Campbell and Jamieson (1978). She made the following point "A rhetorically sound definition of genre must be created not in the substance or the form of discourse but in the action it is used to accomplish" (p. 152). Genres represent "typified social actions"; her definition is thus primarily pragmatic—and only secondarily semantic and syntactic.

Miller's key terms are *action* and *typification*. Action implies both situation and motive. Drawing on Bitzer, she defined situation as a "complex of persons, events, objects, and relations presenting an exigence that can be allayed through the mediation of discourse" (p. 152). But Miller redefined Bitzer's exigence, denying the materialist and determinist implications of his use of the term. She focused on the role of interpretation in exigence: Typified actions reflect commonly constructed interpretations of events.

Central to Miller's argument as well is the peculiar fusion of substance and form implicit in the rhetorical action that is genre. Substance and form, she explained, are hierarchical, so that form at one level is substance at another, and it is their fusion that constitutes the action.

To recapitulate, the central thrust of Miller's argument is that the essence of genre is social action. Such social action manifests itself in regularities of text, both in substance and form, and especially their fusion. Substance and form interrelate hierarchically, so that form on one level implies substance at another.

Place and Play

A second approach to a redefinition of genre builds on speech-act theory and semiotics. In an analysis of genre that is remarkably consonant with, although quite independent of, Miller's, Freadman (1987) developed a conception of genre using the analogy of "game"—based not, however, on the Wittgensteinian model (or at least not limited to the terms of such a model). She placed genres within the context of larger socially constructed frames, which she called "ceremonials." The playing of a game is a ceremony that includes much more than the game itself: It includes the preparations, the choice of partners, the physical venue, the declaration of me winner, and so on. The ceremony situates the games, or to put it another way, the genre is defined foremost by its place within this ceremonial. (The ceremonials themselves are rule-governed and socially constructed in much the same way as the games are.)

Equally important to her discussion is that, as a game, a genre is best thought of as consisting minimally of at least two texts in some sort of dialogic relationship: a debate, for example; or the set of assignment, essay, and feedback. Interaction is at the heart of the genre. The rules that govern these interactions, the rules by which each partner shapes his or her uptake, are best understood as manners or etiquette rather than normative rules. Although the rules of etiquette can sometimes be seen as rules appropriate to a pre-existing situation, they can also be understood as being instrumental in organizing and determining role relations, and in constructing and forming settings.

To sum up, although Freadman develops some notions from speech-act theory, genres in her theory are far more than extensions of speech acts. Linguistic features, either in isolation or in combination, are not the key markers of genre. Place constitutes genre, and place allows for play in several of her meanings of the term.

Freadman's notions therefore complement, extend, and, in some sense, qualify those of Miller. As has already been noted, my goal in this discussion is not to develop a logically consistent and precise theoretic definition of genre, but rather to point to different facets of the notion as it is coming into use in the discipline.

Bakhtin

Although he wrote prolifically from the early 1920s to his death in 1975, Bakhtin's work has only come to be known in the West in general since the late 1960s, and in composition circles in particular in the last 10 years. What is remarkable is the congruence of many of his notions about language with those that have been developed more recently and independently in linguistics and rhetoric. For Bakhtin, the primary unit of analysis in language is the utterance, rather than the word or sentence; he stresses thus the primacy of the communicative function of language. Building on this notion, in "The Problem of Speech Genres" (1986), he argues that whereas

> each separate utterance is individual . . . each sphere in which language is used develops its own relatively stable types of these utterances. . . . Genres correspond to typical situations of speech communication, typical themes, and consequently also to particular contacts between the meanings of words and actual concrete reality under certain typical circumstances. (p. 87)

These notions are consonant with those presented by Miller and Freadman. To complement their discussion, and as background to the analysis of written argument as genre that follows, I highlight three somewhat different takes on the notion of genre that are suggested by Bakhtin. First, he acknowledges not only the active and constructive role of the listener/reader, but also the corresponding recognition by the writer/speaker of this fact: "The entire utterance is constructed . . . in anticipation of encountering this response" (p. 94). Second, Bakhtin focuses on the textual or linguistic dimensions of the typified situations that form the context of genres: "Any utterance is a link in a very complexly organized chain of other utterances." Finally, Bakhtin notes repeatedly that generic forms are "more flexible, plastic, and free" (p. 79) than other forms of language.

Hallidayan Emphases

Yet another stream feeding into the development of the notion of genre is the social theory of language developed by M.A.K. Halliday. Without going into the technical definition of genre developed in the work of Halliday himself (for an overview, see Devitt, 1993), I point to the contributions of a group of researchers and educationists in Australia, working under the influence of Halliday, whose discussions of genre and its acquisition have become the center of an educational debate. The works most prominently associated with this school are those by Gunther Kress (who has more recently been connected to the London Institute of Education) and J.R. Martin, Frances Christie, and Joan Rothery (1987). Although their notion of genre overlaps in significant respects with those presented by Miller and Freadman, there are differences in emphasis. The Hallidayans always root their discussion in their social theory of language. Discussions of context invariably include not just other participants and setting (audience and occasion), but also social and cultural institutions (including economic and educational institutions). The social constructivist implications of the position held by Miller and Freadman are sounded most loudly and explicitly by the Hallidayans.

In addition, the Hallidayans stress that genres "are not simply a set of formal structures into which meanings are poured" (Martin et al., p. 64); genres themselves make meaning. Finally, the Hallidayans pay tribute to the immense shaping force of disciplinary knowledge itself (a point that is made even more centrally by Toulmin and his colleagues as the discussion later reveals). Thus, Kress (1982) wrote: "Texts are determined socially in two major ways; by the effects of the structurings and processes of social occasions leading to generic form; and by organization of meaning/knowledge by and in social institutions leading to the organization by discourse" (pp. 37-38).

Argument Fields

This last point has been developed far more extensively by Toulmin (1958, 1972) and his colleagues (Toulmin, Rieke, & Janik, 1979). Although they make little reference explicitly to the notion of genre, their analysis of the logic of disciplinary and discourse communities underlies much current thinking about disciplinary genres. Since the early 1950s, Toulmin has been investigating empirically what counts for evidence and what counts as successful argumentation within different human spheres. He has been able to identify both common elements underlying most arguments as well as to point to significant variations—in the combination of or weight given to these individual elements by different disciplines or within different discourse communities. The implications of such analyses dovetail with current thinking about genre. There is the same sense of communally sanctioned and socially constructed modes of selecting evidence as well as reasoning from that evidence. Increasingly, those involved in writing research, especially those whose work entails observing discipline-specific writing, have found themselves using the Toulmin model to define generic strategies (see, for example, Currie, Chapter 6, this volume; Herrington 1985).

Swales and "Discourse Communities"

John Swales's monograph, *Genre Analysis* (1990), provides one of the most systematic and comprehensive overviews of genre theory to date.

Most relevant for our discussion at this point is the relationship he points to between genres and discourse communities. "Discourse communities are socio-rhetorical networks that form in order to work towards sets of common goals.... Genres are the properties of discourse communities" (p. 9). The relevant defining features of discourse communities are the following. "A discourse community has a broadly agreed set of common public goals" (p. 24), although these goals may be tacit. "A discourse community has mechanisms of inter-communication among its members" (p. 25). "A discourse community utilizes and hence possesses one or more genres in the communicative furtherance of its aims" (p. 26). And "a discourse community has a threshold level of members with a suitable degree of relevant content and discoursal expertise" (p. 27). Most significantly, Swales argues that although "an academic class is unlikely to be a discourse community at the outset, . . . the hoped-for outcome is that it will form" (p. 32) such a community as a result of what transpires in the course itself.

The precise relationship between specific genres and discourse communities may be theoretically thorny. At a recent conference on genre, for example, participants debated whether discourse communities exist prior to the genres produced within them. Without needing to resolve such issues, introduction of the notion of discourse community can illuminate important aspects of what transpires in the course of acquiring and engaging in the writing of specific genres.

STUDENT WRITING FOR LAW AS A GENRE

In the following pages, I examine an instance of actual student discourse, specifically the writing of arguments for an undergraduate law course, under the light cast by the various reconceptualizations of genre just presented. The specific genre was produced by students in an introductory undergraduate law course. Because their writing for this course had appeared to me, on the basis of informal observation, as an idiosyncratic instance of academic argumentation, I chose to conduct a more formal research study investigating the nature of the writing and its acquisition.

That research is described more fully elsewhere (see Freedman, 1987: Freedman, Carey, & Miller, 1989). For my purpose here, it is enough to say that the course investigated was an introductory undergraduate course in law, aimed at generalists and not intending lawyers, and offered in a lecture and seminar format. The lecture was given to a class of 250 by the course professor, and the seminars, each consisting of 20 to 25 students, were led by teaching assistants. As part of their course work, students were expected to write four 800-word essays, each in response to a precisely worded prompt. For example, one assignment presented students with a hypothetical statute and asked students to discuss the relevance of this statute to various hypothetical situations, using the principles of statutory interpretation. (See Appendix A for the precise wording of this and other assignments.)

To perform the research, my assistants and I sat in on (and taped) the lectures and seminars; interviewed the course professor and the teaching assistant before, during, and after the course; interviewed a group of six students individually for at least an hour once a week throughout the academic year; analyzed the logs of law-related activities that they kept for us; and examined the notes and drafts for all the essays that they composed for the law course as well as all the other academic essays that these students composed over the same academic year. In other words, the research involved both naturalistic observation (including retrospective interviews) as well as textual analyses of the course texts, the lecture and seminar discourse, and the student writing.

Although the students received no explicit directions or guidance as to how to go about writing their essays, and although they were exposed to no models of such writing, the essays produced for the law course showed a remarkable uniformity in macro- and micro-level structure, tone, lexicon, and syntax. At the same time, these law essays were clearly distinct from the other academic writing produced by these same students over the same time period. A distinctive genre was being produced in this class, and our goal was to understand the nature and function of this distinctiveness.

TEXTUAL REGULARITIES

For convenience's sake, my procedure recapitulates the history of genre studies. I begin by pointing to textual regularities and only afterward discuss the writing from the perspective of more recent reconceptualizations of genre. Although recent theories have been concerned to show that such regularities are themselves effects of the social and rhetorical actions undertaken, the fact of these regularities is always acknowledged and, as in this case, often serves as a useful base for discussion.

Textual Analysis

The discussion that follows is organized by the categories of analysis. What is apparent, however, is a difference between Essays 1 and 2 as opposed to Essays 3 and 4. In every instance, Essays 3 and 4 are characterized by all the textual differentiating features that are described later. Essays 1 and 2 display some, but not all, of these features, and as the analysis of syntax suggests, these first two essays seem to represent a midpoint or bridge between the law essays and other academic prose. The significance of this gradation is explored later.

One further point. The analyses were primarily based on the law essays written by the six students we observed in contrast to the other academic prose written by these same students over the same academic year. In order to confirm that the law essays written by these six students were not, in any way, idiosyncratic, further analyses were performed comparing the law essays of the six students in our study to all the other law essays produced in the same seminar section. These analyses corroborated the fact that the students participating in our study produced writing typical of the essays elicited from the seminar section as a whole. In other words, although the following analysis focuses on the work of six students, the description of the law essays applies to all the writing produced in that seminar section.

Lexicon.

The first dimension on which these texts could be differentiated was the lexical. From the first assignment, the papers were characterized by the use of the distinctive specialized vocabulary of law. For example, the following instances of specific legal terminology recur and are only exemplary: *statute, common law, equity, sovereignty,* and *eiusdem generis.* In addition to these legal terms, other lexical items are used in a more specialized sense in the law essays: law, precedent, rule, and civil. The source of these lexical peculiarities is not hard to find: The lectures, the seminar discussions, and the textbook were all characterized by the same language.

Syntax.

Far more significant are the syntactic differences discovered—significant especially because, as will be shown, there were no models for such distinctiveness in the prose the students read. The syntactic analyses included counts of the number of words, T-units, finite clauses, and sentences, followed by computations of the number of words per T-unit, the mean number of T-units per sentence, and finite clauses per T-unit, for the following groupings: all the law papers; Assignments 1 and 2 together; Assignments 3 and 4 together; and all the essays written for all other disciplines over the course of the same year, by these same students. (See Appendix B for a tabular summary of the findings and the statistical analyses.)

To sum up, the law essays as a whole are considerably more syntactically complex (at a statistically significant level) than the other academic essays written by these same students at the same time. Complexity is typically defined by an increase in words per T-unit, a decrease in T-units per sentence, and an increase in clauses per T-unit. The law essays averaged 18.61 words per T-unit (vs. 16.15 for all other essays), 1.15 T-units per sentence (vs. 1.21), and 1.62 clauses per T-unit (vs. 1.48). Furthermore, the syntax became increasingly more complex in the later law assignments: Essays 3 and 4 averaged 20.41 words per T-unit and 1.74 clauses per T-unit.

What makes all this particularly remarkable is that the only conceivable prose model the students were reading was the course text, *Looking at Law*. Two entire chapters of this text were analyzed syntactically, and the same computations were made, revealing that the syntax of this text was considerably closer in complexity to that of the other academic essays written by these students than it was to the syntax of their law essays (see Appendix C).

The explanation for the greater simplicity of the prose in the law text may lie in the fact that its author (the professor for the course) is a very conscious proponent of the plain English movement in law, and consequently of what he deems to be the plain style. Whatever the reason though, neither this text, nor anything in the students' reading for this course, provided a model for the increased complexity of their prose.[2]

Rhetorical Patterns.

In addition to the lexical and syntactic analyses, the papers were compared as to their rhetorical structure. We began broadly with Kinneavy's (1971) classification of aims of discourse. Kinneavy defined six aims, three of which are referential in their primary focus. Writing for law is certainly always referential and furthermore always falls into that specific referential category that Kinneavy named writing "to prove a thesis." In this, the writing for law was similar to most other academic

---

[2]Neither were models sought in other student papers: None of the students whom we observed ever read papers written by other students in their class or by students in preceding years. Occasionally, in their weekly interviews with us, some suggested that looking at other student papers might be a good strategy, and our own response as interviewers was always encouraging. In the end, however, such models were never in fact sought or read; in retrospective interviews at the end of the course, the students all agreed that consulting other students' papers was never a strategy that they employed.

writing. (In contrast, the course text was informative in aim, according to Kinneavy's classification, with the corresponding differences in rhetorical organization.)

Broadly, what characterizes such writing is that the whole is unified by a single thesis, often, although not necessarily, made explicit at both the beginning and end of the piece. The body consists of the proof for this thesis—either in the form of a series of separate points, or one carefully developed train of reasoning, or some combination of both. Sometimes a refutation or counterargument is included.

With this crude scheme as a model, writing for law distinguishes itself from other academic argumentative writing in three ways. First, it differs in degree, that is, it seems to embody the earlier discussed qualities in their purest possible form. Such writing is almost ruthlessly logical, animated as it is by a precisely expressed thesis to which every specific point is clearly and explicitly linked. There is no room for digressions, no tolerance of irrelevant or even semi-relevant points (no matter how elegant).

Second, writing for law differs in that, far more than any other university assignments, it insists on the inclusion of all possible counter arguments. Consequently, there is a characteristic contrapuntal movement to its development that distinguishes it from the other academic writing produced by the students over the same period. In fact, in all the other essays analyzed, counterarguments were almost never introduced, whereas in the law papers (especially assignments 3 and 4), they were introduced at every juncture.

Third, although all academic writing must be logical in the sense that the conclusions must seem to be connected on a reasonable basis to the premises, the emphasis in writing for law is almost entirely on presenting the reasoning processes themselves. Every logical step must be articulated. In other disciplines, logical leaps are possible: Connections are more often accepted as shared knowledge between reader and writer. In writing for law, the whole point of the exercise is to present not so much the logical conclusions, but rather the rationale for these inferences. This point is further developed in the following section.

The Nature of the Argumentation.

Another way of understanding this distinction is through an analysis of the nature of the argumentation in these texts, using a categorization specified by Toulmin et al. (1979). In this system, the following parts of an argument are distinguished: the *claim*—the assertion put forward publicly for general acceptance, that is, the thesis; *the ground*—the specific facts relied on; *the warrants*—the general ways of arguing, that is, the principles for connecting the claims to the grounds; *the backing*—authority for the warrants; *the modalities*—the degree of strength of the claim; and the *rebuttals*. Toulmin et al. argue that although all these elements are at least potentially present in every argument, there is considerable variation in the nature of each element as well as the emphasis given it, depending on the audience, the task, and especially the field or discipline.

Using such a frame of reference to illuminate the distinctiveness of the law writing, it was apparent that, whereas for most of the other academic writing undertaken by our students, emphasis was placed on presenting the claim and clarifying its implications by pointing extensively to the grounds (with the warrants often tacit), the primary focus in the law papers (especially the last two assignments) was on specifying the warrants and their backing in detail and on showing how these warrants applied to the grounds. In the end, it mattered less what claim one made as long as the relationship between the various warrants possible to the grounds, accompanied by the appropriate backing, were all laid out.

Furthermore, the warrants drawn on were far more highly formalized, precise, and exact than those in other academic essays. There are precise rules or principles for statute interpretation, and their use must be specified in each instance. The following excerpt reveals on the microlevel the kind of argumentation that persists throughout the essay:

> The defense in this case would presumably argue that the wall is not a building by definition. Using *eiusdem generis* (of the same kind) canon of interpretation, it is evident that "building" as seen in section 4 refers to the list in section 3: a house, shed, barn, or other structure, which infers the membership of those structures that can be occupied. Therefore, the exclusion of members of the class, fence and wall, imply that they are not included under the meaning of "building." The elements listed that infer building all imply that one cannot occupy them. Since one cannot occupy (in the sense that one cannot enter into it and take shelter) a wall, Brown's boundary marker is therefore not applicable for prosecution under this statute.

Microlevel Rhetorical Patterns.

Another distinct characteristic of these texts can be seen in a recurring pattern on the micro-level. As the previously quoted excerpt shows, there is a characteristic pattern at the level of the conceptual paragraph that involves the following elements ordered in the following way: an elucidation of a central *issue*, the presentation of the appropriate *rule*, its *application*, and a *conclusion*.

Brand and White (1976), in their discussion of the characteristics of legal writing, identified such a pattern and gave it the acronym IRAC (issue, rule, application, conclusion). What is intriguing is the degree to which this pattern recurs in the last two law assignments and only in the law essays, although none of the students consulted Brand and White or any similar rhetoric; nor did the professor or teaching assistant ever make mention of such a pattern in the seminars or classes.

To conclude, these various analyses reveal the degree to which writing for law is distinctive. The lexicon is discipline-specific; the syntax is more complex; the overall rhetorical structure is more purely thesis-oriented, less tolerant of digression, and characterized by a contrapuntal movement; the nature of the argumentation is distinct, focusing on specifying precise warrants, in the context of their backing, and showing their relationship to the grounds; and there are characteristic discourse features at the micro-level, such as the IRAC patterning of conceptual paragraphs.

Furthermore, this distinctiveness is clearly not modeled after any prose the students were reading for this course. Although similar in lexicon, the course text was less syntactically complex. Furthermore, partly because its aim was primarily informative rather than argumentative, the rhetorical and discourse patterns on both the micro- and macro-levels differed radically from those discerned in the student papers.

Staged Development.

As suggested initially, the textual analysis revealed the degree to which the assignments were staged so that all the textual features described earlier were present in every instance of the last two essays, whereas the first two essays displayed some, but not all, of these features (with the second closer in form to the last two than the first). Thus, Essays 1 and 2 were characterized by a lexicon peculiar to law: They shared the same referential aim, the same ruthlessly logical mode of development, and the same intolerance for digressions. In addition, Essay 2 approximated the kind of contrapuntal form that characterized Essays 3 and 4. As for Essays 3 and 4, they displayed all the characteristics specified earlier as well as an emphasis on warrants and backing in the argumentation, in addition to the distinctive, related micro-rhetorical pattern (IRAC). The syntax, in particular, dramatized the gradation: The last two essays were considerably more syntactically complex than the other academic writing performed by these same students over the same year, whereas the syntax in the first two essays represented a step toward such greater complexity.[3]

---

[3]This gradation was carefully—although not consciously—orchestrated by the instructor, as the specification of the course assignments (in Appendix A) suggests. The students' mastery of the new genre was a result of a complex and intricate collaboration between instructor and students, in which the staging of the assignments played a significant role. (Note that the collaboration remained largely tacit: None of the students consulted either the instructor or the teaching assistant for explicit guidance.)

BEYOND TEXTUAL REGULARITIES

Traditional analyses would have begun and ended with the articulation of such textual regularities. What I intend to do now is explore this discourse and these textual regularities using the notions suggested in the earlier discussion of contemporary genre theory as probes. Do these textual regularities derive from some common social action? How does the hierarchic fusion of form and substance accomplish this social purpose? How does place affect the meaning of the text? If genres are best seen as texts in dialogue, how is this interaction maintained or created in these texts? In what sense is the genre a response to, or a product of, cultural or institutional constraints? In what sense is the genre shaped by its discipline, its field of knowledge? The questions overlap and are meant to indicate issues to be addressed rather than to signal the steps in the ensuing argument. I begin by focusing on what the writing of such texts meant for their writers.

The Writer

In his discussion of how children learn to write, Kress (1982) pointed to the "world-ordering" and even the "world-creating" function of "textual structures" (p. 97). The textual features described in the preceding section imply something about the way in which their writers approached or interpreted reality—at least during the writing of those texts. In this section, I tease out the implications of the textual features specified earlier for their writers' stances toward experience and their ways of knowing.

First, however, it is essential to point to the limitations of what can be inferred. The distinction proposed by Toulmin et al. (1979) is illuminating: The form of reasoning presented in these pieces does not replicate "a way of arriving at ideas but rather a way of testing ideas critically" (p. 29), a way of presenting them persuasively to a relevant audience. The steps in the legal arguments do not replicate the mental processes of the writer in determining the solution; instead, they represent the steps by which readers in a certain community can be convinced (or are prepared to be convinced) of the reasonableness of certain claims—claims that have themselves been discovered in as yet ill-understood ways by the writers. In other words, the discovery processes themselves, the internal cognitive operations, cannot be inferred from the products.

What can be inferred, however, is a certain stance toward reality, implied and necessitated by the writing of these specific texts. Thus, the very issues addressed, the phenomena focused on, involve a certain categorization of experience that is different from that of the other academic pieces written by these students (and different from the kinds of categorizations implied in their discussions with us). Specific human situations are addressed, and addressed in a highly specialized way: not from the perspective of the human suffering entailed, nor of the social dynamics involved, not from the perspective of universal moral principles, but rather from the point of view of the relevance of certain specialized legal principles.

This highly specialized categorization of experience is implied not only by the subject matter of the essays, but also by their distinctive lexicon. As we have seen, the language of the essays is characterized by a prolific use of legal terminology: *law, statue, eiusdem generis,* and *precedent.* All these items reveal that the specific phenomena examined are being classified and organized according to the classificatory principles involved in the discipline of law studies. The writers not only look at the kind of phenomena typically analyzed by the discipline, they also use the same lenses. Furthermore, both the boundedness of the texts as well as the intolerance for digressions suggest a concentration of focus that excludes other possible perspectives.

As to the increased complexity of the syntax, the longer T-units and the greater number of clauses per T-unit suggest a more intense interest in the hierarchical interrelationships between propositions: Specific propositions are seen in the context of others, and relationships of cause, effect, condition, and concession are highlighted. On the other hand, simple coordinate relationships within sentences (as measured by T-units per sentence) are of less interest. In an interview at the beginning of the course, the instructor tried to define what he thought of as distinctive in the writing he was eliciting: He spoke in general terms about the need for students "to see the forest rather than the trees." This search for and focus on hierarchical relationships may provide part of the textual instantiation of what the instructor was trying to suggest.

The contrapuntal pattern of the later essays is similarly revealing. Each issue or question, at the micro- and macro-levels, was addressed dialectically: For each point in favor, a corresponding point against was sought. When the array of pros and cons was set out, an attempt was made to arrive at some overarching generalization, taking into account all the arguments on both sides, rising thus to a higher level of abstraction and organizing the specific arguments into a superordinate framework. Here, too, is an example of seeing the forest, of pointing to a pattern that can organize the distinct entities.

This dialectical stance is not unique to law as a discipline; for example, it has important precedents in the history of philosophy. At the same time, certainly it is not the only perspective possible, and not necessarily the best. Coe (1986) pointed to the degree to which a dialectical approach can be limiting. Without arguing for or against the value of any particular stance, it is important to stress that the dialectical stance evinced in these essays represents only one possible stance toward a question—and interestingly not a stance that was represented in any other essay written by these same students over the year in question.

The text analyses also point to a distinctive mode of argumentation. In specifying the pros and cons, the writers argued using highly formalized and specialized modes of reasoning. Without suggesting that such modes of reasoning replicated the students' original discovery processes, I argue that, at the stage of drafting, the students needed to follow through in writing certain kinds of argumentation, that is, to engage in the application of very specialized methods of inference. In other words, they enacted in writing certain modes of reasoning that differed from the modes enacted for other disciplines.

To sum up, in the course of, and as a result of, their writing, the six students we observed began to look at and interpret reality in certain prescribed ways: They focused on certain kinds of phenomena, categorized them in specified ways, took a dialectical stance, searched for hierarchic relationships, and enacted certain formalized modes of reasoning.

Himley (1986) discussed the acquisition of specific genres in the following terms: "We discover new ways to mean, and thus how to participate more fully in the actions of the community. To learn how to write most fundamentally requires learning a social role in an interpretive community" (pp. 139-140). Willard (1982) too pointed to the social dimensions of such interpretive stances. To use Willard's language, through their writing, these students began "to construe certain phenomena in roughly the same way that other actors in the field construe them" (p. 34). In discussing the nature of such fields, Willard made a useful distinction. He differentiated between those fields in which the goals are epistemic (to learn or to know) and those whose goals are action-oriented (involving "ordinary" activities). The field in the case we observed was that of law as a disciplinary activity whose goals are epistemic (as opposed to the action-oriented goals of law as an "ordinary" activity). In writing their essays, the students began to share the stance of, and consequently to affiliate with, a certain argument field or discourse community—that of students of law. The social and the cultural dimensions of what the students learned are explored further in the next sections.

Genre as Social Action.

Miller's (1984) discussion of genre as social action or as "typified rhetorical actions based on recurrent situations" (p. 159) illuminates much that transpired in the law course, if we remember that in this particular instance the recurrence was synchronic. Miller pointed to the "mutual construing of objects, events, interests and purposes" (p. 158), or the "social motive" (p. 159), which results in the creation of those texts that can be differentiated by their distinctive linguistic features. The law essays constitute a specific genre in that they issue from the same social context and are expressions of the same social motive.

Note, however, that although students writing the essays shared the same social motive and responded to the same exigence, their individual private intentions may have varied. Again Miller is instructive:

> Although exigence provides the rhetor with a sense of rhetorical purpose, it is clearly not the same as the rhetor's intention for that can be ill-formed, dissembling, or at odds with what the situation conventionally supports. The exigence provides the rhetor with a socially recognizable way to make his or her intentions known. It provides an occasion, and thus a form, for making public our private versions of things. (pp. 157-158)

The private versions—the individual essays—indeed varied, and the intentions were sometimes ill formed: The essays' grades ranged from As to Ds. Nevertheless, whatever their grades, the essays shared the same social motive and consequently were characterized by similar formal features.

This notion of genre, with its emphasis on context, allows the role of the instructor in the creation of the genre to be acknowledged. More important, such a notion points as well to the impact of the cultural values implicit in the discipline as well as to those underlying the academic institution itself. The social action realized in the genre is in response, not just to a particular assignment specified by the instructor on one particular day, but also to the disciplinary context for that assignment as formulated in the lectures, seminars, and course readings as well as to the implicit institutional values of a university, in which writing is elicited as part of a social contract committed to by students, instructors, the institution itself, and society at large. All of these dimensions form the context and shape the social motive for the specific genre that was realized by the students observed in the Law 100 class.

The Place of the Texts.

Freadman (1987) remarked very shrewdly that "the same propositional content functions differently and thus means something different according to its performative setting. Meaning is not content; it is place and function" (p. 13). If any of the student texts produced in response to Assignments 3 or 4 were retyped using the letterhead of a law firm and addressed to a specific client, their meaning would change fundamentally. We would read these texts as pieces of legal advice, and our interpretation of the whole and each part would be governed by our understanding of this function. In other words, the function or meaning of these law essays can only be understood with reference to their actual setting; that is, these texts were written by students to their instructors, in response to an assignment. It is this place that determined the social action performed by the texts.

Freadman also focused on the interactive nature of genre. Using the analogy of a tennis match, she argued that genre is not the ball, nor the individual shots, nor even the rules of the game, but rather the playing of the game. In Freadman's terms, the genre we observed was the whole interaction—from the assignment (and all that it implied socially and culturally) through the writing to the final feedback. Our observations provided further corroboration of this notion: All the students displayed a sense of lack of closure—until the essay had been returned with a grade. The genre was achieved through a highly orchestrated and subtle interaction of instructors and students—all of whom shared the same goal: to initiate the students into a new discourse community, the community of students of law.

Discourse Community.

Not only Swales, but also a number of researchers and theorists have been looking at academic disciplines as discourse communities and subcommunities, with their own specialized patterns of language use. Such a perspective can offer insights into the interactions observed in the Law 100 class. First, though, it is important to refer to a distinction emphasized by the course instructor in an interview before the course began. He argued that the writing elicited was not the same as that produced by practicing lawyers. It was not "legal writing," in the usual sense. The writing, instead, was characteristic of "students of law," if we think of "students" not in the narrow sense of those enrolled in a specific course, but in the broader sense of those committed to the study of the discipline (as in students of literature). This is analogous to Willard's distinction, cited earlier, between action-oriented and epistemic disciplinary activities.

From the perspective of the literature on discourse communities, the students at the beginning of the year were outsiders to the community, and in enrolling in the course, they in effect stated their intention of becoming, or petitioning to become, members of the community of students of law. Over the course of the year, as a result of and through their writing (with all that the writing implies), the students succeeded in becoming members of that community defined as students of law. That is, their writing both attested to their entry into such a community and more significantly enabled or actualized this entry.

Furthermore, the students' initiation was accomplished collaboratively. The instructor, as well as the teaching assistant, played active roles in the interactions, which, among other things, resulted in the production of the law essays. In his lectures and in the readings he assigned, the professor modeled both the lexicon as well as the persuasive strategies or lines of reasoning that are conventionally accepted as valid in the discipline. In the assignments, he specified and categorized the data to be analyzed and formulated the questions that elicited from the students the kind of responses that could be characterized as a distinctive genre. The teaching assistant, like the professor, modeled persuasive strategies and lexicon, and further, through the grades, validated or confirmed the students' writing as exemplifying the discourse of the community. In other words, the instructor, the teaching assistant, and the students were all active agents in a complex collaboration that resulted in the students' performance as members of a new discourse community. The social goals of the instructors and the students coincided: to initiate the students into a new discourse community, the community of students of law.

To view the interaction as an initiation rite clarifies a great deal that has been troubling to those concerned with writing pedagogy. Typically, as Herrington (1985) observed, the writing that is elicited in disciplinary courses is condemned for its rhetorical artificiality (it asks the students to tell the professor what the professor already knows) as well as for the limited and limiting audience it seems to imply (teacher-as-examiner). However, to suggest that such assignments are pointless because they are artificial rhetorically may be to miss the real point of what is going on. What is going on is best understood as an initiation rite—a rite that is created not just as a hurdle for students to go through, but as a way of experiencing and expressing those qualities and abilities that are necessary for, and characteristic of, the initiates to the community. In tribal initiation rites, feats of endurance and courage may be elicited because such endurance and courage are expected of adult members of that tribe. In the same way, the writing assignments elicit the kinds of habits of mind and stances toward experience appropriate to members of the disciplinary community.

In this context, the gradation in the nature of the assignments and in the formal features displayed is particularly revealing. What we see dramatized thus is a gradual induction, or a very sensitive collaboration, in which the instructor carefully stages a sequence through which students increasingly take on the perspective of the initiated.

DISCUSSION AND IMPLICATIONS

If the textual analysis specified the ways in which the law essays are idiosyncratic, the discussion of the social and cultural dimensions point to the ways in which such writing is typical. My hunch is that further research will reveal that the law essays are typical in their very idiosyncrasy: Much discipline-specific writing can be textually differentiated and distinguished consequently in terms of the kinds of reasoning and stance implied—in precisely the same way as the law essays have been. In other words, my guess is that the social and cultural transactions will be shown to be essentially the same across disciplines, and that writing functions in the same way for each academic discourse community. In each discipline, the instructors' goals are to induct the student writers, and the students' goals are to be thus initiated, into the relevant disciplinary community of scholars. Most important, the initiation takes place through the writing, which allows as well as constrains the students to express the stances to reality appropriate tot he discipline.

In other words, most discipline-specific written arguments produced by students in school or a university are epistemic. Note that I use the word epistemic in a narrower sense than that employed by Willard. The purpose of student writing is not to produce knowledge, in the sense that contributors to learned journals produce knowledge, that is, knowledge that is new to the reader. The goal or social motive of most writing at the secondary or postsecondary levels is epistemic in the sense that the social motive is to enable or constrain the writers to engage in the modes of reasoning and the construction or interpretation or reality characteristic of the discipline being studied.

Teaching Implications

Pedagogically, a number of implications suggest themselves. First, these observations lead to considerably increased respect for what goes on in a disciplinary context. It is facile to dismiss some of the assignments specified in discipline-specific courses as artificial because the rhetorical relationship between student-writer and teacher-reader is not that of informer to uninformed. The goal of such writing is best understood in a broader social and cultural context, in which the functions of discourse extend well beyond those specified in conventional composition taxonomies.

Furthermore, this kind of analysis can only engender a sense of awe at what has been achieved and, more to the point, collaboratively achieved by student and instructors within and through the disciplinary and institution contexts. As researchers, we were struck by the intertextual nature of the creation, the complexity and subtlety of the negotiations among the various players, and the degree to which not just the textual features of the genre but the rules of play and interplay were tacit. For all these reasons, we would warn outside experts (writing-across-the curriculum specialists as well as psychometric consultants) to tread very warily when they suggest "improvements" to courses assignments or pedagogy. Only when the social and cultural dimensions as well as the complex interactive contexts of the writing currently undertaken are fully understood can outsiders suggest modifications or alterations.

Second, this discussion cannot fail to suggest the dangers implicit in reifying genres. Derrida (1980) pointed out that as soon as the word *genre* is sounded, as soon as one attempts to conceive it, a limit is drawn. And when a limit is drawn, norms and interdictions are not far behind. Dixon (1987) too warned against the dangers of reification in the context of education, and, from the outset, Bakhtin (1986) noted the relatively free and flexible nature of generic forms. The point is that norms and interdictions are inconsistent with the essential nature of generic creation as we have seen it. To understand genre as social action is necessarily to acknowledge its inherent dynamism. Genres necessarily change, as cultural and social values shift and as discourse communities redefine their perspectives on reality and their ways of knowing. Cooper (1986) argued for the use of the term *ecology* to capture the dynamism implicit in what is traditionally referred to as *context*.

Third, educationists must ponder the full implications of the social motive thus discerned in school writing for the disciplines. Specifically, we must recognize how much its goal or social action differs from the actions undertaken in most workplace writing or in the realm of public discourse. The social actions undertaken by written arguments in these latter settings are no doubt various and complex, but it is difficult to think of an instance in which the shared social motive would be geared toward the writer's own learning. The fact of this distinctiveness may help to explain much about the difficulty commonly experienced in the transitions between school or academia and the workplace.

Finally, I would contrast the richly textured and consequently constraining power of the kind of context for writing in the disciplinary class with the kind of context more typical of the composition class, in which often assignments are given in a relative vacuum. That is, a very precisely worded assignment may be specified, but that assignment is not contextualized within the kind of complexly interwoven strands of discoursal instantiations (in lecture, seminar, and text) of stance presented in content-area courses. In several studies investigating the writing of argumentative compositions at the elementary and secondary levels, my colleague, Ian Pringle, and I have noted the great variation in structure, tone, and stance of such pieces—in contrast, for example, to the production of narratives by the same students (see Freedman & Pringle, 1984, 1989). In effect, these student writers were selecting their own contexts to respond to in their writing because they were not being constrained or enabled by what had been transpiring to that point in their classroom: Some chose to respond using the hortatory conventions of the persuasive discourse aimed at students concerning drugs, cigarettes, and alcohol; others drew on more expressive exploratory conventions of personal writing; and some few selected topics discussed in content-area classes and wrote carefully reasoned pieces in response, using the generic forms appropriate to the relevant discipline.

This difference—between writing arguments for the disciplines and writing arguments in the composition class—is worth remembering, both when we assess student writing abilities as well as when we set curricular goals for the composition class. We must not feel that our goal in the writing class is to teach some form of "all-purpose argument" in order to prepare students to write effectively elsewhere in the curriculum; they acquire the genres of argument that may need for specific disciplines far more efficiently and effectively within me contexts of discipline-specific courses. If we still wish to elicit the writing of arguments in the composition class, and there are many reasons to do so, we will need to define for ourselves other independent goals, arising perhaps from the desire to help students define values and principles of action for themselves or from the commitment to enable our students to operate more powerfully within the realm of public discourse.

Theoretic Implications

As to the theoretic implications concerning the nature of "argument" in general and generically, we are left with a series of questions. What is common to all kinds of written argument? What does it mean for us as writers to undertake thesis or claim-oriented writing? What is the substance or the meaning created by such form? What is the nature of the social/cultural context that elicits such writing and the social action that is undertaken through this writing? What kind of negotiations or carefully orchestrated collaborations at the educational and the broader sociocultural levels are at play in eliciting and creating written argument?

As we can see, this perspective pushes us inexorably toward those questions addressed in the postmodern and poststructuralist enterprise, concerning the values and methods of Western knowledge, logic, and rationality. These are questions that are dealt with more fully elsewhere in this volume; it is enough here to point to the power of current theoretic reconceptualizations of genre for enhancing our understanding of argument at the most specific and most general levels, for the individuals involved as well as the social and cultural contexts entailed.[4]

APPENDIX A: THE ASSIGNMENTS

First Assignment

The term "common law" is used in four different meanings. Explain briefly, with reference to the relevant history, what these meanings are and how the term "common law" acquired them.

Second Assignment November 1983

"The two main principles in the U.K. Constitution are
  1) Parliamentary Sovereignty, and
  2) The Rule of Law.
  These principles, however, appear to contradict each omer."
Discuss.

Third Assignment: Statutory Interpretation

In January 1984 the following statute, with the short title "The Dilapidations (Highways) Act," is passed by the Ontario legislature. "Whereas it is necessary to provide for the safety of those passing along highways ...

3. If any occupier shall allow his house, shed, barn or other structure to fall into a dangerous condition he shall be guilty of an offense.
4. If any building is by reason of its ruinous or dilapidated condition seriously detrimental to the amenities of the neighbourhood, the local municipality shall within seven days of receiving a report to that effect from its building inspector order its

---

[4]Unexplored as well are the complex political issues implicit in the social action undertaken in the law class. Questions can and ought to be raised concerning a number of political issues. How are such genres, for example, subverted or resisted? Who is privileged and who is disenfranchised through, and as a result of the soical actions described? What regimes of power are reproduced? For a subtle discussion of the political issues associated with genre learning, see Luke (1994).

demolition and if any owner who has received an order to demolish such a building fails so to do within ten days of the receipt of the order he shall be guilty of an offense. Provided that it shall be a defense that the building was one of historic interest or that the owner within two days of the receipt of the order to demolish applied for an extension of time of seven days in order to secure expert advice ...

Advise the accused as to the application of the *Dilapidations (Highways) Act* in each of the following cases:

a) In November 1983 Jones' house becomes dangerous, through lack of repair, to persons using the highway, but he effects the necessary repairs before the end of the month. He is prosecuted under Section 3.

b) Brown has a brick wall which marks the boundary of his property but which is not structurally connected with his house. In March 1984 it becomes dangerous to users of the neighbouring property and he is prosecuted under Section 3. The wall is of great historical interest as the assembling point for the free-men of Leeds Country in their protest against the clergy reserves of Upper Canada.

c) The building inspector of the local municipality on 1st May, 1984, reports to the township council (i.e., the municipal council) that Robinson has painted a rainbow on his house and made it detrimental to the amenities of the neighbourhood. On 15th May the municipality posts to Robinson a letter containing an order to demolish. The letter is delivered to Robinson's home the next day, but he is seriously ill and does not open it until 25th of May. He immediately applies for an extension of time but he receives no answer and on 27th he is prosecuted.

d) Peterson, who operates a shop in the Byward Market, erected a canopy at the entrance to his store to protect plants and flowers which he sells. The canopy has been up for several years and has taken a beating from the elements. He was charged under s.3 of *The Dilapidations (Highway) Act*. When he appeared in Court his lawyer argued that the statute did not apply to commercial establishments but only to private dwellings. Judge X did not accept the argument. He held up an old copy of the "Globe and Mail" and read an article reporting on a debate when the bill was before the Ontario Legislature at which time the Minister of Highways stated the new statute would apply to both commercial and private structures. Judge X found Peterson guilty under the Act.

Fourth Assignment

You are acting for a client shipping corporation which lost one of its vessels on submerged rocks in the St. Lawrence River. The corporation argues that the loss resulted from the negligence of Cartographers Ltd., a company whose sea and river maps are on general sale and widely used by shipping firms. Your clients bought one of Cartographers maps of the St. Lawrence from Shipping Supplies, Ltd., in Toronto, a firm which has since gone bankrupt. They, therefore, want to recover compensation; if possible, from Cartographers, who, they argue, were negligent in not marking these dangerous rocks clearly on their map in the same way that they marked all other submerged rocks in the St. Lawrence. Correspondence with Cartographer's lawyer, however, reveals that Cartographers will argue that they were not negligent because they owed no duty of care to ultimate users of their maps to get all the details absolutely correct. On researching the law, which in this case the parties agree to be the law of Ontario, you find that

(1) there is a duty of care on manufacturers and repairers to the ultimate user to make reasonably sure that the things he uses (e.g., a car, a bottle of ginger beer) are physically safe to use;
(2) there is a duty of care on makers of statements owed to an identified third party (e.g., by an accountant to a specific third party who knows is considering investing in his client's firm on the basis of his—the accountant's—accounts and report prepared for the firm to give to the investor).
(3) with one exception, there is no case that says there is a general duty of care owed by makers of statements (orally, in writing or in pictures like maps) to third parties.

The one exception is the case of Hiker v. Mapping decided last year in the Ontario Court of Appeal. In the case the plaintiff, a hiker, suffered injuries through reliance on a badly prepared map which led him to think that the trail he was using in a certain national park was safer than it was. He sued the defendants who had prepared the map and sold it to him in one of their outlet stores. He sued in the Ottawa County Court for break of contract and negligence. At trial he succeeded on both issues. The defendants appeared and the Court of Appeal gave judgment as follows.

Able J.
    (After reciting the facts). Accordingly, I think the learned County Court Judge was correct to find for the plaintiff in

negligence. Clearly, defendants owed a duty of care to the plaintiff—anyone who prepared material to be used by others, such as a recipe or plan or map, is obligated to take reasonable care not to mislead the user to his detriment. Defendant breached that duty of care. Damage ensued to the user. This is a classic case of negligence. But even if I had not agreed with the judge on this, I would still have found for the plaintiff on the contract point. As to this, I agree with my brother Baker. I would dismiss the appeal.

Baker, J.

I agree the appeal should be dismissed. Plaintiff bought goods—a map—from defendants. Contract law, therefore, and Sale of Goods Act rules require the goods to be fit for the purpose for which they are sold. This map was not fit for that purpose. Accordingly defendants are in breach of contract. I am all the more pleased to agree with the County Court Judge and my brother Able on this because I respectfully disagree with both of them on the point of negligence. Since it is not necessary to my decision to discuss the point, suffice it to say that I do not think Lord Atkin's "neighbour" principle was ever meant to go that far. I, too, would dismiss the appeal.

Chief Justice Charlie

I have the misfortune to find myself disagreeing both with my brothers and with the County Court Judge. Let me say at the outset that I fully accept everything that my brother Baker has said about the contract point. Let me say also that I fully accept everything my brother Able has said about negligence—why, in my view if a cartographer carelessly omitted to mark some submerged rocks on a map subsequently bought by shippers and used by them to their detriment in that they lost one of their ships, that cartographer would be liable to those shippers in negligence. However, neither of my brothers adverted to a point argued by defendants and only briefly dealt with by the County Court Judge, viz. that the plaintiff's action was out of time. (Charlie C.J. then discussed the *Limitation Act*, the cases on it and the County Court Judge's finding, and concluded that the Judge was wrong.)

For those reasons, l would allow the defendants' appeal.

Appeal Dismissed

Question

Since many millions of dollars are involved, you know that if your clients sue you might even end up in the Supreme Court of Canada. Meanwhile, your clients want to know:

1. How far Hiker v. Mapping (whatever it may have decided) would be good authority in the courts.
2. How far Hiker v. Mapping can be said to be authority for the proposition that a duty of care is owed by a map-maker to the ultimate user.
3. What Hiker v. Mapping actually decided in point of law.
4. What is the legal force of Chief Justice Charlie's statement about a cartographer's liability in negligence.

Answer each of these four questions briefly, but giving full reasons for your answers in terms of the applicable rules concerning precedent.

APPENDIX B

Table 5.1. Syntactic Comparison Between Essays Written for Law and Those Written for All Other Disciplines.

	Law Essays 1+2 (N = 12)	Law Essays 3+4 (N s 10)	All Law Essays (N = 22)	All Essays For Other Disciplines (N = 16)
Mean Number of Words per T-Unit	17.1107	20.4104	18.6106	16.1527
Mean Number of T-Units Per Sentence	1.1361	1.1575	1.1459	1.2144
Mean Number of Finite Clauses Per T-Unit	1.5337	1.7365	1.6259	1.4886

The disciplines for which the other papers were written are as follows; Journalism (2); Mass Communications (3); Philosophy (2); Psychology (1); Political Science (2); English Literature (3); and Sociology (3). Note that journal papers were not journalistic essays but rather academic essays about issues in the field of journalism.

One-way analyses of variance were calculated in order to determine the significance of the differences between the means by pairs, showing the following. For words per T-unit, the differences between all law essays versus all other essays, as well as between essays 3 and 4 versus all other essays, were significant, with the F-statistic for all law essays versus all others = 10.009 ($p = .0032$); and for essays 3 and 4 versus all others = 34.573 ($p = .000$). For T-units per sentence, the differences were significant only when all the law essays were compared to all other essays (F-statistic = 4.192, $p = .0480$). For clauses per T-unit, only essays 3 and 4 were significantly different (F-statistic = 6.775, $p = .0156$).

When an analysis of variance was calculated comparing law essays 1 and 2 to essays 3 and 4, it emerged that the differences in words per T unit were significant (F-statistic = 9.744, $p = .0054$), whereas the differences for clauses per T-unit approached significance (F-statistic = 3247, $p = .0866$).

It is important to note too that even when the differences were not significant, the tendency was all in the same direction: That is, the law papers in general, and papers 3 and 4 in particular, have more words per T-unit, fewer T-units per sentence, and more finite clauses per T-unit.

APPENDIX C

Table 5.2. Syntactic Comparisons Between Law Text, Law Essays, and Essays Written for Other Disciplines.

	All Essays	All Law Essays For Other Discipline	Course Text: Looking at Law
Mean Number of Words per T-Unit	18.6106	16.1527	16.36
Mean Number of T-Units Sentence	1.14	1.21	1.9
Mean Number of Finite Clauses Per T-Unit	1.6259	1.4886	1.43

REFERENCES

Bakhtin, M.M. (1986). The problem of speech genres. In C. Emerson and M. Holquist (Eds.), V.W. McGee (Trans.), *Speech genres & other late essays* (pp. 60-102). Austin: University of Texas Press.

Bitzer, L. (1968). The rhetorical situation. *Philosophy and Rhetoric, 1*, 1-14.

Brand, N., & White, J.O. (1976). *Legal writing: The strategy of persuasion.* New York: St. Martin's Press.

Brooks, C., & Warren, R.P. (1970). *Modern rhetoric* (4th ed.). New York: Harcourt Brace Jovanovich.

Bruner, J. (1986). *Actual minds, possible worlds*. Cambridge, MA: Harvard University Press.

Burke, K. (1969). *A rhetoric of motives.* Berkeley: University of Califomia Press.

Campbell, K.K., & Jamieson, K.H. (1978). *Form and genre: Shaping rhetorical action.* Falls Church VA: Speech Cornmunication Association.

Christie, F. (1987). Genres as choice. In I. Reid (Ed.), *The place of genre in learning: Current debates* (pp. 22-34). Victoria, Australia: Deakin University, Centre for Studies in Literary Education.

Coe, R. (1986). *Process, form, and social reality*. Paper presented at the Fourth International Conference on the Teaching of English, Ottawa, Canada .

Cooper, M. (1986). The ecology of writing. *College English, 48*, 364-375.

Derrida, J. (1980). The law of genre. *Glyph, 7*, 17-201.

Devitt, A.J. (1993). Generalizing about genre: New conceptions of an old concept. *College Composition and Communication, 44*, 573-586.

Dixon, J. (1987). The question of genres. In I. Reid (Ed.), *The place of genre in learning: Current debates* (pp. 9-21). Victoria, Australia: Deakin University, Centre for Studies in Literary Education.

Freadman, A. (1987). Anyone for tennis? In I. Reid (Ed.), *The place of genre in learning: Current debates* (pp. 91-124). Victoria, Australia: Deakin University Centre for Studies in Literary Education.

Freedman, A. (1987). Learning to write again: Discipline-specific writing at university. *Carleton Papers in Applied Language Studies, 4*, 95-116.

Freedman, A., Carey, J., & Miller, A. (1989). Students' stances: Dimensions affecting composing and learning processes. *Carleton Papers in Applied Language Studies, 6*, 8~106.

Freedman, A., & Pringle, I. (1984). Why students can't write arguments. *English in Education, 18*, 73-84.

Freedman, A., & Pringle, I. (1989). Contexts for developing argument. In R. Andrews (Ed.), *Narrative & argument* (pp. 73-84). Milton Keynes, UK: Open University Press.

Herrington, A. (1985). Writing in academic settings: A study of the context for writing in two college chemical engineering courses. *Research in the Teaching of English, 19,* 331-359.

Himley, M. (1986). Genre as generative: One perspective on one child's early writing growth. In M. Nystrand (Ed.), *The structure of written communication: Studies in reciprocity between writers and readers* (pp. 137-158). Orlando: Harcourt Brace Jovanovich.

Kinneavy, J.L. (1971). *A theory of discourse.* Englewood Cliffs, NJ: Prentice-Hall.

Kress, G. (1982). *Learning to write.* London: Routledge and Kegan Paul.

Lave, J., & Wenger, E. (1991) *Situated learning: Legitimate peripheral participation.* Cambridge, MA: Cambridge University Press.

Luke, A. (1994) Genres of power: Literacy education and the production of capital. In R. Hasan & G. Williams (Eds.), *Literacy in society.* London: Longman.

Martin, J.R., Christie, F., & Rothery, J. (1987). Social processes in education: A reply to Sawyer and Watson (and others). In I. Reid (Ed.), *The place of genre in learning: Current debates* (pp. 58-82). Victoria, Australia: Deakin University, Centre for Studies in Literary Education. .

Miller, C. (1984). Genre as social action. *Quarterly Journal of Speech, 70,* 151-167.

Swales, J.M. (1990). *Genre analysis: English in academic and research settings.* Cambridge, UK: Cambridge University Press.

Toulmin, S. (1958). *The use of argument.* New York: Cambridge University Press.

Toulmin, S. (1972). *Human understanding.* Princeton, NJ: Princeton University Press.

Toulmin, S., Rieke, R., & Janik, A. (1979). *An introduction to reasoning.* New York: Macmillan.

Wellek, R., & Warren, A. (1977). *Theory of literature* (3rd ed.). New York: Harcourt Brace Jovanovich.

Willard, C.A. (1982). Argument fields. In J.R Cox & C.A. Willard (Eds.), *Advances in argumentation theory and research* (pp. 24-77). Carbondale: Southern Illinois University Press.

CHAPTER 6

*Fullness and Sound Reasoning: Argument and Evaluation in a University Content Course**

Pat Currie

The evaluation of student academic writing is of considerable interest to all teachers, but of central importance to those involved in attempting to prepare students for academic study. In their university careers, it is largely on their writing that students will be evaluated: It is in their writing that students must convince the professor that they have not only learned the basic concepts of that course, but that they have learned to think and argue in ways acceptable to the academic community,

Central to our task of student preparation is an understanding of the nature of academic evaluation. Determining just what is valorized in academic writing, however, is not a straightforward task. It is complicated by at least three factors: (a) the effort of the grader evaluating the text, (b) differences between graders' stated and operational criteria, and (c) differences among the various disciplinary communities.

---

*An earlier version of this chapter was published in S. Anivan (Ed.), *Language teaching methodologies for the nineties*. Singapore: SEAMEO Regional Language Center, 1989, pp. 127-142. Reprinted with permission.

One reason for the elusiveness of evaluation criteria lies in what Shaughnessy (1977a) termed the "dual nature of the relationship" between the student and her evaluator. Whereas on the one hand the relationship is cooperative, in the sense that both student and professor are trying to understand each other, on the other hand it is also a relationship of conflict in terms of the time and effort each is willing to spend on the other. There is, then, a limit to the extent to which the evaluator will try to interpret what the student is trying to say. Thus, if the students is to convince the professor that he or she has mastered not only the course concepts, but also the ways of thinking and arguing valued by that discipline, the student must communicate his or her ideas dearly and appropriately to the professor—largely through the written product, the rhetorical solution to the task.

A second reason why evaluation is hard to pin down is suggested by research focusing on the expectations as stated by the evaluators themselves. Studies by Rose (1979), Johns (1985), and Faigley and Hansen (1985) found discrepancies between what evaluators said they wanted and what they actually did or might do with what they got. In Rose's study, professors who claimed to consider global features of discourse more important than content instructed the teacher assistants (TAs) who were doing the grading to "sift through poorly organized text" for the right answer. If the information was correct, the student got the marks. Johns's (1985) study led her to question some of the evaluators' claims that whereas they considered sentence-level errors irritating, such errors did not influence the grades. Faigley and Hansen (1985) found significant differences between one instructor's stated criteria and those actually applied in grading. Such findings indicate that in our efforts to understand academic evaluation, we need to go beyond the explicitly stated criteria of the evaluators.

Yet another reason why it is hard to pinpoint those features of academic writing valorized by the academic community lies in differences among members of the various disciplines. Researchers (for example, Bazerman, 1981, 1985; Freedman, 1988; Herrington, 1983; and Swales, 1984, 1987; among others) have shown that the shared knowledge, values, perceptions, and beliefs of a given community are manifested in conventions particular to their discipline. Because such conventions, as Maimon (1983) noted, "are expectations in the minds of readers" (p. 112), evaluators are likely to have different, disciplinary-specific expectations. Three separate studies support such a position.

Rose (1979) found differences between the stated evaluative criteria of the English department faculty and those of faculty in other disciplines: The former weighted diction and style more heavily than the latter. Halpern, Spreitzer, and Givens (1978) found similar results: General faculty other than English tended to give higher grades for content than for expression.

In Faigley and Hansen's (1985) study of learning to write in the social sciences, the English instructor and the sociology professor differed significantly in their evaluations of one joint submission. Grading the paper B, the English teacher commented that an A paper would have good sentence structure, with no awkward or wordy sentences and no mechanical problems. The sociology professor, on the other hand, grading the paper A, praised the student's effort and depth of knowledge, noting that he was "more interested in what knowledge the student had acquired than in how well the report was written" (p. 147). The investigators concluded that "people read texts with varying expectations and . . . their judgments of merit vary as a consequence" (p. 148).

Perhaps foreshadowing the current interest in rhetoric, Shaughnessy (1977a) characterized the academic audience and its expectations in terms of its focus on argument:

> The academic audience is, however, the least submissive of audiences, committed as it is . . . to the assessment of new and as yet unproven interpretations of events. The writer is thus expected to make "new" or arguable statements and then to develop a case for them, pushing his inquiry far enough to meet his audience's criteria for fullness and sound reasoning. (p. 240)

Such criteria for "fullness and sound reasoning," of great relevance to any understanding of academic evaluation, are the focus of much of the ongoing research into the nature of argumentation in the different communities.

In her study of writing for law, Freedman (1988, Chapter 5, this volume) found differences between the writing done for law and that done for other academic fields. In law, the emphasis was on "specifying highly formalized and precise . . . warrants and on showing how these warrants applied to the grounds" (1988, pp. 20-21); the text was characterized by a contrapuntal shift back and forth between the two sides of the issue. In most of the other academic writing done by the same students, emphasis was placed on presenting the claim and clarifying its implications by pointing extensively to the grounds.

Further, Toulmin, Rieke, and Janik (1979) noted that an explicit statement of warrants is less common in the world of business than in other communities, because, as they are usually accepted by members of the organization, they are organizational "givens."

Further research into the nature of argumentation needs also to examine how academic evaluators actually respond to students' attempts to imitate the ways of thinking, knowing, and arguing (Bartholomae, 1985) in the academic community and to determine which approximate behaviors are rewarded and which are penalized. We need to explore, for example, what it is in the nature of a student's argumentation that fails to convince the evaluator that he or she has completed the required intellectual task, perhaps even if the right information is actually there. We need to ask which, if any, features of an argument can compensate for weaknesses, perhaps serious ones, elsewhere. Further examination of the nature of argumentation will tease out features particular to individual disciplinary communities as well as those common across disciplines.

This chapter, based on only part of a larger, more extensive study, focuses on the evaluation by the professor of one assignment given in a course on Organizational Behavior (OB), a subgroup or "forum" (Herrington, 1983) of academic business. The results support the notion of differences in argumentation across academic communities and suggest that the degree to which the familiar genre is matched does indeed influence grading, both positively and negatively. Finally, the chapter considers implications for both first and second language instruction.

COURSE CONTEXT

The introductory OB course I examined was a half-credit, required course generally taken in the second or third year of the Bachelor of Commerce program offered within the School of Business in Carleton University's Faculty of Social Sciences. One term (i.e., 13 weeks) consisted of two 1-hour lectures per week—given by the professor—as well as one hour in a seminar group—led by a TA.

It is necessary at this point to stress that the student writing done in this course was not writing for business in the sense of letters or memos, but rather writing about organizational situations and problems for an academic audience. It was, therefore, academic writing for the social sciences.

Apart from the examinations, students wrote nine 2-page assignments graded by the TA, which accounted for 30% of their final grade. Each assignment required the students to apply the OB concepts presented in one textbook chapter and to respond to questions set either by the professor or by the text.

The three students who participated in this study were all non-native speakers of English (NNESs): Leana and Sam, second year students from Hong Kong; and Diana, a third year student from Macao. All had been exempted from further ESL instruction, either by their TOEFL scores or by virtue of their having studied in high school in Canada for more than three years. As well, all three had taken and passed the composition course required of business students who do not achieve a certain standard on a test essay given at the beginning of their first academic year. The course consisted largely of grammar-based instruction.

The process by which the professor (who was also the Course Coordinator and a specialist in OB) provided me with information regarding his evaluation of the assignment was as follows: First, he graded the assignments and briefly rationalized his grades, all in writing; later, in a departure from the normal process, he evaluated them a second time in the course of a more detailed and focused interview with me. Thus, he evaluated each assignment twice. Normally, he would not have graded any of the assignments.

THE TASK AND EXPECTED RESPONSE

The particular question under discussion, based on a case study in the course text, formed one part of Assignment 3, due in the fifth week of the course. In it, the students were required to resolve an issue and argue for the resolution. Unlike many of the questions in the other assignments, which required the students to provide examples or other data to support their statements, this was one of seven such questions requiring them to present an argument in the form of a train of reasoning.

According to Toulmin et al. (1979) observers of organizational operations have identified a standard deliberative process by no means unique to business but very similar to that found in sciences, law, and other fields. The standard procedures for resolving an issue are the following:

1. Facts are gathered
2. Criteria on which the decision will be made are set out
3. Alternative decisions are suggested
4. The best alternative is chosen through careful argumentation.

The rhetorical analysis by Toulmin et al. (1979) also provides a useful framework for the discussion of the evaluation. They divided argument into six major elements that they labeled the *claim*, the *warrant*, the *grounds*, the *backing*, the *rebuttal*, and modalities. For this discussion, only the first three components are relevant. The *claim* is the "assertion put forth publicly for general acceptance" (p. 29; i.e., the thesis—the conclusion you reach, the prediction you make, or the decision you arrive at). The *grounds* are the "specific facts relied on to support a given claim" (p. 33; i.e., the statistics, examples, or details derived from a careful analysis of the situation). The *warrant* is the principle that enables you to use these particular grounds in support of a particular claim.

In the part of the assignment under discussion, the topic was goals, efficiency, and effectiveness. The two companies in the case—

study—Acme and Omega—represented two very different organizations. Acme is a very efficient organization internally, with clear responsibilities and narrowly defined jobs, good vertical integration, and good communication and coordination within the departments. Their goals are profitability and internal efficiency in the high-volume manufacturing of printed circuits.

Omega is a different organization. Where Acme is efficient, Omega is effective. Unlike Acme, Omega is well integrated horizontally with good communication and coordination across departments. At Omega there are no organization charts, as management feels they would put barriers between specialists who should be working together. Omega's goals are not internal efficiency and profitability, but rather the effective use of human resources, creativity, and employee understanding of all aspects of the organization's activities.

In the case study, the firms are competing for a contract to design and produce 100 working models of a prototype of a memory unit for an experimental copier. In part two of the assignment, the students were asked to predict the winner and justify their decision: "Which firm do you think will produce the best results? Why?" The prompt itself provided no criteria for making the decision.

According to the Course Coordinator, it is possible to argue for either company. The arguments are displayed according to the schema outlined by Toulmin et al. (1979). If the students argued for Acme (Figure 6.1a), they needed to warrant their grounds on the basis of the OB concept of *efficiency*, the result of the company's vertical integration (the detailed organization charts and job descriptions) that ensured coordination and communication within each division, and the ability to produce the required 100 prototypes within the specified time limits. Because of the lack of vertical integration at Omega (the absence of organization charts and detailed job responsibilities), it was not efficient. Both options had to be assessed.

If, on the other hand, the students argued for Omega (Fig.6.1b), they warranted their arguments using the concept of *effectiveness*: that good communication and coordination across the functional divisions would enable them to create a good prototype. Unlike Acme, Omega would have the horizontal integration that would enable them to do this.

The warrants involved a definition of the terms *best results* (fast production/a well-designed prototype) as well as a statement of the OB concept (efficiency/effectiveness) that would enable the company to produce these results.

Fullness and Sound Reasoning

ARGUMENT FOR ACME

WARRANT:
Fast production of prototypes achieved through efficiency

OPTIONS:

CLAIM: Acme will get contract

Acme
- Coordination and communication within departments
- Well integrated vertically

  Efficient

Omega
- Lack of org. charts and detailed job description
- Not well integrated vertically

  Not efficient

  GROUNDS

Figure 6.1a. Rhetorical pattern of the argument for Acme

ARGUMENT FOR OMEGA

WARRANT: Good prototype design achieved through effectiveness

OPTIONS:

CLAIM: Omega will get the contract

Omega
- Good communication coordination across departments (horizontal integration)
- Effective use of human resources

  Effective

Acme
- Not well integrated horizontally

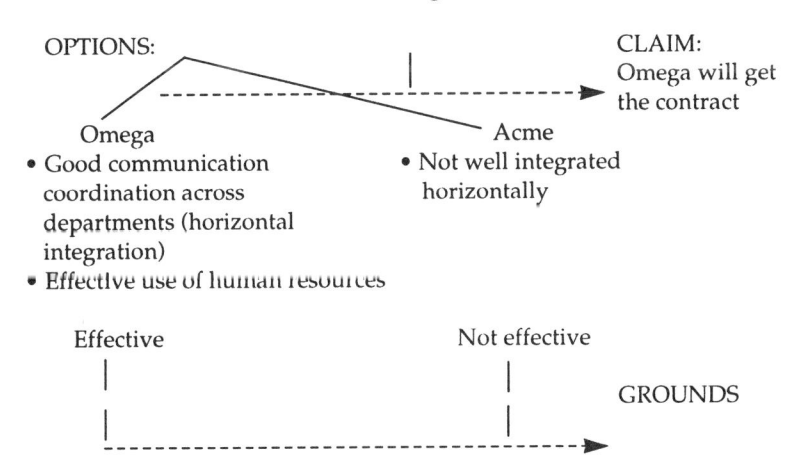

  Not effective

  GROUNDS

Figure 6.1b. Rhetorical pattern of the argument for Omega

THE EVALUATION OF STUDENT RESPONSES

This section examines both the actual, unedited responses of the three students and their evaluations (on two occasions) by the Course Coordinator.

Diana

Diana's response to part two, graded 5 out of 10 in both evaluations, was the following:

> In order to predict either Acme or Omega will provide the best results, we need to summarize the characteristics of the two different organization structure.
>
> Acme is a highly centralized, formalized and specialized organization. They have good vertical and horizontal structural linkages. They have detailed organizational charts and job descriptions. They rely on the formal type of communication where messages are flowed through memos. They are under a closed buffer system. They are confident of their competitive power. By concluding all these factors, we will not deny to admit that Acme will produce the best results.
>
> Omega is a highly decentralized, less formalized and less specialized organization. Even though the President is an expert of that field, he cannot be the only one to make all the credits. They believe that formal communication will act as a barrier against their work. Most of the time will be spent in assisting every employee to be certain of his duty in the organization. This will lead to a time of meeting demands. Their jobs are not guided by rules so they may have conflict about their real roles in the organization. As a result, their performance will be violated. They can be efficient but are not very effective.

In both his first and second evaluations, the Coordinator strongly criticized Diana's answer. His first comment—"Ho hum, here we go again"—provides insight into his limits of time and effort. As he explained, the student was not required to summarize; reading the answer meant reading some unnecessary material. It is also possible that the surface errors signaled less than readily accessible text, which consequently would require more effort.

Second, he criticized the wording of the claim ("We will not deny to admit that Acme will produce the best results"), questioning whether she had really answered the question. In this course, acceptable claims were clear and unequivocal. He decided to accept the claim, but not unreservedly: "I suppose so but she does not say 'why.'" In the interview he explained that he had been referring to the fact that some of her support was either incorrect or irrelevant. For example, the text wrongly described Acme as well integrated horizontally (untrue), and as having a "closed buffer system" (illogical, as buffers operate between the organization and the environment). Such problems also beset her argument against Omega. Again, inaccurate grounds (time in meetings precludes good performance; Omega is efficient but not effective) showed her failure to grasp the situation. Furthermore, some of the grounds were irrelevant ("Acme are confident of their competitive power," and "the president of Omega is an expert in that field").

His main criticism, however, was that she had not stated the criteria by which she was judging the alternatives: "She's missed the 'So what?' part—how this support constitutes an argument for Acme." In Toulmin's terms, she had neither warranted her grounds adequately nor established any criteria for judging this particular warrant applicable in this situation. Consequently, she failed to convince the professor of her ability to think acceptably in the OB community.

Her answer illustrates one difference between writing for OB and writing for business. As noted earlier, according to Toulmin et al. (and later confirmed by the professor), in business it is not common to state warrants because they are generally organizational givens. In the context of this course in the social sciences, however, when you are a university student trying to prove that you understand the concepts and can argue appropriately, warrants are expected.

Leana

Initially, Leana's entire assignment was graded "5-ish"; in the interview, the relevant section was later graded 5-1/2 to 6:

> From all the given facts in the case analysis, it is likely that Acme Electronics will succeed. The reason being that Acme clearly establishes the responsibilities and tasks of all employees so that the jobs will be carried out thoroughly and efficiently. Consequently, timely production is avoided and the firm is able to keep up with the customer's demand. In comparison, Omega Electronics spends a considerable amount of time in meetings. Therefore, the firm is not capable of meeting delivery.

Although the answer contains a linguistically clear and appropriate claim, the rest of the answer contains three major problems. The first problem (one of lexical choice) relates again to the expenditure of time and effort. The Coordinator's initial written comment was "not good—I did not understand the answer." The reason was the phrase "timely production." It can be argued, I suppose, that he might have deduced the intended meaning, either by guessing or by continuing to read, using subsequent clues from the text. This suggestion, however, denies the social context within which the student was writing. In academic writing, the burden of proof of mastery of knowledge rests with the student; the decision about the amount of time and effort spent rests with the professor.

Guessing might present two other problems. First, if he used a common definition—opportune—the meaning would make no sense in the context. If he next tried attributing to "timely" a meaning more directly associated with the word itself—on time—the phrase would still not make sense given that an organization is unlikely to try to avoid punctual delivery. Given the context, however, and the clue that the student was obviously referring to time, the Coordinator could simply have slotted in the meaning that would make the best sense—late. Such a contribution, however, would have been exactly opposite to what the student had actually said, and he, not she, would be answering the question.

His second option was to continue reading in the hope that the meaning would become clear. Here his confusion only increased, as he next queried the word demand. In a business context, demand usually implies an idea of ongoing, whereas this contract involved only one order. According to the Coordinator, the precise term would have been requirements. These two errors in lexical choice, suggesting the student's failure to acquire the language of the community, appear to fit Shaughnessy's (1977a) category of errors that "carry messages which student writers can't afford to send" (p. 12). All students beginning a new discipline must learn the language of that community. For those with less awareness of the subtleties and nuances of language (including but not limited to NNESs), those to whom demands and requirements might seem indistinguishable, the task may at times seem insurmountable. Thoroughly confused, the evaluator simply stopped trying to interpret what the student was trying to say.

The second weakness noted by the Coordinator was the student's failure to explore why at Omega the coordination and communication were done through meetings rather than formalized systems. If a student wanted to make this claim, she at least had to attempt to support it. Further, as nothing in the text indicated that the time spent in meetings led to an inability to meet a production schedule, her grounds were incorrect.

His response to the third major problem highlights two features of warrants in OB: their location and their syntactic form. First, his comments suggest that warrants should precede and be distinct from the grounds. Criticizing the placement of "efficiently," he commented that it should have appeared nearer the first of the sentence, where it would have "located her argument." Before assessing the grounds, he needed to know what only the warrant would tell him—the nature of her argument, the interpretive framework that would make coherent the remainder of the answer. Without that warrant, he was unsure of the relevance and appropriateness of those grounds. In argument, as in decision making, the criteria on which the decision will be made must be clearly established before anything else. Placing the organizational criterion at the end of the sentence may have violated the "given-new" order, or it might have signaled that it was not part of the central warrant but part of the grounds. When asked what his evaluation would have been had the student stated near the beginning that what was needed was an efficient organization, the Coordinator replied that the argument would have been much more acceptable: "It's what I would expect in a good answer."

Studies of reading structure (Meyer,1975) suggest that sentence-initial information is more likely to be recalled than information in sentence-final position. It is possible, given the good reader's strategies of prediction, that he did not even see "efficiently" and so could not deem the argument warranted. It is also possible that having to wait to discover the nature of her argument increased the short-term memory load and thus the effort required to evaluate the answer.

Finally, there is the further possibility that in its adverbial form—efficiently—the warrant was made even less accessible than it would have been as the noun efficiency. Perhaps the combination of these factors—the location and the unexpected syntactic form—made it impossible for him to view it as part of the warrant.

Sam

In contrast to the first two assignments, Sam's initially received a very favorable response—8, with the Coordinator noting that the following section was "very good":

> The major concern on this case is which company can produce one hundred prototypes within the stated period, so the major goal here is fast production. In this case, it does not concern about output level and external environment. Internal efficiency is more important. Inside Acme, coordination and communication between departments would be a problem When problem occurs, it would take time

to solve. On the other hand, inside Omega, each department has better communication with others and departmental activities mesh with one another to have high productivity. Omega would take the advantage of internal organizational health and efficiency. So I think Omega would produce the best results.

In this section, the argumentative structure fits the template of Toulmin et al.; it contains a warrant, a claim, and grounds. As the Coordinator put it, the student "located his argument" in the first sentence by stating the criterion he would use in making his decision ("fast production") as well as the key organizational characteristic ("internal efficiency") that would enable the company to achieve their goal. It is noteworthy that here efficiency appears as a noun, the subject of its own sentence. Sam then assessed each of the two alternatives in terms of its ability to achieve this goal, providing grounds for the fully warranted claim "So I think Omega would produce the best results."

In the more focused and detailed interview, however, the Coordinator found several weaknesses. First, he noted the lack of support for Sam's claim that "when problem occurs, it would take time to solve." The next criticism, far more striking and significant, suggests that a well-formed argument can compensate not only for inadequate grounds, but also for an incorrect claim. Having established the warrant of efficiency, Sam claimed that Omega, not Acme, would produce the best results. Yet Acme was the efficient organization; Omega the effective one.

To explain why the Coordinator failed to see the error, I propose the nature of the student's argumentation. The professor was accustomed to seeing arguments structured in a particular way. This text, which closely matched the familiar genre, enabled him not merely to fill in an information gap, but to reconstruct what was actually there to suit his expectations. Because of his prior knowledge of the structure of an acceptable argument, he was led to believe that his expectations of content would be fulfilled.

The Coordinator did, in fact, regard this as a very plausible explanation of what happened; schema theory shows us that the rhetorical organization of a text interacts with the schemata or prior knowledge of the reader to help him or her create meaning out of that text. I would guess that this evaluator is not alone, that other evaluators of student papers have practiced similar strategies with similar results.

One contributing factor to his adoption of predictive reading might well have been the time and effort he felt he would have had to spend on the text of a second language writer. Once the argumentative structure was so clearly highlighted, and the initial content deemed correct, he may not have troubled to read thoroughly the less accessible grounds.

It appears, then, that in this introductory OB course, an acceptable argument includes a warrant: a statement of the chosen criteria, the concept being applied to the given situation, and, if not specified in the prompt, an explanation for the selection of that concept. The argumentative structure may further require that, in order for writers to locate their arguments, warrants both precede the grounds and be explicitly signaled as distinct from such grounds, thus enabling graders easily and efficiently to assess their relevance and appropriateness. Regarding the location and form of that warrant, a well-formed argument may need the concept realized in its own sentence, perhaps even in a particular syntactic form. It may also be the case that the claim is less important than the grounds and warrant.

With regard to the importance of warrants, one final point has yet to be made: the ability of the concept to determine the relevance of the grounds. In her argument for Acme's predicted success, Diana wrote that Acme was confident of its competitive ability. Because the concept of efficiency does not include the notion of confidence, her grounds were rejected as irrelevant.

With regard to commonalities and differences among communities, the nature of argumentation required for these assignments is different from that required for law. In OB there was no contrapuntal shift back and forth, but a more linear progression through warrant and grounds.

As the OB assignments under discussion here were very task-specific, requiring the students to resolve an issue and argue for the resolution, comparisons cannot be made to the other, typical academic writing observed by Freedman (1988, this volume).

Finally, despite similar procedures for resolving an issue, the writing of arguments in OB differed in one significant way from writing for business: In the context of this university course, warrants were not "givens" to be omitted from the display, but required indicators of acceptable reasoning.

IMPLICATIONS

One basic question this study sought to answer was what criteria this evaluator, the Course Coordinator, actually applied in evaluating the students' responses to the task. The overriding criterion appears to have been the degree to which the argumentative nature of each text matched the genre familiar to him, followed by the accessibility of the text. In the first evaluation, Sam's answer, which most closely approximated that genre, received an 8 (Sam appears to have been lucky; on no other occasion did he structure an argument as well as he had here); Leana's response, which matched his argumentative expectations less closely, but in language that obstructed the meaning, received a grade of "5-ish"; Diana, whose answer looked least like the familiar genre, received 5.

Thus, it appears that the students' grades depended less on their ability to complete the conceptual task than on their ability to argue acceptably—to construct a rhetorical solution that matched what the evaluator had in mind. In one interview Diana captured the essence of the student's task: "It's easy to get an A if you can read through the mind of the professor."

What do such results suggest for both first and second language writing pedagogy? First, in conjunction with the results of Rose (1979) and Faigley and Hansen (1985), they suggest the need for a shift in the traditional focus of the classroom. Because it appears there are mistakes our students can afford to make, especially if they occur within a well-reasoned answer, I suggest there is a need for us to concentrate less on errors that offend our English teachers' perceptions of accuracy and grammaticality in order more profitably to spend our time and energy on the errors that a student cannot afford to make—errors such as lexical choice that put evaluators in a situation in which they have to do the work of the student.

Second, given that studies besides this one (e.g., Freedman, 1988; Herrington, 1983) report that university students are required to write arguments, classroom materials need to address this requirement. To date many classes and textbooks have focused on the typical modes of organization, such as comparison/contrast, cause/effect, and chronology, to the exclusion of argumentation. Furthermore, the same neglect holds for what the rhetoricians tell us are "standard procedures" for resolving issues in fields such as business, science, and law.

Students who do not understand what Shaughnessy (1977b) termed "rituals and ways of winning arguments in academia" have great obstacles to overcome in their efforts to succeed at a university, a task perhaps even more difficult for second language students. For us in first and second language writing, then, it becomes even more important that we attend to the calls of scholars such as Maimon (1983) and Bizzell (1982) to make academic discourse more accessible than is currently the case.

Yet, although it is safe to say that university students are frequently required to write arguments, the nature of the expected argumentation appears not to be monolithic: Probable pitfalls in trying to generalize about the nature of argumentation in academe are signaled by the substantial differences between organizational behavior, law (Freedman, 1988), and chemical engineering (Herrington, 1983). It is quite possible that differences also exist within disciplines and departments (for example, in biology, between entomologists and plant physiologists; or, in psychology, between the clinicians and the neuroscientists) and between individual professors.

In the face of such diversity and ambiguity, then, what is the classroom teacher to do? I suggest that one place to start is in our own writing classes, in collaboration, if possible, with instructors of content courses. Together, the writing teacher and content instructor might devise a task requiring the students to resolve an issue and present a written argument defending their conclusions. Here students could engage in the "standard procedures" identified by Toulmin et al. (or in procedures specified by the instructor). Ideally, the content expert would also participate in the evaluation, perhaps with the class or perhaps alone with the classroom teacher, who could discuss the evaluations with the class, indicating which features pleased, which irritated, and why.

Even without such expert resources, however, our classrooms can still provide students with materials and activities that require tasks of resolution/argumentation and the evaluation of student attempts. At the very least the students would learn procedures for resolving an issue, the components of argumentation, and the awareness of genres.

Following Maimon, Belcher, Hearn, Nodine, and O'Connor (1981), students might examine important issues, questions, and writings of a variety of fields. The issue of capital punishment, for example, might be viewed from the perspectives of law, history, anthropology, and sociology, with writing assignments reflecting the diversity of views.

The classroom teacher could use the vehicle of academic journalogs employed by Johns (1990), who trained her students in the ethnographic skills necessary to examine the writing required in a Western civilization course they were taking along with their academic skills course.

Classes of university students from diverse disciplines could extend journalogs to examine the issues, questions, expectations, and writing in their current courses. Students might also answer questions from earlier examination papers in their major subjects, asking their professors to comment on their attempts.

Differences between genres learned in the writing class and those expected in other courses need not be seen as indications of the teacher's lack of knowledge, but rather as a means of heightening student awareness of disciplinary expectations.

Approaches such as these teach students the concepts, skills, and terminology needed in their explorations. Perhaps even more importantly, they teach them skills and strategies to figure out the nature of disciplinary expectations and go a long way toward addressing the need to focus on the student as an individual. At the same time, they also relieve the classroom teacher of the unrealistic burden of knowing all the answers, placing the responsibility for his or her learning squarely on the student.

Despite ambiguity and uncertainty regarding academic argumentation, what is clear is that research and teaching need to go hand in hand. Research is needed into the similarities and differences across and within disciplines and departments as well as among the individuals within these communities. We also need to learn more about how successful students, especially second language speakers, both figure out and meet the expectations of their communities. It is in this area in particular that teachers are well placed to do the needed research.

If we continue on both fronts, we will all benefit—ourselves, our colleagues, and our students. As teachers of writing, we will reap not only an expanded awareness of the universe of discourse, but also the satisfaction that we have helped initiate our students into the rites of academe.

For our colleagues, the advantages include, perhaps, a more conscious awareness of their own values and expectations as well as more effective ways of helping their students meet those expectations.

For our students, the benefit can be a forum for the development of the skills necessary to their growth as individuals and to their full and successful participation in the academic community.

REFERENCES

Bartholomae, D. (1985). Inventing the university. In M. Rose (Ed.), *When a writer can't write* (pp.134-165). New York: Guilford Press.

Bazerman, C. (1981). What written knowledge does: Three examples of academic discourse. *Philosophy of the Social Sciences, 11*, 361-388.

Bizzell, P. (1982). College composition: Initiation into the academic discourse community. *Curriculum Inquiry, 12*, 191-207.

Faigley, L., & Hansen, K. (1985). Learning to write in the social sciences. *College Composition and Communication, 36*(2), 140-149.

Freedman, A. (1988, May). *Looking at writing for law: The social and cultural dimension of learning a new genre*. Paper presented at the Institute of Teaching and Learning, University of Chicago.

Halpern, S., Spreitzer, & Givens, S. (1978). Who can evaluate writing? *College Composition and Communication, 29*(4), 396-397.

Herrington, A.J. (1983). *Writing in academic settings: A study of the rhetorical contexts for writing in two college chemical engineering courses*. Unpublished doctoral dissertation, Rensselaer Polytechnic

Institute, Troy, NY. (Dissertation Abstracts International, ADD-84-09508).

Johns, A.M. (1985). *Writing tasks and evaluation in lower division classes: A comparison of two- and four-year post-secondary institutions.* Unpublished manuscript.

Johns, A.M. (1990). Coherence as a cultural phenomenon: Employing ethnographic principles in the academic milieu. In U. Connor & A.M. Johns (Eds.), *Coherence in writing: Research and pedagogical perspectives* (pp. 209-226). Alexandria, VA: TESOL.

Maimon, E.P. (1983). Maps and genres: Exploring connections in the arts and sciences. In W.B. Horner (Ed.), *Composition and literature: Bridging the gap* (pp. 110-125). Chicago: University of Chicago Press.

Maimon, E.P., Belcher, G.L., Hearn, G.W., Nodine, B.G., & O'Connor, F.W. (1981). *Writing in the arts and sciences.* Boston: Little, Brown.

Meyer, B.J.F. (1975). *The organization of prose and its effects on memory.* Amsterdam: North-Holland.

Rose, M. (1979). When faculty talk about writing. *College English, 41*(3), 272-279.

Shaughnessy, M. (1977a). *Errors and expectations.* New York: Oxford University Press.

Shaughnessy, M. (1977b). Some needed research on writing. *College Composition and Communication, 28*(3), 317-321.

Swales, J. (1984). Research into the structure of introductions to journal articles and its application to the teaching of academic writing. In R. Williams, J. Swales, & J. Kirkman (Eds.), *Common ground: Shared interests in ESP and communication studies* (pp. 77-86). Oxford: Pergamon.

Swales, J. (1987). Utilizing the literatures in teaching the research paper. *TESOL Quarterly, 21*(1), 41-68.

Toulmin, S., Rieke, R., & Janik, A. (1979). *An introduction to reasoning.* New York: Macmillan.

CHAPTER 7

The Nature of Argument in Peer Dialogue Journals

Chris M. Anson
Richard Beach

To introduce their research on the development of argumentative thinking among children, Stein and Miller (1990) describe two theoretical perspectives for understanding the nature of argument. In the *disputative* perspective, the participants "mutually attribute argumentative intentions to each other," assuming that their assertions are incompatible and that their strategy must be to "win," that is, to prevail in a rhetorical battle (p. 265). In the *evaluative* perspective, participants espouse positions, claims, or beliefs that are then substantiated with supporting evidence. This second form of argument does not enact "an explicit conflict between two positions" (p. 266), the overriding goal is no longer disputative or adversarial, but evaluative: to avoid logical flaws in (or potential objections to) the line of reasoning. "Opponents" need not even be invoked. In contrast to the embattled disputator clinging loyally to his or her claims and beliefs, the arguer may even modify or abandon certain positions after further reasoned investigation. The seeming social autonomy of such argumentation is often used to support what Brandt (1990) calls "strong-text" theories of written discourse.

Stein and Miller (1990) suggest that real-world interactions rarely reflect either disputative or evaluative argument in their pure forms. Rather, social argument is usually characterized by both a reasoned course of argument and a more personal commitment to a position. This third, *interactive* form is more immediate and less textually autonomous. The social nature of such argument encourages participants to weigh positions, negotiate, and accommodate one another's perspectives.

Interactive argumentation serves two basic functions:

> First, it *facilitates social interaction*, inasmuch as arguing allows individuals to negotiate, to resolve differences, and to generate codes that regulate the conditions under which actions and beliefs can be maintained.... Second, [it] *facilitates learning*, in that it almost always forces the two parties to acquire new information about the specific conflict under consideration. (p. 267; emphasis added)

Because it takes place interpersonally (in immediate social and familial contexts), interactive argument seems likely to develop at an early age. Whether or not students have learned successful strategies for engaging in disputative or evaluative argumentation, they all come into academic settings with extensive practice in social forms of argument. To engage in that practice over an extended period of time, students need a relatively safe social environment that encourages them to tentatively expound ideas and opinions without fear of ridicule or rebuke. We believe that journals and other expressive forms of writing provide such an environment.

In this chapter, we examine the nature of interactive argument in a highly social variety of expressive writing—the peer dialogue journal. Peer dialogue journals typically involve pairs of students in a sustained exchange of informal journal-like entries focusing on the domain of knowledge or experience in an academic course. Several other forms and uses of dialogue journals are described in the pedagogical literature on writing to learn (see Anson, Schwiebert, & Williamson, 1993), most notably dialogues between children and their teachers (Atwell, 1987; Reed, 1988), "internally" dialogic journals written to the self (e.g., Andrasick, 1990), or journals used among special populations such as the deaf, the learning disabled, or migrant youth (see Davis, 1983; Gaustad & Messenheimer-Young, 1991; Johnson & Hoover, 1989; Kluwin & Kelley, 1991; Staton,1985). For purposes of our analysis, we focus on written dialogues between students who exchanged entries on a regular basis in class and responded to each other's ideas without the intervention of a teacher. Rather than simply writing to themselves as in a solo journal or "learning log," students who exchange entries with each other have a social purpose and motivation to explore and extend their responses to course material.

Research on the development of argumentative thinking also shows that strategies usually associated with specific genres of argument may appear in other forms of writing. Berrill (1990), for example, found that 16-year-old students tended to write exposition when called on to write argumentation. On closer analysis of the rhetorical moves in their exposition, Berrill discovered that many of the students were "exploring the underlying assumptions which are brought to the argument, possibly trying to establish a common ground for understanding which is necessary before rational argument can take place" (p. 84). From a Bahktinian perspective, such expository exploration might well reflect attempts to acknowledge opposing views as part of a global strategy of accommodation and social interaction not yet entirely replaced by oppositional discourse. Similar claims have also been made for argumentation in narration (see Fox, 1990; Wilkinson, 1990) and in letters written in role-play situations (Beach & Anson, 1988). Because dialogue journals invite the world of discourse (ranging from personal narratives and observation notes to long, impassioned pleas for one or another view), they manifest richly various forms of "argumentation," all as a function of the interaction they require.

In analyzing peer dialogue journals in several academic courses from junior high to graduate school, we have begun to appreciate the uniquely social nature of argument in the context of Stein and Miller's mutual functions of interaction and learning. First, we explore the nature of peer dialogue journals as a hybrid genre incorporating the characteristics of both face-to-face oral interaction and more formalized academic writing. Next we examine the variety of forms that disagreement takes in dialogue journals—not always overtly argumentative, but, we claim, very often as intellectually and developmentally useful as traditional argumentative writing. Finally, we suggest some of the benefits of taking a more highly social and contextual view of argument in academic settings, one that might eventually parallel in importance or perhaps even replace the more traditional presentation of written argument that presupposes a victor or the scrutiny of an evaluator searching for logical or rhetorical flaws.

PEER DIALOGUE JOURNALS: A HYBRID GENRE

Unlike more historically stable types of writing, peer dialogue journals invite multiple modes of discourse in academic settings. To begin to understand the unique nature of argument in this hybrid form, we describe some of its rhetorical features and the ways in which these are shaped by its purposes and typical school contexts.

As illustrated in Figure 7.1, the peer dialogue journal combines the characteristics of formal written essays, oral conversation, solo journals, and teacher-student dialogue journals. As a hybrid genre, it draws on features of argument unique to each mode.

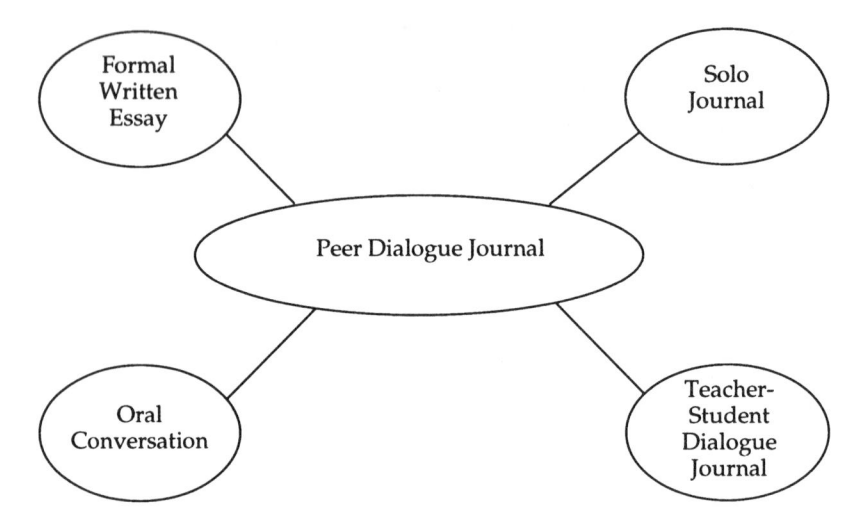

Figure 7.1. Peer dialogue journals as a hybrid genre

In formal essay writing, students' argument is often guided by a logical "thesis/support" textual structure. For example, in writing about the problems and benefits of recycling, students formulate a hypothesis about recycling and then support it with facts and opinions. Typically, the writing is evaluated on the basis of the amount and quality of supporting evidence. Driven by these criteria, students assume that they need to feign authority or take a definitive position. Standard writing guides and textbooks often reveal this position metaphorically by suggesting that writers should "arm" themselves with the appropriate "rhetorical weapons" and "prove" themselves as authorities on the topic in order to "win over" their audience. Students may assume that revealing any doubts about the validity of their position undermines this projected sense of authority. Although students need to develop confidence in expressing their ideas, they are often intimidated by having to assume a definitive stance, particularly when they are ill informed or have some ambivalent feelings about a topic. Given their difficulty writing critically or analytically (Applebee, Langer, & Mullis, 1986), they are driven to accumulate and mechanically display factual information without exploring it and integrating it into what they already know or think. For example, McCann (1989) found that whereas there were no differences between 6th, 9th, and 12th graders in their use of supporting data in persuasive essays, older writers were better able to state claims or use warrants. In a related study, Knudson (1992) found that 4th, 6th, 9th, and 12th grade students all had difficulty writing opposing views or responding to those views, features of argument prevalent in oral conversation. Students may be so concerned with projecting a definitive stance that they may not consider their audience's potential response.

In contrast, students experience considerably less anxiety engaging in oral conversation or journal writing because they can explore their responses in a more informal, tentative way. Instead of taking a definitive, omniscient pose, students can explicitly explore doubts, questions, and contradictions as they arise. Through their informal writing, they discover and construct their position rather than restate something they have heard but have not carefully considered. For example, in discussing a difficult scenario about a language issue, Carmen, an undergraduate student, wrote the following:

> Victor: I had a tough time on this scenario! I realize that getting a media job would be great for the guy in the scenario, but then I got puzzled about whether he should get rid of his Brooklyn accent to get the job or else assert his rights. . . . I just don't know where the source of the problem is. It should be the audience, because they should understand all the various accents of the states—but then why would we even have all the accents that we do? This does get complicated, doesn't it? . . . I guess my advice to the guy in the scenario would be to go ahead and enroll in the accent eradication course. I mean, it can't hurt him, and he can always use his old Brooklyn accent at home and at the ball game. What do you think?

To which Victor, her journal partner, responded:

> Carmen: I agree totally (not with your confusion!). I think there are two problems here. One is whether the guy should do certain things (like changing his accent) to get a job. The other is whether the media should have accent as a requirement for the job. The first seems like a short-term problem for the guy in the scenario, and I think, why not, go ahead and take the course. . . . Now the other issue is tougher because it's long term. I think this is where I feel your confusion, because should the media exclude people on the basis of their accents. And it's even tougher when you think that maybe there are subtle dialect things like what we've been studying

about Black English vernacular that could exclude whole groups from consideration, and that's just plain discrimination. (Anson & Wilcox, 1992, p. 26)

Such talk has an honest, informal, searching flavor. Both Carmen and Victor were exploring their responses without the formal constraints of written essays. Carmen was not trying to prove her points in order to "win over" Victor. She was actually willing to admit that she was not sure about her feelings (something rarely found in formal essays) when, in addressing Victor, she said, "I just don't know," "I had a tough time," and "it gets complicated, doesn't it?" Carmen was not only seeking verification of her intellectual struggle (which, at least in this entry, she gets), but also posing certain positions as if she were testing the intellectual waters before taking the plunge into a strong position. Although Victor seemed a bit more assertive (perhaps related to his traditionally invoked gender role or his discovery of a dichotomy), his language still suggested tentativeness—confusion about the long-term part of the problem.

This written exchange draws on the features of oral conversation. As Shuy (1988) claims, the reciprocity of dialogue journals is "closer to talk written down than any other school writing" (p. 81). Conversational exchanges of such an interactive nature, according to Halliday (1979), reveal an unfolding process, whereas formal essay writing is more preoccupied with finished products. Halliday notes that "writing creates a world of things; talking creates a world of happening" (p. 93).

By engaging in a conversation, students are continually receiving comments from their partners. When students write an essay or "solo" journal entry, they generate their own ideas without the immediate response of others. In fact, in most traditional academic settings, response comes only in the form of teacher evaluation (often focusing on the logical progression of ideas). In contrast, oral or written conversation compels the participants to follow certain conversational maxims (Grice, 1975) that allow for the unfolding of thought, the mutual constructing of a point or idea (Vipond, Hunt, Jewett, & Reither, 1990). Standards for successful reasoning may be no less stringent in oral or written dialogue, but each assertion receives consideration online, resulting in something more like a tennis game than a lone player practicing serves against a wall.

The fact that students can anticipate and/or receive some supportive reaction to their ideas often bolsters their willingness to explore tentative ideas. Because students are engaged in a conversational exchange, they are expected to follow Grice's (1975) maxim of quality: that they believe what they are saying to be true, that they are sincere about their beliefs in the truth, and that they have evidence to support their positions. At the same time, they are exploring a tentative position or "passing theory" (Dasenbrock, 1991), momentarily entertaining an idea without being totally committed to its truth. They may therefore frame their arguments as opinion, a conversational move that suspends truth claims and invites audience reaction.

Based on her analysis of conversation, Schiffrin (1990) notes that it is difficult to distinguish between statements of opinion and statements of fact simply on the basis of linguistic cues. An utterance, "The government is bankrupt," could be taken either as a statement of opinion or as a statement of fact. To determine whether someone is stating an opinion requires examination of the speaker's own "internal, evaluative position" (p. 244). This means that opinions cannot be substantiated by external evaluation; they represent subjective positions.

Schiffrin notes that in prefacing a statement with the phrase, "in my opinion," a speaker is addressing his or her degree of commitment to the words. Saying "in my opinion" may decrease a speaker's commitment, implying, "I'm not sure," or increase that commitment, implying "I don't care what anyone else thinks" (p. 245). In both cases, the speaker is mitigating the commitment to the truth by focusing on his or her own stance. As Schiffrin notes, "opinions free the speaker (as author) from a claim to truth, by emphasizing the speaker's claim (as principle) to sincerity" (p. 245). Because speakers are freed from a claim of truth, their audience cannot deny them the right to express their opinion, but can challenge their opinion.

By formulating a position as tentative, a student may be seeking a journal partner's verification—asking for validation or response. Rather than implying, "I don't care what you think," the student is implying, "I'm not sure about this . . . what do you think?" Anticipating some positive verification for an opinion, the student may be motivated to explore various ramifications of the opinion without fear of being "shot down."

The timing of written exchanges also sets dialogue journals apart from direct, face-to-face communication. Depending on the rate at which students exchange entries (from the "instant" sharing on networked computer systems to the several days between typical college class sessions), peer dialogue journals may lack some of the immediacy of oral conversation. Yet, the lag time in response may have its advantages.

Written exchanges at some remove from the interlocutor may reduce students' fear of asserting themselves in conversation. Mabrito (1991), for example, compared college writers' exchanges on electronic mail and in face-to-face groups. The high-apprehensive writers offered more directions for revisions in the electronic mail exchanges than in the face-to-face groups. The electronic mail served as an "equalizing force" for the high-apprehensive writers. This equalizing force may also help to reduce gender differences common in verbal interaction. As Mulac (1989) showed, male college students subliminally wish to assert authority; in face-to-face interactions in mixed-gender groups, males tend to dominate the discussion. Although the previous entry shows greater assertiveness by Victor than Carmen, in a group discussion Carmen may have ended up saying very little or been reluctant to challenge Victor's views in a subsequent comment. Even rough word counts of journals written in mixed-gender pairs or groups shows that women are not as likely to be silenced as they are in oral conversation. If anything, the journals give them voice (see Gannett, 1992).

The permanence of print suggests another advantage of written versus oral dialogue. Given the pace and nonverbal interaction of oral exchanges, students may too readily accede to a writer's claim without careful reflection. In a written exchange, a partner has more time to mull over or critically assess an opinion in order to formulate some specific reactions. Mabrito's apprehensive writers were more likely to use comments suggested by electronic mail than comments given to them orally because they retained more of the information from reading than from listening (Mabrito, 1991). Victor's entry may have been prompted in part by Carmen's assertions, assertions he may not have reacted to as thoughtfully in face-to-face conversation, when many other dimensions of social interaction (including the constraints of time) influence the nature of reflection.

The opportunity to reflect is particularly important for younger students. For example, in the following exchange between two ninth-grade students, Rachelle and Lynette, Rachelle argued against proposed legislation restricting adolescents under age 16 from working:

> Rachelle's entry: I think that a law forbidding high-school students from holding jobs is about the stupidist thing I've ever heard. I don't understand the reasoning at all. Why would they do this? To give kids more time to study? Like they would use their free time studying! They'd probably just goof off after school, watching "Duck Tales"! No, I'm sorry, but that is just stupid. A lot of kids need those jobs to help earn money for their families. They might be the biggest source of income. Besides, even if it wasn't crucial to your family for you to get a job, how could you do anything without money? How could you buy a car? Go to college? For most kids, these are reasons they get jobs, and they couldn't have these things without it. Besides, whatever happened to a job teaching you responsibility? This idea is so ridiculous, it would never go through. Wait, I just thought of another reason. Kids that really need the money would drop out of high school to get a job and support their families.

> Lynette's entry: Rachelle, I'm not sure I agree with you on the law forbidding high-school students from having jobs. I should say I agree and disagree. I know some kids get a job to help support the family. I think that is great. I also think it;'s okay to want extra money to save up for a car and college. I don't think having a job is okay when it starts to interfere with your studies. I think it is so important to get good grades, and I won't let anything get in the way of letting that happen.

Rachelle is openly able to explore various reasons for her opposition with an eye to gaining some reciprocal agreement from Lynette. Because Lynette can read over Rachelle's entry, she can respond to—and agree or disagree with—several aspects of her argument.

As in oral conversation, a partner may not explicitly state his or her agreement or verification. Agreement may be signaled by a partner taking an equivalent or parallel position (Goodwin & Goodwin, 1990). This often occurs with shared narratives reflecting an implicit position, with one narrative triggering a reciprocal response. In written exchange, however, it may be more likely that a partner can take the time to infer an implied position in a narrative in order to formulate a parallel narrative. For example, in another exchange between Lynette and Rachelle, Lynette related her experience of being arbitrarily punished for missing a practice:

> Lynette's entry: I don't know if you guys are going to write anymore, but if you do I want you to respond to this. On Monday, Anne C & I were walking to swimming. I looked up & 2 guys turned around. It was my boyfriend Shane & Anne's boyfriend Pat. They had come to watch our swim practice. As we walked in our coach Nicole had a cow because they were there. We didn't know that they were coming. They had come from A___. What were we supposed to do? Tell them they were supposed to leave when they would have done no harm? If anything Anne and I would have worked harder to try and impress them. We turned around and walked out. Nicole said we had to be back in 3 minutes. We didn't come back. Anne decided not to go, and then I kind of followed her decision. That night I told my parents what I had done. I asked my mom if she would write me a note to excuse me so I would swim in the meet. Nicole had told the team that she might not let us swim in the meet. When we got to swim practice on Tuesday the coaches had a long talk with us. The reason why we left was because they didn't give us a chance to prove that we could perform well with them there. They had decided not to let us swim in the meet. I understand why they didn't let us swim, but they are punishing the team more than they are punishing us. Anne & I get first, seconds, &. thirds. We have beaten C___ before 89 to 82. We ended up losing the meet 69 to 102.

> Rachelle's entry: I know what you mean, and I have a perfect example. On Wednesday the A___ team had a game (for softball), so we had practice. Some people didn't show up for the practice, so they didn't get to play in Thursday's game. We only had 8 players then, so we used two outfielders and lost 21-4. (Don't laugh, they were really good.) Maybe not being able to start or something would have been a better punishment, instead of punishing the whole team.

One motivation for Lynette to share her narrative is the anticipation of receiving some sympathetic verification from Rachelle for her implied position. As a student in their class noted, 'It seemed as though I was really communicating with someone and they cared about my thoughts. Receiving responses was like waiting for a letter in the mail. I was always very curious to find out what the other person thought." Students also noted that they were particularly concerned about their writing. As another student remarked, "When I was writing, I 'talked' to my partner and wrote better because I knew someone else was going to read it. I seemed to be more careful about *how* I wrote as well as *what* I wrote."

Because they anticipate responses that may or may not verify the validity of their positions, students may be less definitive, expressing doubts about their position or posing thoughtful, self-examining questions to be answered by their partner. Had Carmen written her ideas in an essay or solo journal, she would probably not have confessed confusion or sought verification by asking Victor what he thought. In many ways, teachers' orchestration of classroom discussions models ways for students to extend their thinking. Ironically, these strategies, encouraged by ongoing feedback in the "softer" social exchanges in the classroom, may not be as readily practiced in the more "rigorous" task of essay-writing.

Although students seek verification, they also need to be challenged by their partners. In arguing a position, given their level of intellectual development (Perry, 1970), students often adopt a dogmatic, absolutist stance characteristic of dualistic thinking in which they fail to entertain alternative perspectives (Anson, 1989; Lunsford, 1980). For students to move from a dualistic stance to accepting multiple perspectives, they need to challenge the limited nature of their own positions and assumptions. As hermeneutic theorist Gadamer (1976) argues, students need to continually reexamine their existing beliefs or prejudices. By entering into a dialectical exchange with their partner, students are challenged to explore and clarify their positions, which often leads to self doubts and an examination of their assumptions.

Based on dialogic approaches to communication, Haswell (1991) proposes a theory of development or "transformation," beginning with "an initial state of internal instability [which] is shocked into . . . unlearning and revising old knowledge or skills" (p. 131). For Haswell, there are four phases of this transformation, phases we apply to the dialectical exchange between partners.

1. *Self-contradictions.* Rather than perceiving growth as simply tensions between developmental stages, current theorists also focus on the student's inner conflicts or self-contradictions. For example, in his freshmen composition course about the Vietnam War, Kroll (1990) provided his students with disparate accounts of the same battle. The students then wrote their reactions to these accounts in their journals, exploring their own conflicted responses to such opposing versions of reality. Underlying many of these tensions during adolescence is a basic developmental conflict between the need for autonomy and independence versus social acceptance and dependency on conventional world views (Kegan, 1982).

Rather than perceiving students as in a state of "readiness" or fixed in a particular stage, Haswell (1991) argues that students are already in a state of self-contradiction. For students who are completely satisfied with their lives, teachers may need to create instability or incongruities. By openly sharing their own doubts with their partner regarding a position, students begin to entertain self-contradictions.

2. *Alienation.* Having recognized their own inner tensions, in the phase of *alienation*, a term Haswell takes from Gadamer, students are challenged by some external force or perspectives. This leads to a sense of alienation from their own familiar beliefs and assumptions, a sense that, as ethnographers note, the familiar is strange. Without some external prod, students are unlikely to reflect on their own beliefs or prejudices. As Haswell (1991) notes, "the inner developmental state of students is necessary but not sufficient to promote most learning" (p. 141). In a dialogue journal, a reader may challenge a partner's positions, creating a sense of alienation. At the same time, consistent with Vygotsky's (1962) concept of the "zone of proximal development," students need to be challenged without being overwhelmed to the point of resistance.

3. *Re-action.* Students' experience of alienation leads to a "reaction" in which they reexamine their beliefs. For Haswell (1991), "change then proceeds as much backward as forward" (p. 143). In sharing their beliefs with their partner, students are "risking the very prejudices that make our world and articulate our truth" (Crusius, 1991, p. 38), particularly when they realize that their evidence no longer supports their beliefs.

4. *Appropriation.* In the final phase, students adopt or appropriate a new, alternative perspective or set of beliefs. In order to affirm their new beliefs, students need further verification from their partner.

THE INFLUENCE OF SOCIAL RELATIONSHIPS ON ARGUMENT

Haswell's phases revolve around the dialectical challenges inherent in genuine, meaningful dialogue. The quality of that dialogue depends on the social relationships established between partners through their writing. Ideally, that relationship involves one of equal social status. Such is not the case with teacher-student dialogue journals (de la Luz Reyes, 1991; Peyton & Seyoum, 1989; Schatzberg-Smith, 1988; Staton, Shuy, Peyton, & Reed, 1988). Research comparing peer- and student-to-teacher dialogue journals show more positive results when students write to each other (de la Luz Reyes, 1991). Students may be more intimidated by writing to a teacher than to a peer. Schatzberg-Smith (1988), for example, found that only 12 of 38 college students dialoguing with their teachers ever asked questions, and did so rarely. In contrast, secondary and college students create in their dialogue journals a system of social support that leads to a kind of intellectual confidence and reciprocity not seen as fully in student-teacher dialogues. Peyton and Seyoum (1989) also found that when teachers asked questions without engaging in other contributions, students wrote only simple answers. Although younger children may need and appreciate instructional feedback in journals (Kreeft, 1984), with age comes a greater reluctance to share feelings with or confess ignorance to a teacher, who is perceived as an evaluator (Britton, 1970).

If students perceive their partner as superior in status, they may be reluctant to disclose doubts or invite verification. They may also perceive disagreements as an attempt to maintain authority as opposed to a desire to engage in genuine dialogue. To avoid "face threats" (Brown & Levinson, 1987) or conflict, they simply agree with the positions posed. Or, they may simply not respond. For example, after a session at a conference (Ruddell, 1992), a group of four female academics agreed to share journal entry responses to the book, *Women's Ways of Knowing* (Belenky, 1986). After one year, there were no exchanges. When asked to reflect on the lack of exchange, the academics cited a number of reasons relating to their social roles and relationships. They noted that they were reluctant to share matters of a personal nature with colleagues they did not know well. Given their unfamiliarity, they lacked a sense of trust. Sensing some academic competition and the need to protect their professional reputation, they felt vulnerable and even inadequate expressing doubts and concerns.

In our research on partners' exchanges at various grade levels, we find that these social dimensions play an important role in shaping the degree to which students are willing to express self-doubts or challenge each others' positions. To illustrate the influence of these social dimensions, we turn to some exchanges by two pairs of dialogue partners enrolled in a graduate composition methods course for present and prospective teachers. All students were required to keep a dialogue journal with at least one other member of the class. Both pairs exchanged disks with word processing files to which they added text and responded to their partner's entries whenever they could (for information on "networked" computer systems used for interactive writing, see Batson, 1989; Hawisher & Selfe, 1991, 1992; Selfe & Meyer, 1991). Both pairs had initially established positive social relationships through self-disclosures and sharing of personal experiences. Later, we contrast these exchanges with those of undergraduate students (most of them education majors) in a course on English language and literacy, exchanges reflecting less positive social relationships.

Our examination of the experienced writers' exchanges revealed a number of argumentative strategies employed in the context of social reciprocity. We describe these strategies categorically, as distinct colors in the fabric of dialogic learning. In so doing, we do not want to suggest the exclusiveness of each strategy; reading entire dialogue journals shows how interconnected all the strategies are in the ongoing exchange. For purposes of analysis and further research, however, we found that some modest classifications can be useful and illuminating (Anson & Beach, 1990).

Raising Challenges/Evoking Contradictions

In a written essay, a writer organizes an argument around a central point. As Geisler (1990) argues, the writer may engage in considerable internal dialogue, for example, by entertaining and trying to refute counterarguments. Such thinking is typical of Stein and Miller's (1990) "evaluative" mode of argument and has a long tradition in rhetoric. In contrast, oral conversation creates a mutual exchange of opinions (Schiffrin, 1990) or "passing theories" (Dasenbrock, 1991), from which a point begins to emerge. The conversation may then revolve around this point for some time. According to the Gricean maxim of relevance, participants "stick to the point" or deviate by "getting off the point." As they negotiate their way around the topic, participants also begin to entertain self-contradictions, experiencing a sense of Haswell's alienation that leads to dialectical challenges. While they are challenging each other, they continue to make positive comments, hedges, and acknowledgments that hold the social relationship together.

In the following excerpted exchanges, Gretchen and Kate discussed some speakers who attended their class. The topic emerging from the dialogue is an evaluation of the speakers (a guest teacher who brought along two 18-year-old students) and the session they conducted:

> Gretchen's entry: . . . I also thought that L___'s situation was a bit too unique for the mainstream ant it didn't feel that she as "expert" had/has thought much about how to help translate this stuff down either from a class with high motivation to one with low motivation or given a situation where teachers have to work within grading constraints. . . .
>
> Kate's entry: True, but I think you have to give her a break here, Gretchen. It's her summer, she came in as a favor to us, and she is used to focusing on her CIS curriculum. I know I don't take the time to consider how the activities I create could be translated for the higher grades.

What we see in these excerpts (of a longer exchange) is an evaluative assertion by Gretchen about the quality of the presentation. Typical of spontaneous writing, Gretchen's assertion came from a self-contradiction or "felt difficulty," a sense that not everything the presenter said was useful or relevant. When Kate responded, she began with an expression of assent ("true") that seems to function here much more as a social "buffer" than as real agreement. The rest of the entry essentially contradicted the force of Gretchen's assessment. What Kate provided, however, was not an argument against Gretchen's claim about lack of relevance, but an explanation for the content of the presentation.

As Gretchen continued her evaluation of the session, she maintained her affective tone:

> Gretchen's entry: I guess I'm saying I felt some frustration here. I also was interested in the student's response when I asked them if this experience has affected their writing . . . the young man's response was that it has helped him organize and that was it until Linda began to prompt him. The young woman agreed with the young man, but also talked about time management skills and learning about another culture and how that will carry with her and how she's learned a method of looking at the world that she can now employ when she sits down to write.
>
> Kate's entry: Yes—but he's an eighteen year old kid who was speaking to a group of 25 TEACHERS. I was amazed that the two of them didn't need more prompting.

Again, Kate used the same strategy: rhetorically nodding in agreement (a politeness phenomenon typical of maintaining "face"—see Brown & Levinson, 1987), but then—this time even more forcefully—contradicting Gretchen's evaluation by explaining away its small inadequacies. In an examination of agreement and disagreement in conversations and letters between professional biochemists discussing their work, Mulkay

(1985) shows that although statements of agreement are simple and direct, "disagreements are more varied in form":

> Almost two-thirds of disagreements are prefaced by some kind of agreement, and the other kinds of preface, which prepare the way for disagreement, tend to displace the responsibility for its occurrence and to explain and justify its expression. . . . There is some indication that strong disagreement is easier to declare in writing than face to face. (p. 201)

Hedges of several kinds are used in direct contradiction to soften the blow of disagreement. In an exchange between Mike and Ross, Ross prefaced his remarks with a light-hearted third-person introduction. Mike had expressed interest in using portfolios in his classroom; one entry could be a letter by the student describing how he or she wants to improve:

> Mike's entry: Then I will expect them at the end of the trimester to be able to show me how they have improved in that area. I think I will also ask them how it is that they see me being able to help them.
>
> Ross' entry: (Ross interjecting here with some skepticism: Doesn't this imply that students want to improve?)

A similar hedge takes the form of a "feigned" position as devil's advocate. In an exchange between Gretchen and Kate, Gretchen responded to a reading in the course that focused on students' writing processes:

> Gretchen's entry: Jenny seemed to be the one individual truly interested in the topic of the paper and she conveyed to me her sense of curiosity and enthusiasm about it.
>
> Kate's entry: Devil's advocate: How do you know she meant it? Maybe she has mastered the art of conning people with her writing. Does it matter that the kids seem truly invested in the topic?

As becomes clear in subsequent entries, Kate was not in complete agreement with Gretchen here. She was not, in other words, "playing" the role of devil's advocate for the sake of raising an interesting question. But her prefatory remark had the effect of softening her disagreement (in comparison with a bald statement such as "I disagree. She couldn't have meant it. She has simply mastered . . . "). While posing direct contradictions, these students consistently added a word or phrase reducing the face threat of the disagreement. At the same time, they were raising some troubling issues, such as Ross's question as to whether students "want to improve," leading to a sense of alienation from set beliefs.

Posing Questions

Partners also challenge each other by posing questions. In the context of a dialogue journal, it is not always clear whether the questions are meant to be rhetorical ploys to introduce counterassertions without confrontation, or whether the question is genuinely asked in expectation of an answer. In the following exchange, we again see Gretchen evaluating the class presentation:

> Gretchen's entry: The most serious piece I felt was lacking was the feeling good about writing or that they had pleased some reader with their work, even if it had been their group members.
>
> Kate's entry: Do you think highly motivated students in high school think of writing in terms of its entertainment value? My experience has been that they, like most other students, view it as a chore. The difference is that they can complete the chore more effectively than can other kids. A twelve week project is awfully big for any kid. I can understand how easily they might lose sight of making their writing pleasing and instead focus on time management and meeting the required criteria.

In the context of the earlier evaluative statements by Gretchen and counterstatements by Kate, we see both participants moving steadily toward a more reflective exploration and application of the ideas from the presentation. Gretchen's initial affective response has opened a door now to Kate's generalized question about high school students' writing. What we see Kate doing, then, is challenging Gretchen's expectation that high school students should find entertainment in writing; but Kate's question moves the discussion toward principles of teaching (the focus of their coursework).

Creation of Alienation

As a dialogue continues, one partner is challenged to reexamine his or her position to the point of alienation—a self-denigrating awareness of the limitations or strangeness of the position. The other partner may then reciprocate by either agreeing with his or her peer's self-examination (in a move that rhetorically suggests a mild victory) or contradicting it (a socially important way of repairing cognitive dissonance and disjunction experienced by the confessional partner). As Gretchen and Kate's dialogue about the presentation continued, they returned to their original evaluation in a "looping" typical of oral conversation. Gretchen had, by now, rethought the force of her original objections:

> Gretchen's entry: . . . Perhaps I'm being too critical. I think I'm sounding like a doomsayer instead of open and enlightened one, but if this is the result I can expect . . . is it worth the effort?
>
> Kate's entry: I think you might be [being too critical]. I think you had much higher expectations of their presentation than I had. Perhaps that's why I'm not so disappointed. Keep in mind that they finished the project at the very end of the school year. They had tons of senior activities in which to participate. It's been two months since graduation. Maybe this explains some of their "unformed" answers to your questions. [end of entry]

In spite of Gretchen's obvious shift in position, Kate relentlessly pushed on with her justifications of the presentation, and had the last word in this series of exchanges. In traditional argumentative terms, Kate "won" the debate. But instead of two adversaries still clinging to their original positions, we see changes taking place in both women's thinking: Both had explored the quality of the session (and the reasons that might explain their responses), and both had engaged in a discussion about how high school students view writing as entertainment. In traditional argumentative writing, Gretchen might have sought reasons for her critical judgment of the session (as "support" for her "thesis"), but she may not have seen her judgment from such a critical perspective as that encouraged by Kate's reactions.

Extension/Elaboration

After one writer makes an assertion, his or her partner may latch on to this line of thinking and then be carried forward with it, perhaps providing more support or examples, relating the ideas to other areas of knowledge or experience. In this sense, the original idea is "appropriated" by the partner and integrated into his or her own thinking. Although on the surface the dialogue may seem consensual, the very process of "taking over" someone's thought and reinterpreting it can lead to intellectual challenge. For both writers, the result is a kind of collaborative invention, in which one idea is seen or understood in several ways.

After a long entry by Kate in which she expressed disdain for grammar instruction but a personal love of grammar ("relishing in the lessons I had in schools when I was in sixth grade"), Gretchen responded by making a distinction (which Kate had not) between grammar instruction and reading:

> Kate's entry: I know that my students were taught the same grammatical rules, etc. in the previous year as I will teach them this year. They forget it all immediately after they're tested. And why should they remember it? How practical is it, really, when it's taught the way many of us teach it?
>
> Gretchen's entry: During class today and then after when Ruth and I talked about grammar I became even more convinced than ever that it's not grammar instruction but reading that helps us internalize it. And the more variety in the types of reading the better. [continues for 150 words]

In extending and elaborating Kate's comments about grammar into a controversial area (the effects of consistent reading on students' internalized "grammars"), Gretchen potentially challenged Kate's thinking. That is, Kate may have elaborated her assertion in a different direction ("we should abolish grammar from the schools"; "I have another, better way to teach grammar"; "although they have no use for it, they can come to love it like I did"; etc.). Gretchen's mutual ownership of Kate's assertion allows for potential dissent, even if this is hidden from view beneath the seeming alignment of their positions.

Elaboration can also take the form of one partner "resolving" another's tentativeness of opinion. Looking again like a kind of agreement, this response has the effect of a challenge: it compels the first writer to "test" a stronger position. In the following, Mike and Ross discussed their evaluations of student papers. Reflecting the initial phase of self-contradiction, Ross was conflicted about the genuineness of the student writer's feelings:

> Ross' entry: I like the personal connection this writer made with T., although for a while I wondered if this connection were going to be made. The sentiment is a little over done with the use of exclamation points and there is a sense that the story might be a little too pat, maybe even contrived to a degree. Still, it's fairly well written (I would of changed "would of").
>
> Mike's entry: Oh, please, all of these responses are contrived. Who are you trying to kid?

In a sense, Mike's rather assertive response challenged Ross to take a stronger position about the paper. But Ross did not have to have Mike make up his mind for him; equally likely is a more defensive stance

("No, there is something genuine about the paper") or, for that matter, a productive reexamination of the paper in order to confirm or disconfirm Mike's more radical statement.

Expression of Confusion

In oral discourse, interlocutors may express confusion either honestly (i.e., they do not understand a statement) or strategically, as a way to point out logical flaws or garbled thinking. In dialogue journals, the former use of confusion predominates; we have only rarely encountered the more adversarial strategic employment of confusion, probably because the need to maintain the social ties of the ongoing exchange outweighs the desire to "win" at words. Regardless of the underlying motivation, a reader's confusion has the same effect of disrupting and challenging a partner's complacency of thought, leading to further learning. In subsequent entries, the original writer must clarify his or her thinking and explain it, optionally, to the partner.

In the following excerpt, Ross explained to Mike how he liked to respond to assigned readings in his journal:

> Ross' entry: Well, hey, we're once again "on line" and writing in the journal. I'm going to try to cover the "dog-eared" pages and the underlining first. That has become my mode of responding to readings of late. I dog-ear a page or underline and then whenever I get back to writing I try to remember just why it was that I thought a particular passage was especially poignant or repugnant.
>
> Mike's entry: Huh? I'm confused!

Although Ross saw no need later to clarify his reading/reflecting process for Mike—this is, after all, not an important intellectual point—Mike's puzzlement reminded Ross that he must explain contexts and disambiguate personally expressed ideas. In a similar vein, after Ross had written a series of rather disjointed, associatively organized paragraphs, Mike began his response with, "You do seem to be Rambling Ross today." Again, the lightheartedness of Mike's entry served to soften the impact of the criticism.

The preceding strategies for argument are among many other types of responses noted in the dialogue journals of mature learners, responses that include enthusiastic assent ("Yup!" or "I agree totally"), jokes and asides, personal comments not related to the subject matter of the course, suggestions, and the like. Even some of the oppositional strategies described earlier can function to bond the two participants. For example, after Mike had spent one of his entries discussing an educational method of having students conduct ethnographic interviews, Ross extended Mike's entry and then suggested that the two of them come up with a "Seventeen Steps of Ethnography" document and "give it a slick name and go out and give workshops and stuff." In focusing on those features that seem most "argumentative" in challenging or pressuring a partner's assumptions, however, we suggest that far from consistently reinforcing already held beliefs, dialogue journals can lead to the sorts of intellectual dissonance (and subsequent learning) often associated with more directly adversarial modes of writing.

VARIETIES OF DYSFUNCTION IN DIALOGUE JOURNALS

Many social and pragmatic features of classrooms doubtlessly affect the nature of students' interactions in dialogue journals. In courses in which students meet daily, the sheer frequency of exchanges creates a stronger social relationship much faster than in courses in which as much as a week goes by between sessions. Age, ethnicity, gender, and other differences between partners may also affect the nature of the exchange, particularly if either writer has strong prejudices or suspicions. Coursework that is intellectually stimulating may lead to more speculative and imaginative entries (which might precipitate more dialogue) than coursework that involves rote memorization of facts. And courses with little or no intervention in the process of journaling, no models of successful interaction, or no suggestions for topics may yield more sterile dialogue than courses in which the teacher plays a central role in shaping the nature of dialogue. Left entirely to their own devices, some students may quickly establish a productive relationship and carry on a useful dialogue, whereas others may flounder and produce material of little use to each other.

To examine cases of dialogue journals that do not encourage the critical, "argumentative" reflection we described earlier, we turn to some samples written by pairs of students enrolled in an undergraduate course on English language and literacy. In this class, students were asked to keep dialogue journals focusing on lectures, readings, and personal responses to the course material. The class was large (over 75 students), provided only occasional opportunities for students to interact (except through the journals), and offered almost no guidance about keeping dialogue journals.

To determine the nature of the social exchange, we simply categorized whether or not the students invited a response from their partner and responded to their partner. If, during an entry, the students issued even one invitation or made one response to their partner, that entry received a positive ranking. The students' entries were also categorized in terms of whether they were simply summarizing the readings, employing narratives to illustrate ideas, or metacognitively reflecting on their own learning. The results indicated little extensive social exchange. No more than 25% of the students invited a response from their partner or responded to their partner. Although about two-thirds of the students went beyond simply summarizing the material, only about one-third reflected on what they were learning. Further analysis of individual pairs points to a number of specific social characteristics that restricted the extent to which students engaged in dialectical thinking of the sort described earlier.

Nondialogic Assumptions of Audience

One characteristic of less dialogic journals was a lack of mutual commitment to social exchange. Many students, especially initially, simply ignored each other, treating their teacher as their real audience. Whereas students with more positive relationships began writing to each other immediately, with little sense that an authority figure (the teacher) would eventually read and assess their exchanges, students with less positive relationships seemed torn between writing to each other and writing to the teacher. Linguistically, many such dialogues referred to the partner using names and third-person pronouns. The dialogue, therefore, consisted of two monologues, each partner talking about the other to a kind of rhetorical "moderator." These students may have wished to give the impression that they were fulfilling their tasks of responding to the assigned readings instead of engaging in dialogue with their partner. As a result, they treated their writing more as a routine assignment of summarizing and reacting to the readings without challenging each others' ideas.

Occasionally, both the teacher and the partner were addressed in the third-person, turning the dialogue journal into a solo journal much of which was a response to other people's words and ideas. Laura, for example, wrote "about," not "to," her partner Terry: "After reading Terry's entries I found I wasn't the only one who had a hard time finding the "perfect" article to summarize." In her very next entry, Laura then referred to her teacher in the same voice: "In class today when Prof. C___ discussed the lexical dialect differences a very funny situation became clear to me. Earlier this summer. . . ." Because both Terry and the professor would see these entries, Laura's writing set up an odd rhetorical situation in which true dialogue and the resulting intellectual challenges we described earlier were, to some extent, sealed off.

Reluctance to Challenge

In many instances, students were reluctant to challenge their partner. If they did respond, they often simply agreed with their partner's position:

> Lee's entry: After reading and rereading today's assignment I'm struck by how logical the linguistic system is . . . .
>
> Gail's entry: . . . I agree that the linguistic system is very logical.
>
> Lee's entry: I was intrigued in class today by the juxtaposition of prescriptive and descriptive grammars and the difference between conscious and tacit rules.
>
> Gail's entry: Lee—I too was intrigued about class lecture on prescriptive and descriptive grammar.
>
> Lee's entry [recounting a lunch meeting]: What this all leads up to is that our social, economic or professional status does color other people's impressions of what we say.
>
> Gail's entry: Lee—I agree that the way in which people (especially professionals, speakers, etc.) talk influences people's opinions of them.

As is clear in these excerpts, throughout Lee and Gail's interactions Lee made assertions and Gail agreed with them. In fact, the over 100 pages of text these two students turned in contained not one instance of Gail initiating an idea with which Lee then explicitly agreed. Furthermore, Gail addressed Lee directly, using his first name, three times as often as Lee addressed Gail directly. In addition to illustrating the dysfunctional nature of constant agreement (in this case, by Gail), this set of exchanges also shows an interesting social dynamic perhaps relating to gender (Lee is male, Gail female) and/or to each partner's assessment of the other's intellectual prowess. Gail was much less likely to initiate an exploration of an idea and much more likely to let Lee do the creative thinking while she responded, usually favorably, to his ideas. Notice, for example, that in her zeal to agree with Lee (in the third excerpt), Gail even went along with a different idea from what Lee had proposed. An examination of the entire dialogue journal, however, shows Gail addressing Lee less directly toward the end of the course than at the beginning, and venturing many more of her own creative ideas. Thus, in spite of the limited dialogic quality or the journal, Gail at least seemed to have been influenced by Lee's very creative and speculative mode of thought.

Some students may be reluctant to challenge each other because they are just beginning to establish a social relationship. Because they do not know each other at the start of the dialogue, they may be concerned about alienating their partner with what were perceived to be challenges to their positions. Students in the language course were predictably reluctant to disclose to unfamiliar partners their own doubts, questions, and self-contradictions.

Younger students may also lack the sophisticated skills required to balance disagreement with "politeness" strategies that maintain relationships. Scholars of peer group conferences suggest that young undergraduates lack the metacognitive and social skills needed to discuss each other's writing critically. Instead, when asked to comment on the rough draft of someone in the group, students tend to make platitudinous statements in order not to seem combative ("I liked it; it was good"; or "Nice paper, flows well"). Rhetorically face to face with a classmate they do not know, many students may have chosen to be "nice," to agree with their partner's ideas just for the sake of keeping the channels of communication open.

Lack of Integration with Prior Knowledge

Another explanation of the lack of dialectical exchange has to do with the larger social context of the classroom and requirements of this linguistics course. Because much of the students' grade depended on their performance on tests, they generally used their journals to summarize and clarify the often complex material of the course. They were therefore less likely to raise critical questions or examine underlying assumptions of the course content. Or, if students did engage in arguments about the meaning of certain concepts, the arguments revolved around the degree to which optional definitions were the correct ones.

Such functions of learning, because they appear to be so "internal" and personal, may have the effect of silencing others' contributions to the exchange. Exchanges between Laura and Terry, for example, show much less reciprocation when either partner wrote an entry whose purpose was to commit something to memory or express difficulty understanding a concept:

> Julie's entry: What exactly is an auxiliary verb? What am I looking for? Subject, what exactly is a subject? There are so many different question rules and reformulations of the previous ones. I need to find out what an auxiliary verb is first before I can go on. OK, is am are was were are the forms of the verb be—these words is am are was were are like also question words—am this? Is that? ect. ect. Have had had, do. . . .

Such entries most often forcibly shut down dialogue when the writer appeared to be grappling with and perhaps solving his or her own intellectual problems. In some cases, genuine puzzlement led to greater response simply because the entry was a literal cry for help, addressed as a genuine question to a partner. Kelly, for example, used her dialogue journal as an opportunity to learn from her partner, Heidi:

> Kellys entry: Heidi, at the end of Chapter 3 there were some key words one of which was *word formulation rule*. Do you know the meaning of this? I put down to build up complex words from base morphemes and affixes, does that sound ok? This can almost interest me in how the vocal chords work but I'm not going to get overexcited.
>
> Heidi's entry: Kelly, you seem to have the general gist of it as I understand it. Look on p. 76 & 77 for some good examples. It's just a basic description of how adding affixes to base morphemes changes the words in predictable ways.

In focusing on several ways in which productive dissonance in dialogue journals was limited by the nature of the relationships between participants, we do not want to suggest that all the journals were unsuccessful. Many pairs of students, as illustrated in the following exchange between Curt and Patti, wrote journal entries in which there was clear and constant intellectual growth by virtue of engaged dialogue and disagreement. For example, after Curt spent several pages claiming that a visiting family from Colorado had little noticeable accent, Patti responded as follows:

> Interesting, Curt. To tell you the truth, I didn't notice all that much of an accent out in Colorado. . . . The community I lived in out in Colorado was Hispanic. Now, most likely, any accent I detected was laced with a hispanic sound. . . . Something you may want to think about is that possibly this family had an accent from living somewhere other than Colorado. My guess is that the parents are from another state etc and they chose to move to Col. The children were brought up in Colorado and *that's* why they don't have accents nearly so strong.

The differences between fully dialogic (even productively contestatory) journals like this one and others that displayed little mutual reflection and interaction clearly have many sources, both internalized in students' psychologies and externalized in the context of the classroom, teacher, and coursework We conclude, then, with some remarks about pedagogy and future exploration of this unique genre.

LEARNING AND DISAGREEING: DIALOGIC ARGUMENT IN THE CLASSROOM

In a classroom in which students are constructing their own knowledge, they may be more likely to raise critical questions or engage in a dialectical exchange. Teachers may treat course material as open for question or debate, asking students to share entries during class discussions as a way to demonstrate different perspectives. For example, Harris (1992) asked students to identify a problem posed by a specific scene in the Spike Lee movie, *Do the Right Thing*. As the students shared their writing, they were exposed to different comments about the film and subsequently reconsidered and revised their interpretations. In the process, they began to examine the limitations of their own assumptions relative to other competing perspectives.

Similarly, in teaching a unit to college freshmen on the question as to whether homosexuals should be allowed to teach, Crusius (1991) found that whereas many of his students initially were opposed to the idea, they began to reexamine their beliefs after some research and discussion. By "deconstructing and reconstructing under the pressure of what is known and in response to key questions" (p. 89) students began to perceive the limitations of "disabling prejudices" such as those associated with homophobic attitudes about teachers. Crusius posed the question, "When should we change our minds? . . . when the preponderance of the evidence suggests that our opinion just does not hold water" (p. 89). In discussing their views, students may recognize that they can no longer defend their previously held beliefs.

To help students reflect on the ways in which positions are related to social identities, they can also review their journal entries and reflect on the following questions:

> Who is speaking and in what voices?
> What attitudes and beliefs are being espoused?
> What are the motives for assuming a certain voice?
> How do these voices reflect my gender, class, or race?
> How do these voices serve to define relationships with others?

In reflecting on their social roles, students may note tensions and conflicts between their different voices. They may, for example, note that their role of "rebel" as reflected in their criticisms of school policies differs from their role of "good student." It is important that students recognize that these tensions and conflicts are a healthy, normal part of development.

Teachers can also use journals themselves to reflect on self-contradictions in their ideas and pedagogical beliefs. In her study of six teachers who wrote dialogue journals in exchange with her, Miller (1990) found that they were able to explore their own constraints, tensions, uncertainties, and voices associated with teaching. The dialogue journal provided a much more deeply reflective context for the teachers than might have been provided in oral conversation. One teacher, Beth, wrote about her difficulties being a mathematics department chair who, for the time being, no longer had the satisfaction of creating her own classroom environment:

> I don't think it is the need to go back and be a teacher again but to find a space that allows me to be me, to feel that what I have to say is important. The only place there is for me where I can be me to the greatest degree is our teacher-researcher group. I wonder if in administration that environment is dropped because of self-interests taking a priority, because of the fear of being shown as an incompetent, because of a false self built upon successfully landing a job? I do not own this job yet and cannot "see" what that could mean. The struggle is either with me always having to ask, or with the subtle controls emanating from those who are my superiors. (p. 124)

In a later entry, she delved deeper to try to clarify her struggle between internal and external expectations of job success:

> The biggest change for myself that I have felt in a long time came from our last research meetings where Katherine went on about her project with the two teachers and her situation with the new teacher in school. Here I was looking for dependency but wanting independence inside. Her scenarios helped me to see this in myself, and I know that it's a constant battle. Her actions have helped me to stand taller and to not fear it all so much. (pp. 124-125)

In her response to Beth, Miller wrote:

> I can see how you are struggling with all aspects of this job right now. The job itself seems to bring a lot of issues to the surface for you. And I know that you fight that shutting down and shutting out that the pressures sometimes force you to do. You talk about trying to resist the compartmentalized, sequential, logical aspects of your job as the only ways to do it, and yet, sometimes, maybe your shutting down is an intuitive way of protecting your sanity, of knowing where you have to stop pushing, for the moment, anyway! (p. 125)

In a later meeting, Beth told Miller how her own writings and voice had helped her grapple with her role:

> Your question to that teacher, "What would you do?," has changed my life in some ways, I think. All I could think about was how much I was like that woman, in wanting the model to follow for my job, and in wanting approval that I was doing it "right." I know that I have been talking about the "right answer" issue for a while, but that situation really made me step back and look at myself in ways that you were seeing that woman. (p. 125)

In this process, Beth was able to grapple with the tension between dependency and independence, between needing approval and operating on her own. By sharing their own self-contradictions with students, teachers are modeling ways of perceiving the limitations of one's own thinking.

Teachers can also model ways to respond with "reader-based" reactions to each others' entries. In providing "reader-based" descriptive feedback to students' responses, teachers are describing their own online reactions to their writing—the ways in which they, as readers, are engaged, confused, perplexed, intrigued, involved, or moved by the students arguments. Teachers may also react by posing counter-arguments, creating a sense of disequilibrium between their own and the student's positions.

These and other instructional possibilities open up many new channels for teacher-based and empirical research on the nature of argument in journal writing. One strand of research, for example, might compare differences between students' (or professionals') use of argument in oral versus journal writing. Such a comparison might illustrate how these different modes shape the structures and other discursive characteristics of argument.

Gender based studies, of increasing importance to pedagogical theory, might examine in more detail the types of interactions between same- and different-sexed dialoguing partners or groups. Schwegler and Shamoon (1992), for example, found no gender-based differences between freshman college students' tending to write either "context driven" or "principle-driven" arguments (see Belenky, 1986); yet, they found a significant degree of agreement among raters who, oblivious to the gender of the writer, categorized student essays on the basis of these two modes. Their research suggests that certain modes of discourse, especially in collaborative contexts such as the dialogue journal, may not have their origins in essentialist distinctions of sex, but in broader social and cultural forms of knowledge and ways of learning.

Finally, we need to know much more about the influence of various teaching techniques on the nature of dialogical thinking. Instructional ideology, for example, can have a profound effect on students' ways of writing in response to the same task as Mosenthal, Davidson-Mosenthal, and Krieger (1981) found in their study of fourth grade students' narratives written on the same prompt in classrooms of teachers with different views of teaching and learning. Controlled and naturalistic studies might examine more closely the differences between dialogue journals written in different classes in the same subject area. And, perhaps more critically for the writing-to-learn movement, con trolled experimental research might compare the intellectual gains made by students with similar profiles in different sections of the same course, one that uses dialogue journals and one that does not.

Through these and other investigations, we may be able to support more empirically what most teachers who have used journal writing in their classes strongly believe: that writing used in the full spirit of collaboration, connection, and social reciprocity creates a more dynamic and open classroom while moving students significantly forward in their intellectual, moral, and personal development.

REFERENCES

Andrasick, K. (1990). *Opening texts*. Portsmouth, NH: Heinemann Boynton/Cook.

Anson, C.M. (1989). Response styles and ways of knowing. In C. M. Anson (Ed.), *Writing and response: Theory, practice, and research* (pp. 332-366). Urbana, IL: National Council of Teachers of English.

Anson, C.M., & Beach, R. (1990, March). *Research on writing to learn: The interesting case of academic journals.* Paper presented at the Conference on College Composition and Communication, Chicago, IL.

Anson, C.M., & Wilcox, L.E. (1992). *A field guide to writing*. New York: HarperCollins.

Anson, C.M., Schwiebert, J.E., & Williamson, M.M. (1993). *Writing across the curriculum: An annotated bibliography*. Westport, CT: Greenwood Press.

Applebee, A.N., Langer, J.A., & Mullis, I.V.S. (1986). *The writing report card: Writing achievement in American schools*. Princeton, NJ: National Assessment of Educational Progress.

Bakhtin, M. (1981). *The dialogic imagination: Four essays*. (M. Holquist, Ed.). Austin: University of Texas Press.

Batson, T. (1989). Teaching in networked classrooms. In C. Selfe, D. Rodriguez, & W. Oates (Eds.), *Computers in English and the language arts*. Urbana, IL: National Council of Teachers of English.

Beach, R., & Anson, C.M. (1988). The pragmatics of memo writing: Developmental differences in the use of rhetorical strategies. *Written Communication, 5*(2), 157-183.

Beach, R., & Anson, C.M. (1993). Using peer dialogue journals to foster response. In R. Durst & G. Newell (Eds.), *Exploring texts* (pp. 191-210). Norwood, MA: Christopher-Gordon.

Belenky, M. F. (1986). *Women's ways of knowing*. New York: Basic Books.

Berrill, D. (1990). What exposition has to do with argument: Argumentative writing of sixteen-year-olds. *English in Education, 24*(1), 77-92.

Brandt, D. (1990). *Literacy as involvement: The acts of writers, readers, and texts*. Carbondale: Southern Illinois University Press.

Britton, J. N. (1970). *Language and learning*. Harmondsworth, UK: Penguin.

Brown, P., & Levinson. S. (1987). *Politeness: Some universals in language usage*. New York: Cambridge University Press.

Crusius, T. (1991). *A teacher's introduction to philosophical hermeneutics*. Urbana, IL: National Council of Teachers of English.

Dasenbrock, R. W. (1991). Do we write the text we read? *College English, 53*, 7-18.

Davis, F. A. (1983). Why you call me emigrant? Dialogue journal writing with migrant youth. *Childhood Education, 66*(2), 110-116.

Fox, C. (1990). The genesis of argument in narrative discourse. *English in Education, 24*(1), 23-31.

Gadamer, H. (1976). *Philosophical hermeneutics* (D. Linge, Ed.). Berkeley: University of California Press.

Gannett, C. (1992). *Gender and the journal: Diaries and academic discourse*. Albany: State University of New York Press.

Gaustad, M. G., & Messenheimer-Young, T. (1991, Spring). Dialogue journals for students with learning disabilities. *Teaching Exceptional Children*, pp. 28-32.

Geisler, C. (1990). The artful conversation: Characterizing the development of advanced literacy. In R. Beach & S. Hynds (Eds.), *Developing discourse practices in adolescence and adulthood* (pp. 93-109). Norwood, NJ: Ablex.

Goodwin, C., & Goodwin, M.H. (1990). Interstitial argument. In A. Grimshaw (Ed.), *Conflict talk: Sociolinguistic investigations of arguments in conversation* (pp. 85-117). New York: Cambridge University Press.

Grice, H.P. (1975). Logic and conversation. In P. Cole & J.L. Morgan (Eds.), *Syntax and semantics 3: Speech acts* (pp. 41-58). New York: Academic Press.

Halliday, M.A.K. (1989). *Spoken and written language.* New York: Oxford University Press.
Harris, J. (1992). Reading the right thing. *Reader, 27,* 29-47.
Haswell, R. (1991). *Gaining ground in college writing: Tales of development and interpretation.* Dallas: Southern Methodist University Press.
Hawisher, G.E., & Selfe, C. (1991). The rhetoric of technology and the electronic writing class. *College Composition and Communication, 42*(1), 55-65.
Hawisher, G. E., & Selfe, C. L. (1992). Voices in college classrooms: The dynamics of electronic discussion. *The Quarterly of the National Writing Project and the Center for the Study of Writing and Literacy, 14*(3), 24-28.
Johnson, S.E., & Hoover, J.H. (1989). Using dialogue journals with secondary learning disabled students. *Academic Therapy, 25*(1), 75-80.
Kegan, R. (1982). *The evolving self: Problem and process in human development.* Cambridge, MA: Harvard University Press.
Kluwin, T. N., & Kelley, A. B. (1991). The effectiveness of dialogue journal writing in improving the writing skills of young deaf writers. *AAD, 136*(3), 284-291.
Knudson, R.E. (1992). The development of written argumentation: An analysis and comparison of argumentative writing at four grade levels. *Child Study Journal, 22*(3), 167-184.
Kreeft, J. (1984). Dialogue writing: Bridge from talk to essay writing. *Language Arts, 61*(2), 141-150.
Kroll, B. (1990). Teaching English for reflective thinking. In R. Beach & S. Hynds (Eds.), *Developing discourse practices in adolescence and adulthood* (pp. 287-217). Norwood, NJ: Ablex.
Lunsford, A.A. (1980). The content of basic writers' essays. *College Composition and Communication, 31,* 278-290.
de la Luz Reyes, M. (1991). A process approach to literacy using dialogue journals and literature logs with second language learners. *Research in the Teaching of English, 25,* 291-313.
Mabrito, M. (1991). Electronic mail as a vehicle for peer response. *Written Communication, 8,* 509-532.
McCann, T.M. (1989). Student argumentative writing: Knowledge and ability at three grade levels. *Research in the Teaching of English, 23*(1),
Miller, J.L. (1990). *Creating spaces and finding voices: Teachers collaborating for empowerment.* Albany: State University of New York Press.
Mosenthal, P., Davidson-Mosenthal, R., & Krieger, V. (1981). How fourth-graders develop points of view in classroom writing. *Research in the Teaching of English, 15*(3), 197-214.
Mulac, A. (1989). Men's and women's talk in same-gender and mixed-gender dyads: Power or polemic? *Journal of Language and Social Psychology, 8,* 249-270.

Mulkay, M. (1985). Agreement and disagreement in conversations and letters. *Text, 5,* 201-227.

Perry, W.G., Jr. (1970). *Forms of intellectual and ethical development in the college years: A scheme.* New York: Holt, Rinehart & Winston.

Peyton, J., & Seyoum, M. (1989). The effect of teacher strategies on students' interactive writing: The case for dialogue journals. *Research in the Teaching of English, 23*(3), 310-333.

Reed, L. (1988). Dialogue journals make my whole year flow. In J. Staton, R. Shuy, J. Peyton, & L. Reed (Eds.), *Dialogue journal communication: Classroom, linguistic, social and cognitive views* (pp. 56-73). Norwood, NJ: Ablex.

Ruddell, M. R. (1992, December). *Negotiating ambiguity and risk: Scaffolds for proficient reading and writing.* Paper presented at the National Reading Conference, Palm Springs.

Schatzberg-Smith, K. (1988). *Dialogue journal writing and the study habits and attitudes of underprepared college students.* Unpublished doctoral dissertation, Hofstra University, New York.

Schiffrin, D. (1990). The management of a co-operative self during argument: The role of opinions and stories. In A. Grimshaw (Ed.), *Conflict talk: Sociolinguistic investigations of arguments in conversation* (pp. 241-259). New York: Cambridge University Press

Schwegler, R.A., & Shamoon, L.K. (1992). *Gender and argumentative style: Is there a connection?* Unpublished manuscript, Department of English, University of Rhode Island, Kingston, RI.

Selfe, C., & Meyer, P. (1991). Testing claims for on-line conferences. *Written Communication, 8,* 163-192.

Shuy, R.W. (1988). The oral language basis for dialogue journals. In J. Staton, R.W. Shuy, J.K. Peyton, & L. Reed (Eds.), *Dialogue journal communication: Classroom, linguistic, social, and cognitive views* (pp. 73-87). Norwood, NJ: Ablex.

Staton, J. (1985). Using dialogue journals for developing thinking, reading and writing with hearing-impaired students. *Volta Review, 87*(5), 127-154.

Staton, J., Shuy, R.W., Peyton, J.K., & Reed, L. (Eds.). (1988). *Dialogue journal communication: Classroom, linguistic, social, and cognitive views.* Norwood, NJ: Ablex.

Stein, N. L, & Miller, C.A. (1990). I win—you lose: The development of argumentative thinking. In B. Dorval (Ed.), *Conversational organization and its development* (pp. 265-309). Norwood, NJ: Ablex.

Vipond, D., Hunt, R., Jewett, J., & Reither, J. (1990). Making sense of reading. In R. Beach & S. Hynds (Eds.), *Developing discourse practices in adolescence and adulthood* (pp. 110-135). Norwood, NJ: Ablex.

Vygotsky, LS. (1962). *Thought and language.* Boston: MIT Press.
Wilkinson, A. (1990). Argument as a primary act of mind. *English in Education,* 24(1), 10-12

CHAPTER 8

Reframing Argument from the Metaphor of War

Deborah P. Berrill

THE "ARGUMENT IS WAR" METAPHOR

In their influential book, *Metaphors We Live By*, Lakoff and Johnson (1980) demonstrate how metaphorical understandings underpin the basic concepts by which we live our lives. As they said;

> The concepts that govern our thought are not just matters of the intellect. They also govern our everyday functioning, down to the most mundane details. Our concepts structure what we perceive, how we get around in the world, and how we relate to other people. (p. 3)

For their major illustration of this idea of metaphors framing our understandings and actions, Lakoff and Johnson showed how the metaphor of war frames the concept of argument. They first noted common phrases associated with argument, phrases that emphasize the combatative, battlelike aspects of argument. Some of these include the following:

Your claims are *indefensible.*
He attacked *every weak point* in my argument.
His criticisms *were right on target.*
I *demolished* his argument.
I've never *won* an argument with him.
If you use that *strategy,* he'll *wipe you out.*
He *shot down* all of my arguments. (p. 4)

As we pause to consider the language used in relation to argument, we become aware that we speak of strategies of arguments, of mounting arguments, of *going on the offensive,* of *taking defensive positions,* of *defending our position,* of *rallying* with a *counterargument,* of *maneuvering, choosing our ground, digging in, making a stand,* and *retreating.*

Persons involved in argument are seen as opponents who attempt to triumph over the other, with *victory* recognizable when the opposition is *demolished, vanquished, obliterated,* or *silenced.* The difference of opinion that has resulted in argumentative *war* is thus seen to be resolved by a *winner* who has *mounted the stronger campaign* against a *loser*: The winner's position triumphs, and the loser's position no longer exists.

Lakoff and Johnson (1980) wrote:

We see the person we are arguing with as an opponent. We attack his positions and we defend our own. We gain and lose ground. We plan and use strategies. If we find a position indefensible, we can abandon it and take a new line of attack.

Many of the things we do in arguing are partially structured by the concept of war. Though there is no physical battle, there is a verbal battle, and the structure of an argument—attack, defense, counterattack, etc.—reflects this. It is in this sense that the ARGUMENT IS WAR metaphor is one that we live by in this culture: it structures the actions we perform in arguing.

Try to imagine a culture where arguments are not viewed in terms of war, where no one wins or loses, where there is no sense of attacking or defending, gaining or losing ground. Imagine a culture where an argument is viewed as a dance, the participants are seen as performers, and the goal is to perform in a balanced and aesthetically pleasing way. In such a culture, people would review arguments differently, experience them differently, carry them out differently, and talk about them differently. . . . Perhaps the most neutral way of describing this difference between their culture and ours would be to say that we have a discourse form structured in terms of battle and they have one structured in terms of dance. (pp. 4-5)

Thus, in Anglosaxon culture, we traditionally understand and engage in argument in terms of war. We act in warlike ways, attempting to dominate the topic at hand with our own formulation and evaluation of the issues, destroying positions that are different from our own. In so doing, we approach argumentative questions in a monological fashion, insisting that one position is right and the other is wrong.

My concern with war as the metaphor that underlies argument is that it frames argumentative processes in ways that unnecessarily restrict those processes. I now briefly review what is meant by argument.

ARGUMENT AS A DIALOGIC PROCESS

To define the term argument, I return to rhetoric and, as Hairston (1978) has done, to Ruby's definition. Ruby (1954) wrote:

> By "argument" we shall mean the basic unit of reasoning. The proof of any statement or belief is always presented in the form of an argument, defined as "a unit of discourse in which beliefs are supported by reasons." Our interest henceforth is in argument . . . insofar as arguments are an indispensable element in the quest of truth. Argument in this sense is the heart and soul of the rational enterprise. (pp. 104 105)

According to Ruby, argument is not a process of winning or losing, but rather a rational process of enlightenment; as Wilkinson (Chapter 1, this volume) said it is a process of "evidenced thinking."

By argument, then, I refer to a reasoning process. It is the way(s) of thinking about an issue, thinking about it differently, that is of interest to me. In argument, we seek to evaluate the degree of truthfulness of different points of view and of various types of evidence (see Berrill, 1990a). The war metaphor of argument does carry the "difference of opinion" essence of argument, as does our common use of the word. However, the war metaphor seeks to eliminate differences, and in doing so posits a single way of understanding. Lamb (1991) noted the monologic way that "most (all) of use were taught to conceptualize arguments: what we want comes first, and we use the available means of persuasion to get it. . . . We may acknowledge the other side's position but only to refute it" (p. 13). This is in contrast to classical, dialectical argument that seeks to explore differences and to build new understandings on the truths found in alternate positions. The war metaphor does not easily allow for this kind of exploration.

Unlike the way many of us were taught to conceptualize argument, a crucial aspect of argumentative reasoning is the reception of differences, the recognition that alternative viewpoint may have legitimacies of which we have been unaware. Therefore, in dialectical argument (and some would say, in what is truly a Aristotelian dialectic), a Bakhtinian dialogic process must take place, wherein each different position is received and understood *in the way the person holding that position intends it to be* before the position is evaluated.

If we were to outline argumentative processes of this sort, we might come up with something like the following:

1. Generate alternative viewpoints.
2. Receive those viewpoints, acknowledging the validities that they hold.
3. Evaluate the relative legitimacies of alternate viewpoints on the basis of their validities and their omissions.

As Michael Basseches (1984) stressed in *Dialectical Thinking and Adult Development*, the dialectic process attempts to create a new order, building on orders or understandings that are recognized as incomplete. He wrote of dialectic as a rational process that attempts to create order "through efforts to discover what is left out of existing ways of ordering the universe, and then to create new orderings which embrace and include what was previously excluded." (p. 11). In this understanding of argument, a fourth process would be added to the previous three: create new orderings or understandings that include what was previously excluded from either or both viewpoints.

This understanding of argument is quite different from argument that is framed in the metaphor of war, for dialectic processes can only work if opposing viewpoints are received and investigated intact. Destruction of opposition leaves no possibility of building new orders that include aspects of alternative understandings, of those considerations that were "previously excluded" in Basseches's words.

Interestingly, world events of the past several years underscore the recognition of the importance of ensuring that opposing points of view are heard. Few people would propose that resolution of opposing points of view is easy: Building new orders has never been simple. But Western democracies continue to reiterate the importance of hearing opposing voices rather than silencing them. Many have viewed events in states of the former Soviet Union, in the former Yugoslavia, and in the Mideast as particularly dismaying, for the warfare in these areas has signaled a strong will to silence the opposition. Again, it is the vocalization of opposition, of alternatives, that is the pivotal element. The silencing of opposition through the engulfing of ideas by a single individual runs contrary to notions of democratic process—which, I would argue, are those of dialectic/dialogic argument.

It is the process being able to hear opposing points of view and to explore the validities of alternatives that is central to creating new orders, to finding solutions that allow decisions to be made. And when resolution is not possible, the explicit voicing of difference is also often the key to agreeing to live with those differences, at least temporarily.

Monological processes that do not allow for reception of alternatives obstruct the possibility of identifying differences both on an interpersonal level and at the state level. The same voicing of opposition that is important interpersonally is the essential feature of argumentative debate on which democracies pride themselves for political decision making. As Currie (Chapter 6, this volume), Anson and Beach (Chapter 7, this volume). Watson-Gegeo (Chapter 9, this volume), Carter (Chapter 10, this volume), and Lamb (Chapter 13, this volume) intimate, argumentative processes may well be more important than argumentative form.

With argument, then, we refer to reasoning processes that rely on exploration of alternative points of view, usually with an attempt to accommodate alternatives somehow in a final formulation of a new order. Connotations of argument as war carry assumptions of silencing of opposition which hinders that exploration. In this chapter, I look at how the writing of 16-year-olds, often assessed as "nonargument" in international testing, manifests more argumentative processes than a war metaphor acknowledges.

STUDENT ABILITY TO WRITE ARGUMENT

What happens in school with regard to argument? Various local and international studies have revealed that students have difficulty in argumentative writing (Applebee, Langer, & Mullis, 1986; Conry & Rodgers, 1978; Crowhurst, 1987; Freedman & Pringle, 1984; Gorman, White, Brooks, MacClure, & Kispal,1948). These studies look especially at the form of the argumentative scripts, following the assumption that argumentative form represents argumentative processes, argumentative thinking.

A number of hypotheses have been put forward as to why students cannot write satisfactory argument. Various scholars have noted the cognitive difficulty of argument (see, for instance, Bereiter & Scardamalia, 1987; Bruner, 1975; Peel, 1971), and others have pointed out that we do not share enough models of written argument with our students (see, for instance, Applebee, 1984; Pringle & Freedman, 1985). As Wilkinson (1990) noted, we read bedtime stories to our children, not bedtime arguments. Yet, as he also pointed out, children exhibit an ability to argue at a surprisingly early age. Crowhurst (Chapter 3, this volume) and Lynch (Chapter 2, this volume) also agree with this statement, encouraging educators to involve young writers in meaningful argumentative writing.

How We Teach Written Argument in School

In addition, however, it may be that we are approaching our teaching of argument in ways that hinder its development. With reference to the writing of university undergraduates, Ritchie (1989) noted that her students wrote "as though language is monological." Looking closely at three writers in a first-year writing workshop course, she wrote that:

> [The students were] proficient at what they described as "informative, factual, and logical writing." But, like many students, they had little experience either with speculative, exploratory writing or with writing which assumed a dialogue with one's readers. The first essay Becky brought to the writing workshop . . . is typical of the school writing students become good at. . . .
>
> In this paper, Becky simply repeats what authorities say about adolescence. She does not engage in a dialogue with these authorities nor does she allow her subject, adolescence, to become charged with the qualities of "hero" one might expect when the writer is herself an adolescent. Furthermore, she does not assume a reader who will interact with her, a reader who will question her authorities, or who will expect some new or personal insight on her subject. She writes as though language is monological, to use Bakhtin's term . . .
>
> But there is more going on here. Becky believed that writing is a matter of conforming to the conventions of academic discourse, of imitating and reproducing the ideas and information of authorities on a given subject. She had never written about herself or about her own opinions and ideas. (pp. 159-160)

Applebee's (1984) study, *Contexts for Learning to Write,* and Barnes and Barnes's (1989) *Versions of English* both support Ritchie's (1989) conclusion that

> The chief function of writing in schools is seldom heuristic and is usually evaluative, to test mastery of subject matter or conformity to institutional rules. Students then leave school conceiving of writing as an act of retrieving a fixed body of information and putting it into a correct form to meet the requirements of the teacher and institution. (p. 159)

In a similar vein, Dixon and Stratta (1982) call for a clarification and reevaluation of what we mean by argument, especially in relation to teaching argumentative writing. They corroborate and extend Ritchie's concerns about how we teach writing to focus on how we teach argument. They wrote:

> A tradition has grown up that argument implies contention, confrontation and the desire to win. In this version adversaries are engaged in a duel. Each advocates, asserts, and justifies one point of view while attempting to refute, challenge, rebut and negate the opponent's. Each seeks to confound the other, and it is not always a matter of persuasion by reasoning. . . . However, we would maintain that it is a closed form that shuts off alternative uses for argument in everyday life.
>
> In everyday life there may well be two sides, but they may need to negotiate and reach an agreed decision. Argument will be involved, but so will something broader which we have to call discussion. . . . The kinds of process we are thinking of include raising questions heuristically, examining and critically scrutinising alternative positions, making tentative proposals, investigating and studying the grounds for generalised opinions, coming to conclusions or deciding that the issue cannot be completely resolved for the moment. (p. 10)

It is possible that our present framing of argument in the metaphor of war may restrict reasoning processes, such as the heuristic exploration of issues, examination of alternative position, and investigation of the grounds or underlying assumptions for opinions as noted by Dixon and Stratta and Berrill (1991) and that our framing of argument in the metaphor of war may exclude the very dialectic processes that we value as part of argument. Ritchie (1989) and Dixon and Stratta (1982) contend that the writing framework that we presently use in the teaching of argument does not allow students to employ the argumentative processes outlined earlier. Yet, adolescents may already include some of the dialectical/dialogical processes in their argumentative writing that are central to argumentative reasoning: It may be, however, that we do not recognize these processes in our concern to see developed theses.

STUDENT ARGUMENTATIVE WRITING

I now look closely at some examples of student argument. The following papers were written by 16-year-olds in response to the question,"Should parents be able to control the lives of their teenage children?" The students had opportunity to discuss the question in small groups that were as heterogeneous as possible to facilitate the probability of hearing a different point of view on the topic. Thus, in some classes, the small groups were composed of students from different ethnic and racial backgrounds (Asian, Afro-Caribbean, Anglosaxon) and in others students were in mixed- gender groupings. After their discussions, students wrote individual papers in response to the argumentative question.

Many of these papers did not satisfy traditional norms of argumentation (see Berrill, 1990b), for they lacked a central unifying thesis. Instead, many of the papers had only a loose focus about them in which all of the writing was on the same topic, but in which there was no single position that was being put forth. In many ways, the papers more resembled exposition than they did argument (see Berrill, 1990b; Freedman & Pringle, 1984). Yet, it may be that the papers revealed a developing argument that sought to be dialogic, acknowledging validities of alternate points of view, rather than being monologic as Ritchie (1989) found undergraduate writers to be.

I now look at a few extracts from papers in an exploration of the thinking processes involved. About halfway through her paper, 16-year old Aneela wrote the following:

> My parents are really strict. This is probably due to the fact that I'm a girl and I come from a country with different rules and cultures than British ones.
>
> My parents are overprotective with all of us. That is my two sisters and brother. I'm the youngest.
>
> My parents don't let me go out by myself. If I want to go out to the shops, for example, I have to go with my sister.
>
> I can't go out late unless I am with my parents.
>
> So my time is mainly spent at home cooking and cleaning.
>
> This makes me feel imprisoned in my own home. I tell my mum how I feel and she says its not good for young girls to be out on the streets. When faced with this kind of situation some girls accept it but other girls rebel and argue with their parents or they do the things which their parents stop them from doing, behind their backs.
>
> So parents shouldn't stifle their children because they might find their children being dishonest behind their backs.
>
> I get sick of my mum and dad telling me what to do.
>
> They even go to the point of telling me what to wear and how to have my hair.
>
> I tend to ignore them and curse them behind their backs.
>
> Sometimes I buy clothes and things, and wear them behind my par-

ents back because I know they won't like the clothes, but I do. My parents don't understand that experimenting with clothes is all a part of being a teenager. If my parents understood a little bit more, I wouldn't do things that they'd disapprove of behind their backs.

If I say to my mum "Why can't I wear this" she'll say "what will people think if they see you dressed like that. What will they say?"

Alot of parents restrict teenagers from doing things, which may be harmless, on account of what people may say.

I respect that because I know it can be difficult for a parent to hear people saying bad things about their children but some parents use this as an excuse to get their own way and to make their children feel a little guilty . . .

My dad tells me all the things he used to get up to, like bunking school and going out and enjoying himself. When he tells me how much he used to enjoy himself I wonder why he's so strict with us.

I think teenagers should help their parents to understand and talk to them if they can. But parents have to be prepared to listen to what their children have to say.

I do love my parents, but because my parents control so much of my life, I feel like leaving home. I've told a lot of people that I want to leave home when I'm old enough. I know this would make my parents angry, and they'll try to make me stay, but I know that if I do, I'll probably end up hating them.

I don't always like being told what to do, but sometimes I'd like advice. So up to a certain point parents should control their teenagers lives, but they shouldn't rule them.

A parent shouldn't control teenagers as such, but should guide them and give them advice, because teenagers are on the brink of maturity and adulthood, so you should let them feel it.

Tell them if you think they are wrong, ask them if they agree or not. You'll find your child will have more respect for you.

Contrary to Ritchie's (1989) example of Becky who merely "conforms to the conventions of academic discourse" (p. 160), Aneela's paper was charged with her own knowledge, her own expertise of what it is like to be a teenage daughter in a minority culture. The degree of parental control she experienced, she said, "makes me feel imprisoned in my own home." She recounted her side of the issue, showing her anger. Yet she also recognized that her parents have certain legitimacy when she wrote, "I respect that because I know it can be difficult for a parent to hear people saying bad things about their children." Despite her desire to leave home and have more control over her own life, Aneela acknowledged that parents have an important role to play in the lives of their teenage children. She said, "A parent shouldn't control teenagers as such, but should guide them and give them advice, because teenagers are on the brink of maturity and adulthood, so you should let them feel it."

In her exploration of the issues involved in this question of parental control, Aneela explored her own feelings and attempted to reconcile her position with that of her parents. For her, this was a very difficult task. Yet, even given the depth of her feelings, Aneela did recognize that parents have a certain amount of experience that qualifies them as "guides." She explored her own position and the reasons she holds that position, and she began to explore her parents' position and possible ways in which they may have legitimacy. Aneela recognized that a resolution of the conflict she and her parents are experiencing may be possible through a different relationship that might be created to satisfy both her needs and theirs. ("I think teenagers should help their parents to understand and talk to them if they can. But parents have to be prepared to listen to what their children have to say.") Although Aneela's position could easily be a monological one that sought independence from her parents, it is not. Aneela's writing is, indeed, exploratory, identifying her own position and seeking broader issues that may allow the conflict to be put into a wider context for different perspective. Despite the strength of her feelings, Aneela's paper did not attempt to silence the alternate point of view of her parents, but rather to engage them. ("I wonder why he's so strict with us". ". . . sometimes I'd like advice.")

Most of the 16-year-olds who wrote on this topic showed an even greater recognition of the parental (the "other") point of view than did Aneela. Priti wrote the following:

> As there are two different types of people being discussed in this subject, there may be two different types of answers with varying opinions in each answer. For this writing, different points of view have to be stated fairly so both sides of the subject can be commented upon. If a parent had been asked the same question, he or she would give a different answer in comparison with a teenager having been asked the same question.
>
> We teenagers cannot identify with the situation easily as we have not gone through the stage in our lives of being teenagers. We have not experienced the gap of being teenagers and adults. We have not fully experienced being adults and having children of our own. We have not gone through the stage of being adults faced with the problems our children will come up with. (Priti, 16 years)

Priti wrote very explicitly about the different cultures of teenagers and parents ("there are two different types of people being discussed") and said that we should expect at least two different types of answers. She discussed reasons why parents have validity in their point of view by

Reframing Argument From the Metaphor of War 181

delineating experiences that parents have had but teenagers have not, showing how their cultures differ. This process is closely akin to a mediating process that Lamb made explicit by drawing on Ruddick's (1989) *Maternal Thinking*. Lamb (1991) wrote "[In conflict resolution] it is critical that one already has and retains a sense of one's self. The process requires, ultimately, more recognition and honouring of difference than it does searching for common ground" (p. 16).

We read both Aneela's and Priti's papers, seeing them, gaining a sense of their own positions, formulating them in words. As well, however, there was an honoring of the differences between their own positions and those of their parents (which were validated by the reception and formulation of their parents' positions into words).

In contrast to Aneela, Priti was willing to go along with parental control to a large degree. Yet, she also wrote the following:

> Parents should give advice rather than control their children's lives by telling them what to do and what not to do. Teenage children should be given room to grow up. Parents should only view their child's problems not decide and come to a decision for them.
>
> Some parents don't know how to let go of their children especially if they have never been separated from them. Some parents may want their children by their side all the time, never letting them go on a school holiday, to stay at a friend's place or even on a low basis of going shopping. Children should be given independence. They should not rely on their parents as a guide for the rest of their life. Parents are the only sole people who will be able to tell their children that they should do somethings and not others. They don't want their children to make the same mistakes as they had when they were the same age as their children.
>
> Parents always seem to refer back to when they were young. They seem to know what's best for their children. Sometimes they don't understand that things they did before are different from what teenagers do now. They always seem to tell their children, in their time they wouldn't have dreamt of doing some of the things teenagers do now.
>
> Teenagers should show respect and appreciation of what they have got compared to their parents and be glad of some of the things they haven't got like stricter parents. Through a teenagers eyes, they see their parents controlling the;r lives, but in the parents view they believe they are only trying to be more helpful. Nevertheless, parents do often overtake their teenage children's life but considering that they want to help and show their concern maybe teenager's shouldn't be offended by their parent's actions. If the teenagers think their parents are over-controlling their lives they should sensibly tell them. They should not cause an argument, but discuss the

situation in a proper manner, maybe as a small family meeting, with just the parents and the teenager present. (Priti, 16 years)

In international studies of argument, this writing might well be assessed as nonargumentative. Priti seemed to go back and forth, first giving credence to the parental point of view and then to the teenager point of view. There was thus no clear thesis that structured the whole and that served to guide the writer in selecting the topics to be discussed.

Yet, many of the reasoning processes that we look for in argument are present. Priti explicitly recognized alternative positions, and she generated specific examples of issues that were part of the larger topic. She explored the validity of each position in relation to the point of view of that person. Her tone was remarkably reasonable, recognizing validities of each position. ("Through a teenagers eyes, they see their parents controlling their lives, but in the parents view they believe they are only trying to be more helpful.") Much of Priti's paper continued in this same tone, oftentimes agreeing with the validity of either the parent or the teenager, but almost always explaining her understanding as to why the opposing site has certain legitimacy as well. This writing is dialogic in its acknowledgment of legitimacies of opposing points of view and in the exploration of the differences between opposing points of view.

Priti's final suggestion promoted a continuation of the same process—an exploration of both points of view. She wrote: "[They should] discuss the situation in a proper manner, maybe as a small family meeting, with just the parents and the teenager present." This suggestion strongly corroborates Watson-Gegeo's thesis (Chapter 9, this volume), which shows argument to be a way of maintaining relationship among the Kwara'ae. Also, as Lamb (Chapter 13, this volume) suggested, the process of argument that Priti outlined keeps open the possibility of a continuing conversation between people with alternate points of view. As Priti said, the dialogue must be "in a proper manner," presumably with politeness and true listening and reception of others' views. As well, this was to be "a small family meeting" in which a relationship already exists and in which the processes of argument would be allowed to occur because of the preexisting relationship.

What presents itself as problematic with the writing from a traditional point of view is that the evaluation of positions is conducted on a per-situation basis rather than from a single abstract statement of truth, leaving the reader uncertain as to what criteria serve as the basis of the evaluations. However, Priti implied that each situation might well have to be worked out individually. We may be looking here at a different way of approaching decision making—one that is akin to that described by Gilligan's *In A Different Voice* (1982). Gilligan demonstrated that the females in her study often felt that decisions could not be made without full understanding of the contexts surrounding those decisions. Rather than seeing this process as reflecting arrested moral development (as they would in a traditional Kohlbergian approach, in which the best decisions are made in relation to a universal truth), Gilligan showed this process to be different—not "less than." Priti posited the same approach.

I now look at just one more example of writing in relation to this topic. Jeganthi wrote her paper in a way that she felt reflected the opinions of the whole group that discussed the question. For instance, she wrote:

> When we want to listen to the radio and television, we receive questions like, "Haven't you got homework?" or "How can you work with this on?" If we want money, we get asked, "What do you want this for?" or "Oh my God, your not going to buy that utterly disgusting orange jumper are you?"
>
> Nowadays, the fashion is to wear bright coloured clothes, which are very casual and a lot of make-up. We all receive things like "When I was your age, I wouldn't dare be seen in those clothes" and "My parents wouldn't never allow it."
>
> Our parents also seem to question us about our friends. For example, they say, "Are you sure she is a polite girl," and "Does she come from a nice home and background." There is also moans about studies. They say, "Are you sure you get enough homework? In my day we were glued to our seats with homework" and "When are you going to realise, homework is the foundation of your career."
>
> All this annoys you, but it is what a person has to do to be a parent. The questions are very humiliating on occasions like when you get interrogated about your friends. The group agreed on these points and we found out that our parents were alike in many ways.
>
> We think parents, very often reflect back to their childhood days and, try to bring us up the way that they were brought up. They always compare their lives to ours, even though they know that times have changed. Many teenagers get annoyed and upset with their parents, when they don't see eye to eye. It is only when they grow up that they realise there parents were often right. I don't really mind nowadays, when I don't agree with my parents, because now I know that they are doing it for the best.
>
> There are many influences on our lives, which affect the way we think. Teenagers, well I know the people in our group do tend to care more about what their friends say. For example, if you buy a new coat, you ask your parents what they think about it and they like it. This is only because they don't want to upset you. Then, when you ask your friends what they think and they laugh and say, "Oh you look really stupid!" Therefore, we tend to care more about what our friends say and go by their words.

> People who follow very strict religions, seem to have more problems than people who don't follow strict religions. I am a Hindu and this happens to be a very strict religion. Fortunately, my parents aren't strict and I don't follow my religion thoroughly. Hindu people have to have arranged marriages and I absolutely hated this idea. I just didn't want to go through with it, because it seems like a ridiculous arrangement. I talked to my parents and they didn't mind. They preferred me to have an arranged marriage, but they said that the decision was entirely up to me. And, of course, I said "NO!"
>
> Although I am relieved, I give my deepest sympathy to anyone who is forced to have an arranged marriage. When you have to follow a strict religion and completely obey strict parents, it is very difficult and can bring grief to the person involved. Therefore, religion plays an important part as an influence on why parents and teenagers argue. Whether the person obeys their parents or refuses to fulfill their duties is entirely up to them. . . .
>
> Our conclusion is that life would not be normal without arguments. It is only natural for arguments to arise between the teenager and the parent. This is because they belong to two different age groups and the age groups each relate to different backgrounds, reasons and influences. (Jeganthi, 16 years)

Like the other extracts discussed, Jeganthi's paper may seem at first to be nonargumentative. Her paper is exploratory, identifying specifics of her own point of view and giving that view greater legitimation through corroboration of her group. Her examples are thus representative of a wider teenage public. Yet, she also explored the alternate point of view, receiving the other point of view and even honoring those differences. Her last paragraph, in particular, highlighted her recognition of differences between teenagers and parents as a "natural" phenomenon: "This is because they belong to two different age groups and the age groups each relate to different backgrounds, reasons and influences." Like Priti, Jeganthi wrote of the different cultures of those involved in these conflicts of opinions. For these writers, being able to converse about the differences seems more important than bringing the argument to resolution. What is especially apparent is their desire to be voiced, to be heard, to have their positions received.

CONCLUSION

At the center of the papers of these writers is a dynamic process that Dixon and Stratta (1982), Lamb (1991), and Watson-Gegeo (Chapter 9, this volume) seek to reestablish in argument. This type of argumentative process is not one that seeks to silence its opposition, but rather is one that seeks to enter into dialogue with it, exploring alternate viewpoints, evaluating the relative legitimacies, and establishing a new order that includes aspects of both viewpoints. Lamb (1991) said that we must learn how to "articulate the place of conflict" (p. 18). Priti corroborated this, saying: "If the teenagers think their parents are over-controlling their lives they should sensibly tell them. They should not cause an argument, but discuss the situation in a proper manner." Alternate views must be received; their legitimacies acknowledged. This articulation is central to argumentative processes and is in great contrast to the silencing of opposition that the war metaphor of argument carries.

These developing writers do not have central theses in their papers, but their writing reflects many reasoning processes already at work. First, there is explicit recognition of difference of opinion, one of the significant features of argument (Govier, Chapter 4, this volume). In addition to naming their differences, the writers attempted to recognize the legitimacy of opposing points of view and to negotiate new orders that include both positions or at least that honor the validities of their differences.

It may be that it is more difficult for persons in positions of power to become aware of alternate points of view ("places of conflict" in Lamb's terms); for, whether or not it is the intention, the words and actions of the powerful often silence those who are less powerful and who disagree. Where in our mainstream culture do we ensure that the voices of the powerless are not silenced?

It may be no coincidence that these papers were all written by young women of visible minority cultures. They wrote in their papers that they were not of the majority. (Jeganthi: "I am a Hindu"; Aneela: "My parents are really strict. This is probably due to the fact that I'm a girl and I come from a country with different rules and cultures than British ones.") Lamb (1991) wrote: "As a culture, we learn much more about how to repress or ignore conflict than how to live with and transform it" (p. 18). It may be that only those in the majority can ignore conflict: Possibly those who are in positions of greatest powerlessness (such as youth, female and persons of color in a white society) must learn how to live with conflict and, if they are lucky, transform it.

These writers may provide particularly striking examples of attempts at dialogue because of their social and political identities. Nevertheless, they also serve to alert us to the fact that argument need not only be seen in a framework of war and that, in fact, the silencing that accompanies the monological war framework is antithetical to reasoning processes many of us wish to foster in argumentative writing.

REFERENCES

Applebee, A.N. (1984). *Contexts for learning to write.* Norwood, NJ: Ablex.
Applebee, A.N., Langer, J.A., & Mullis, I.V.S. (1986). *The writing report card: Writing achievement in American schools.* Princeton, NJ: The National Assessment of Educational Progress.
Barnes, D., & Barnes, D. (1989). *Versions of English.* Portsmouth, NH: Heinemann.
Basseches, M. (1984). *Dialectical thinking and adult development.* Norwood, NJ: Ablex.
Bereiter, C., & Scardamalia, M. (1987). *The psychology of written composition.* Hillsdale, NJ: Erlbaum.
Berrill, D.P. (1990a). Adolescents arguing. In A. Wilkinson, A. Davies, & D. Berrill (Eds.), *Spoken English illuminated* (pp. 63-75). Milton Keynes, UK: Open University Press.
Berrill, D.P. (1990b). What exposition has to do with argument. *English in Education, 24*(1), 77-92.
Berrill, D.P. (1991). Exploring underlying assumptions: Small groups work university undergraduates. *Educational Review, 43*(2), Special ed.
Bruner, J.S. (1975). Language as an instrument of thought. In A. Davies (Ed.), *Problems of language and learning.* London: Heinemann.
Conry, R., & Rodgers, D. (1978). *B.C. assessment of written expression: Summary report.* Vancouver, Canada: B.C. Ministry of Education.
Crowhurst, M. (1987). Cohesion in argument and narration at three grade levels. *Research in the Teaching of English, 21*(2), 185-201.
Dixon, J., & Stratta, L. (1982). Argument: What does it mean for teachers of English? *English in Education, 16*(1), 41-54.
Freedman A., & Pringle, I. (1984). Why students can't write argument. *English in Education, 18*(2), 73-84.
Gilligan, C. (1982). *In a different voice.* Cambridge, MA: Harvard University Press.
Gorman, T.P., White, J., Brooks, C., MacLure, M., & Kispal, A. (1988). *A review of language monitoring 1979-1983.* London: Assessment of Performance Unit, HMSO.
Hairston, M. (1978). *A contemporary rhetoric* (2nd ed.). Boston: Houghton Mifflin.
Lakoff, G., & Johnson, M. (1980). *Metaphors we live by.* Chicago: University of Chicago Press.
Lamb, C.E. (1991). Beyond argument in feminist composition. *College Composition and Communication, 42*(1), 11-24.
Peel, E.A. (1971). *The nature of adolescent judgment.* London: Staples Press.
Pringle, I., & Freedman, A. (1985). *A comparative study of writing abilities*

in two modes at the grade 5, 8, and 12 levels. Toronto: Ontario Ministry of Education.

Ritchie, J.S. (1989). Beginning writers: Diverse voices and individual identities. *College Composition and Communication, 40*(2), 152-174.

Ruby, L. (1954). *The art of making sense*. New York J.B. Lippincott.

Ruddick, S. (1989). *Maternal thinking*. Boston: Beacon Press.

Wilkinson, A.M. (1990). Argument as a primary act of mind. *English in Education*, 24(1), 10-22.

CHAPTER 9

*Argument as Transformation: A Pacific Framing of Conflict, Community, and Learning**

Karen Ann Watson-Gegeo

> Disentangling discourse is . . . a critical focus for understanding the processes—conceptual, communicative, and institutional—through which people continually create and transform the realities in which they live. (White & Watson Gegeo, 1990, p. 3)
>
> As a culture, we learn much more about how to repress or ignore conflict than how to live with it and transform it. (Lamb, 1991, p. 18)

In the past few years, traditional ways of teaching writing, first criticized because of schools' growing failure to produce competent writers, have

---

*Research on Kwara'ae language and culture was partially supported by grants from the National Institute of Mental Health, the Milton Fund, the Spencer Foundation, the National Science Foundation, and Fulbright. Our gratitude goes to the Kwara'ae families who participated in our study for the trust and help they extended to Gegeo and myself. Although bearing only my name, this chapter would have been impossible to write without Gegeo's collaboration—a collaboration across mind, culture, and gender! The chapter also greatly benefited from a fortuitous, completely coincidental conversation about argument and gender with Stephen T. Boggs and Jack Bilmes in Hawaii, Summer 1992.

increasingly been challenged by minority scholars and feminists as culturally and sexually biased and as silencing other (nonmainstream white, nonmale) voices. Feminists have eloquently challenged the dichotomy between argumentation and autobiography embodied in the model of writing-as-product typically found in schools, that is, the valuing of the expository essay over the more exploratory autobiographical or narrative composition (e.g., Caywood & Overing 1987; Lamb 1991). Lamb (1991) proposed that more useful than a distinction between expository and autobiographical writing is that between (monologic) argumentation and mediation or negotiation. Her model for writing, consistent with a "feminist pedagogy" (Belenky, Clinchy, Goldberger, & Tarule, 1976, hooks, 1989; Mandziuk, 1992), is one in which knowledge is "cooperatively and collaboratively constructed." A mediated solution to the presupposed conflict in argument finds its base in "attentive love" and interdependent relationships (Bateson 1989; Ruddick, 1989). The emphasis is shifted from product to process in writing, and power becomes "mutually enabling" (Lamb, 1991, p. 21; the discussion is further elaborated by Lamb, Chapter 13, this volume).

My purpose here is to explore the monological model of argumentation typically emphasized in American writing instruction and the feminist alternative of Lamb and others from an anthropological and sociolinguistic perspective. I draw comparative material from Kwara'ae, a Pacific island society in which my husband David Welchman Gegeo and I have conducted research for 14 years. Pacific island societies are known for their strong traditions of individual oratory and often elaborate forms of systematic argumentation (Watson-Gegeo, 1986). Skills in debating and public speaking enhance individual reputations and are often crucial to gaining or maintaining social status and resources—among men in some societies, among both women and men in others. Nevertheless, an essential if not primary goal in "disentangling" strategies for dealing with conflict throughout the Pacific islands is community connectedness, the search for common ground, and both individual and social transformation (Watson-Gegeo & White, 1990). Definitions of and boundaries around concepts of community, compromise, common ground, argument, female/male, knowledge, and power are cultural. Cross-cultural comparison is important for clarifying the cultural assumptions in our concepts and for revealing what may or may not be universal in human gender assumptions and behavior.

The Kwara'ae, a rural Melanesian people of Malaita island in the Solomon Islands, offer a good point of comparison because of their well articulated concepts of person and relationship, detailed process for settling disputes, and systematic strategies for socializing children into forms of oral argumentation via a symbolically important teaching event. Most Kwara'ae live in rural villages, supporting themselves on marginally fertile land by subsistence gardening. Adults typically have low (or no) literacy skills.

In the spirit of writing as interpretive account, I use Kwara'ae cultural practices to examine several issues. One is the nature of argument, knowledge, and related concepts and ways of dealing with conflict. Another is the extent to which notions about these concepts and concomitant patterns of behavior and thinking may be gender-based and/or associated with other socioculturally constructed identities—raising the question of notions of person and relationship. Additional insight on all these concerns is realized by examining the way that children are socialized into patterns of thinking and arguing.

KNOWLEDGE, ARGUMENTATION PROCESSES, AND CONFLICT

Argument has been defined in at least two ways in the literature relevant to our discussion: (a) as "the basic unit of reasoning," that is, "a unit of discourse in which beliefs are supported by reasons" or evidence (Ruby, 1954, pp. 104 105; used by Berrill, Chapter 8, this volume); and (b) as "ways to proceed if one is in conflict with one's audience" (Lamb, 1991, p. 11).

Although both characterizations place argument firmly within the province of rhetoric, they have differing implications. "Argument as reasoning" points toward forms of reasoning, toward dialogical and dialectical processes in search of truth and the creation of knowledge (see Berrill, Chapter 8, this volume). Under this definition, multiple propositions or points of view might be examined, and all, some, or none of them supported or rejected. "Argument as reasoning" is neutral with regard to the stance taken by the arguers. "Argument as conflict," however, implies disagreement and an adversarial stance on the part of arguers or arguer and audience. In English the term *argument* includes both meanings, making it easy to conflate them when discussing argument in writing, whichever definition is initially offered. However, the two meanings of *reasoning and conflict* do not necessarily co-occur in a language's argument lexicon. In Kwara'ae, for instance, terms equivalent to "argument as conflict" would be translated as *dispute* in English and are separate from those concerned with "argument as reasoning," although systematic reasoning processes are essential to negotiating disputes or deciding cases in local court in which disputants are adversaries.

In her summary of recent feminist perspectives on writing, Lamb (1991, p. 13) labeled the (American) status quo academic conceptualization of the generation and testing of knowledge through argument as *monologic:* The author was adversarial and monovocal and acknowledged counterpositions only to refute them (p. 13; see also Fort, 1975). This construal of argument as conflictual or adversarial and reasoning as linear—together with congruent assumptions about the purpose of writing and narrow expectations for form ant content—under lies teachers' notions of "the school composition/essay" and is taught from the elementary grades through high school, often in the face of supposed innovations such as the "process writing" approach (Ulichny & Watson-Gegeo, 1989). Expository writing is expected to have "a clear thesis" and "a substantiating set of logically developed points and/or illustrations attempting to prove this thesis," that is, minimal argumentative structure (Freedman & Pringle, 1984, p. 26). As one would expect, the foregoing portrayal finds its fullest expression in academic writing (Frey, 1990).

The linking of reasoning processes with an adversarial stance in the search for knowledge or truth is embodied in the American cultural proposition "ARGUMENT IS WAR" (Lakoff & Johnson, 1980). In pointing out that "ARGUMENT IS WAR" is a *cultural* proposition and probably not universal, Lakoff and Johnson (1980; see also Berrill, Chapter 8, this volume) urged readers to imagine a culture in which the underlying metaphor for argument is "dance" rather than "war," and the implications this difference might have. In her examination of the implications of "ARGUMENT IS WAR" for literacy and writing instruction, Berrill (Chapter 8, this volume) specifically showed how framing argument as war restricts argumentation because it shifts attention from exploring to eliminating differences, makes the possibility of considering or elaborating alternatives problematic, and hampers the development of reasoning processes.

We should be careful not to assume causal relationships between behavior and metaphors or lexical items, and "ARGUMENT IS WAR" is not the only metaphor underlying American cultural conceptions of argument, even if it is the most important one. Relationships among lexical items in a language and commonly used metaphors may influence thinking, however, and, perhaps more importantly, they reveal the make-up of cultural models and schemas[1] that organize thinking and behavior. In contrast to English, in which "winning" and 'losing" arguments is a major aspect of the "ARGUMENT IS WAR" metaphor, traditionally there were no primary lexical items for "win" or

---

[1]Cultural model refers to the "entirety of a prototypical event sequence embedded in a simplified world." Schema refers to a "reconceptualization of a given cultural model, or component of a model, for a particular cognitive purpose" (Holland & Quinn 1987, p. 25). That is, schemas are the application of models to particular circumstances—and schemas themselves are learned "packages" of behavior. Knowledge encoded in cultural models is brought to bear on specific cognitive tasks in the form of proposition schemas and image schemas (Lakoff,1984, p. 10). An example of an important Kwara'ae proposition schema is "FAMILIES SHARE

"lose" in Kwara'ae, only expressions based on positional metaphors, such as "go ahead of or above," "go behind," and so on, with no underlying implication that the current outcome is a final condition. With modernization, "win" and "lose" terms have been borrowed directly from English into Kwara'ae (as *winim* and *lusim*, via Solomon Islands Pijin). The lack of primary terms for win and lose may well have to do with assumptions about the nature of conflict as something to be *contained* more than *resolved*, and of the *outcome* (e.g., "settlement") of conflict as *temporary* rather than *final*. Although one can succeed or fail in gaining one's point in a contested argument in Kwara'ae, with very concrete results (e.g., loss of land), the Kwara'ae's conceptualization of argumentation processes is grounded more in a theory of knowledge, truth, and community than of conflict.

In Kwara'ae, the primary metaphors underlying *argumentation processes* are drawn from nonwar kinds of activity in everyday life, especially from the domain of gardening. Terms for discourse registers[2] are themselves drawn from gardening. The formal register of the language, "high rhetoric," is called *ala'anga lalifu*—"importantly rooted" (i.e., speech that carries important sociocultural meaning). High rhetoric is also said to be "heavy," just as a heavy pig or piece of taro root is the more valuable. *Lalifu* speech is contrasted with "low rhetoric," or *ala'anga kwalabasa*—"vine-like speech." The latter refers to ordinary, informal talk involving ideas that wander (e.g., are connected by association, with frequent changes of topic, punctuated by teasing and joking), leading to no culturally important point (however, a "monological" standard is not being applied here). Such talk is "light" in weight. Public debate, formal meetings, and all talk about cultural topics of great importance (philosophy, religion, marriage, etc.) occurs in high rhetoric, skills in which is essential for both men and women. Ability to speak well involves learning not only a variety of grammatical, lexical, and stylistic features, but also learning how to argue systematically and logically, supporting each point with evidence. This sort of talk and reasoning is described as *saga*—"straight"—a multivocal metaphor implying being congruent with cultural values, coherent and cohesive with regard to discourse structure, and guided by logical principles.

FOOD WITHOUT EXPECTATION OF RETURN" (see Watson-Gegeo, 1992). An example of an important image schema directly related to this proposition schema is EXTENDED FAMILY MEMBERS ARE ALL ONE HEARTH" (or one basket, one garden etc.). "ARGUMENT IS WAR" is an image schema.

[2]*Register* refers to "a variety of language defined according to its use in social situations," as in a scientific register, a religious register, a formal English register, and so on (Crystal, 1991, p. 295). As expressed by Hudson (1980, p. 49), your "dialect shows who (or what) you *are*, . . . [your] register shows what you are *doing*." High and low rhetoric are the only registers in Kwara'ae given indigenous labels.

Thinking and behaving "straight" involves examining the evidence, reasoning logically, and deducing action correctly from the evidence, from cultural postulates, and from the common-sense knowledge that together serve as common ground in the community. The thesis or point being argued may be explicit, entirely tacit, or indirectly presented, and in many cases indirection is preferred. Whether or not the "rhetoric of indirection" actually distinguishes female from male writing in America (Smithson, 1990, p. 9), it aptly describes a common mode of oral presentation by both men and women in Pacific island societies. Narratives of events and personal experiences, and expressions of personal feeling, all "count" as evidence to be weighed and evaluated. Narrative, autobiographical, and exploratory accounts offered in such discussions and debates may or may not be overtly linked via causal or other logical connectors realized in the grammar (e.g., *because, so, then*). A culturally knowledgeable discourse analyst can readily supply the intended connections—which may be metaphorical or via links within and between cultural models or schemas—as can any competent member of the Kwara'ae community.

The most commonly used Kwara'ae metaphor for systematic reasoning is *"ini te'ete'e sulia—"* inch with the fingers along it"—a gardening metaphor for how, in a tangle of potato vines, the end of a particular vine is located by feeling along it carefully with the fingers; the metaphor implies locating truth or coming to a reliable conclusion by systematically reasoning through a tangle of evidence and possibilities. Vines typically twist and turn, wind around themselves and each other, and may branch into one or more lesser vines—following a vine does not imply an entirely linear approach to evidence or to logic. It does imply that a solution, answer, or decision can be reached. The metaphor also applies to the systematic consideration, one by one, of alternative interpretations. Another important metaphor is *didi sulia*—"chip to produce a design"—drawn from manufacturing stone tools in earlier times; it implies the carefully chipping away with arguments one by one until a conclusion is reached. Here, the metaphor suggests that truth, knowledge, or decision involves many facets, each of which depends on the others for is angle and shape, but which together produce an integrated and useful design.

Someone who makes a strong point or argument that effectively ends a debate or dispute may be described as having "pinched it off" (*ini musia*, as in pinching back a growing vine ore leaf bud to stop its growth) or "struck it off" (*kwa'i musia*, implying a single slash with a machete, as when cutting through brush or vine).[3]

---

[3]The Kwara'ae are not without more aggressive expressions for debate or dispute. If a verbal dispute is prolonged or unusually intense, a disputant whose

In argumentation processes, arriving at the truth is the explicit aim for the Kwara'ae, who see knowledge as the result of reflection on experience, the experience of individuals and groups over time. *Falafala*—"tradition, culture"—consists of representations of that experience in cultural models, schemas, prototypes, examples, values, and oral art. *Falafala* has a human voice and human face: "*Falafala* says . . . :" "in the eyes of *Falafala*." *Falafala* is not a monolithic entity, for when applied to differing kin groups, villages, and even individuals, *Falafala* refers to varying beliefs and patterns of behavior that together with the voices of the past constitute the ongoing conversation (Burke, 1967) that is Kwara'ae culture.

In sum, the metaphors used for argumentation show that systematic logical reasoning is highly valued in Kwara'ae, and that the Kwara'ae acknowledge multiple perspectives on truth. This acknowledgment is built into their conceptual schemas.

Kwara'ae metaphors underlying dealing with conflict have to do with avoiding something negative (a social split, damage, pain, shame, etc.) or with not renewing a hurt, rather than with physical combat or war. These metaphors are consistent with the primary goal in dealing with conflict, that is, restoring social relationships. In small, kin-based communities such as Kwara'ae, people are often less concerned with resolving a conflict than they are with containing it, even if they hold to a cultural ideal of resolution. Resolution may be divisive (e.g., awarding compensation may prolong feelings of anger rather than remove them), whereas containment permits ongoing dialogue. Complex or serious disputes are handled through a multistage process involving private and public counseling as well as other varieties of mediation, and several formal strategies are available, including court proceedings.

In Kwara'ae as in many other Pacific societies, argumentation processes and conflict processes share the "straight vs. entangled" metaphor (Watson-Gegeo & White, 1990). Thus, in place of the American "ARGUMENT IS WAR" metaphor, in the Pacific islands "CONFLICT IS ENTANGLEMENT," and "ARGUMENT(ATION) IS STRAIGHTENING OUT." More specifically, confused, problematic, or conflicted ideas, circumstances, or relationships in Kwara'ae are said to be *firu*—"entangled" as in a tangled fishing line or tangled potato vines in the garden. "Entangled" ideas and circumstances can be *fa'asaga*—

---

latest move or speech was particularly effective in swaying the argument his or her way might remark in giving an account to another, "I struck him/her" (English equivalent: "I whipped him/her") or "We did good work on him/her" (English equivalent: "We worked him/her over")These metaphors are drawn from individual fist fighting rather than from war, and are not linked to a larger war frame. They are also not the primary metaphors underlying talk in a verbal dispute or about disputes and argumentation.

"made straight" through talk. "Straightening out" does not imply a "monological" course to the talk, for in a dispute-handling event, problems and perspectives are typically examined in a holistic fashion, and all involved have their eyes on the primary goal of restoring relationships and community harmony.

In summary, the differences between American and Kwara'ae surface metaphors for argument reflect differing cultural models of knowledge, argument, and conflict.[4] These, in turn, involve differing concepts of person, relation, and community, to which we now turn.

PERSON, RELATION, SOCIALIZATION, AND TRANSFORMATION

We need to examine the Kwara'ae conception of person and relationship in some detail in order to understand how it differs from Anglo-European conceptions and gender assumptions and why the differences are meaningful with regard to argument and conflict. In Kwara'ae world view, a person is constructed of physical, mental, emotional, spiritual, intellectual, and behavioral characteristics, even as a mosaic might be constructed of small tiles or as the Kwara'ae express it, the person is a "wasp's nest of many chambers."[5] Each "chamber" is called *kula*—"part, point, or place." A variety of metaphorically based expressions are used to describe the interrelationships among the parts of a person. A particular *kula* may be "correct" or "wrong," in the sense of being "entangled." It may "fit" or "not fit," in the sense of cultural expectations for personal health or behavior. A person who has one or more *kulas* so described is called "incomplete," or more seriously, "half," in contrast to "complete."

A "complete" person is one who embodies the key or "ultimate values" (Firth, 1964, p. 174) forming the basis of Kwara'ae culture.[6]

---

[4]Gegeo (personal communication, June 1993) suggested that the "ARGUMENT AS WAR" metaphor and its absence in Kwara'ae may reflect the contrast between state and nonstate social formations. In the past, war in Kwara'ae consisted of raids and limited skirmishes, and there were no armies, only bands of closely related ordinary men led into hand-to-hand combat by a particularly strong fighter who occupied the social position of *ramo*—warrior—in a clan. Such battles were small scale, and a single death or wounding were sometimes sufficient to declare the contest decided. Institutionalization of the state and its military, and the prominent role played by armies in Anglo-European history of the past several hundred years, may have given rise to war metaphors in Anglo-European argumentation.

[5]Note that a wasp's nest does not carry the negative connotations for the Kwara'ae that are present for many English-speaking Americans.

[6]The eight key values are (alphabetically): *alafe'anga*—"love"—including obliga-

These values emphasize helping and sharing and clue us to how the Kwara'ae conceive of the connection between personal characteristics, social relationships, and community. Distortions or imbalances in one's personal mosaic of *kulas* have *social meaning* because of their effect on social relationships. The Kwara'ae regard the person as only one *kula* in a set of concentric spheres of *kulas* beginning with the individual at its core, moving outward to the nuclear and then extended family, to the village, the descent group, clan, or tribe, and finally the whole society.) On the one hand, the *kula* model situates the individual person in a complex supportive network and is a statement of community connectedness; respect for individual differences and views, and tolerance for eccentricities as well, are included here. On the other hand, given that all *kula* levels are interdependent, the *kula* model is a statement of how every act of an individual has the potential of affecting and involving *all* of the relationships connected in the social network of *kula* spheres, one's own and those of everyone else. It is in this latter sense that conflict is seen as the result of personal and interpersonal relations becoming behaviorally "'"entangled" and needing to be "straightened out."

Clearly, then, the Kwara'ae *kula* model is important to an understanding of "argument as conflict." But what has it to do with "argument as reasoning?" A great deal, because the Kwara'ae believe that "straight thinking" leads to actions and feelings that are also "straight" (i.e., in line with cultural expectations and in harmony with self and others). Here we see that "straight," a metaphor that could be mistaken as "monological" when applied to reasoning, is in fact thicker and richer because it is grounded in assumptions about social relations and community interdependence.

All of these points come together in a symbolically important event called *fa'amanata'anga*, in which the *kula* model of the person and relations is introduced, reinforced, and evoked persuasively in public and private teaching, counseling, and dispute-settling sessions at varying levels of social organization. *Fa'amanata'anga*, the general term in Kwara'ae for the teaching of knowledge and abstract skills, literally means "causing to think" or "shaping the mind." In its narrower sense, it refers to a highly focused, symbolically significant, interactional event in which intellectual instruction, counseling, and social conflict resolution may all co-occur (Watson-Gegeo & Gegeo, 1990). In this

---

tions to kin as well as feelings of affection; *aroaro'anga*—"peace, peaceful behavior"; *babato'o'anga*—"emotional and behavioral stability, maturity, dependability; *enoeno'anga*—"humility, delicacy, adaptability, gracefulness, tranquility, gentleness"; *fangale'a'anga*—"sharing, giving and receiving"; *kwaigwale'e'anga*—"welcoming, comforting, hospitality"; *kwaisare'e'anga*—"feeding without expectation of return"; and *mamana'anga* [cognate of "mana"]—"honesty, truthfulness power."

teaching/counseling event, the *kula* framework just discussed guides the main speaker(s) and listeners toward a holistic approach to intellectual, personal, and social issues. It is the holistic approach to knowledge and problems that makes it possible for *fa'amanata'anga* sessions to include multiple functions (e.g., teaching information or intellectual skills, counseling about behavior, and handling interpersonal conflicts).[7]

Fa'amanata'anga begins in simplified form when a child is about 18 months and continues throughout life within the family.[8] Sessions are also held across families, primarily to counsel or resolve disputes among adults,[9] although "tutorials" on bodies of cultural knowledge (e.g., myth, genealogy) are also common. At the village or district level, *fa'amanata'anga* always closes conflict-handling meetings and proceedings as a way of reinforcing cultural values, recognizing the validity of personal feelings, repairing social relationships, and teaching about culturally appropriate ways to deal with similar situations.

In childhood, *fa'amanata'anga* sessions are used to teach children intellectual skills and cultural knowledge and to counsel them on their behavior and relationships with others. Through these sessions, children come to understand and operate within the framework of the *kula* model for person and relationships. These sessions are also the primary teaching event through which children learn forms of logical reasoning and oral argumentation in high-rhetoric skills, which as adults they will need to competently participate in culturally important events and conflict-handling activities. In *fa'amanata'anga* sessions tape-recorded and analyzed by Gegeo and myself, children as young as 3 years old demonstrated their metalinguistic awareness and knowledge of reasoning forms through their correct use of logical reasoning particles (Watson Gegeo, 1992).

---

[7] We can see here that the Kwara'ae notion of "straight thinking" leading to "straight behavior" and relationships bears a strong resemblance to cognitive therapy (Beck, 1976; Ellis, 1971).

[8] More complete treatments of Kwara'ae children's socialization are found in Watson-Gegeo and Gegeo (1986a, 1986b, 1989,1992).

[9] One of the difficulties in talking cross-culturally about conflict-handling events and processes is the indeterminate meaning of *mediation*. Mediation involves the intervention of a third party to help deal with a dispute or conflict. Beyond this essential characteristic, however, mediation takes many forms with various ideological underpinnings. In the United States, organizations and agencies attempting to deal with conflict may have very different approaches to it and yet gloss their activities as *mediation*, without defining it (Adler, Lovaas, & Milner, 1987). That the teaching of writing should have a mediative rather than argumentative focus (e.g., Lamb, 1991) requires first that we clarify what we mean by *mediation*.

However, the goal of this teaching/counseling event is not to teach children how to debate well in order to win. Nor is "winning" the goal behind the systematic reasoning and argumentation in *fa'amanata'anga* used for mediation or in connection with other conflict handling activities. Rather, the goal is to use and to teach the use of argumentation forms to bring about personal and social *transformation*, so as to create, strengthen, and/or restore social relationships and community.

The transformative aim is reflected in how sessions are structured and in the stance taken by speakers and listeners. A *fa'amanata'anga* session is typically led by a senior person, male or female (within the family, a parent or grandparent; within a larger social unit, an elder or mature person), who organizes and controls the speaking floor. Listeners are silent, eyes averted or focused in midspace, facial expressions serious or affectively blank, and in focused meditative concentration. Whether or not a given speaker is targeting his or her message to a specific individual, all are to reflectively examine their personal and interpersonal *kula* systems and be asking themselves, "How does this [what the current speaker is saying] apply to my *kula*s?" Two cultural assumptions underlie the expectation of personal and social transformation through *fa'amanata'anga* : talk shapes thinking, and "straight" thinking leads to behavior and relationships that are "straight."

Fa'amanata'anga is metaphorically described as "heavy words" and "important silences," the latter referring to reflective seconds of silence with which speakers segment their talk. These silences are said to clear the mind as if approximating a prebirth condition, so that negative ideas may be uprooted and new ones planted. Periods of silence also help to focus consciousness: One is to see either pitch darkness or pure white light, and no other color or image, behind one's partially closed eyelids. This meditative level of concentration helps to create the deeply spiritual, sacred quality of *fa'amanata'anga* sessions and to make intellectual and emotional transformation possible. Under these conditions, the talk of the various participants can indeed be formative for thinking and relationships.

Returning to the American dichotomy between argument and mediation discussed earlier, then, we see that in Kwara'ae the opposition is not argument in *contrast* to autobiography or mediation, but argument *in the service* of autobiographical or mediating functions (social relationships, community interdependence). What, then, is the role of gender?

ARGUMENT, DISCOURSE STYLE, AND GENDER

Feminist studies and treatments of both oral and written argument in Western societies have demonstrated systematic differences between females and males in their use of language and discourse forms (e.g., Belenky et al., 1976; Caywood & Overin, 1987; Prey, 1990; hooks, 1989; Mills, 1987, Ruddick, 1989). In a recent study of undergraduate science teaching, Lamiel (1992) corroborated many of these points by examining over the course of a semester, the classroom discourse of two relatively inexperienced young American university teachers in introductory biology courses.

Lamiel (p. 20) characterized the male teacher's pedagogical strategy as "distancing," nicely embodied in his statement, "I am here to show you the way research works." His stance vis-à-vis students was authoritative, with himself as source of knowledge and students as empty vessels ("he wants to *insert* information he knows into their *underdeveloped* brains"). His primary metaphors and expressions were remote and aggressive ("away," "out there," "over there," "enter," "manipulate," "approach," "attack," "rip this apart," "flush it out"). Lamiel characterized the female teacher's teaching strategy as "connected," well expressed in her saying to her (freshman) students during the course of an early session, "but you now realize as zoologists. . . ." Her stance vis à-vis the students was collaborative, with herself as the instrument or conveyor rather than source of information, and students as knowledgeable foundations from which to build ("she wants to draw out from with in, and to share the knowledge around us and within the students and their developing brains"). Her primary metaphors and expressions were proximate and nonaggressive ("come," "here," "in," "with us," "around us"; physiological processes were explained from a perspective inside the animal's body rather than probing it from the outside). The pronoun usage of the two teachers is particularly revealing. The male teacher's "we" meant "I and the experts in my field," in contrast to "you," the students, who were excluded from "we." The female teacher's "we" referred to herself and the students, in contrast to "they," the authorities in the field.

Lamiel's careful discourse analysis confirms what we intuitively know about American gender patterns in teaching. Here, again, there are interesting comparisons to be made with Kwara'ae. *Fa'amanata'anga* is authority-oriented, and a cursory glance at transcripts from recorded sessions can give the impression that the primary speakers are lecturing at the listeners, especially when dealing with behavior; for example, "My son, I do not want to see that kind of *kula* [of a damaged kula]." However, here the "I" refers to *falafala*, for one of the useful available options in *fa'amanata'anga* is for the senior speaker(s) to speak as *falafala*, that is, *falafala* speaks through them in the meditative context of the session (and, in this way, because *falafala* consists of the evolving discourse of the generations, an emotional link is made between past and present). This stance is not merely a male prerogative, for women take it as easily as men in *fa'amanata'anga* sessions.

With regard to pronouns, in Kwara'ae as in Pacific languages generally, pronouns are conveniently marked for inclusion and exclusion of addressee, and further marked for immediate group versus larger, more external group (the boundaries being dependent on the context of usage). In *fa'amanata'anga* sessions, "we, inclusive of addressee" forms are predominate. Most general statements of knowledge, appropriate behavior, and cultural propositions are incorporated in sentences or phrases using the form for "we, inclusive," incorporating the larger group (clan or tribe, or the whole of Kwara'ae society). The effect is that the target individual(s) of a lesson is or are distanced neither from the teacher/speaker nor from the larger community. Often these generalizations are abstract and indirect, requiring the hearer to do considerable interpretive "work." Thus, for instance, "Our older sibling is our older sibling" is an abstraction about the unity of the family and of mutual obligations between older and younger siblings. Such "we" statements are shorthand ways of evoking complex sets of cultural propositions, and help give *fa'amanata'anga* sessions their condensed, indirect, and poetic quality. In part, the "we inclusive" stance of Kwara'ae teaching grows out of Kwara'ae assumptions about the human mind. "Students"—children and others are assumed to have working minds and real-world knowledge, and to be capable of reasoning and reflection at a young age, whatever their gender.

Because each person is recognized as potentially having some what differing habits, preferences, or ideas from others (having her or his own *falafala*), *fa'amanata'anga* sessions are rich for the variety of strategies the best teachers (as rated by the Kwara'ae themselves) use. Sessions typically include both distancing and collaborative strategies, with the overall goals of generating and/or transmitting knowledge; transforming minds, feelings, and behavior; and strengthening community ties. The goals to be reached and the strategies through which to gain them, then, are shared across gender in Kwara'ae.

CONCLUSION

The Kwara'ae's view of the nature of argument, knowledge, and related concepts, and ways of dealing with conflict, differs from that of mainstream American culture. These differences depend to a great extent on notions of person and relationship. The differences are clearly manifested in childhood socialization practices—and, for that matter, in socialization practices across the life span.

The Kwara'ae's case also indicates that notions of argument and concomitant patterns of behavior and thinking need not be gender based as they appear to be in mainstream American society. In Kwara'ae, argumentation involves an integration of careful, culturally articulated logical processes of reasoning and evidence with cooperative and collaborative construction of meaning, knowledge, and decision making. As it is based in and congruent with Kwara'ae rather than American culture, this integration may or may not be fully congruent with what American feminists are calling for in the teaching of writing. Nevertheless, it is clear that the Kwara'ae construal of argument depends on socioculturally constructed notions of person, mind, behavior, and community rather than on gender identity. Those notions differ from the dichotomy between "women's rootedness in a sense of connection and men's emphasis on separation and autonomy" (Belenky et al. 1976, p. 45) that apparently typifies the American mainstream. The Kwara'ae thus offers one example of an alternative way of conceptualizing argument, with implications for community building.

REFERENCES

Adler, P., Lovaas, K., & Milner, N. (1987). *The ideologies of mediation: The movement's own story*. (Program on Conflict Resolution Paper No. 1987-1). Honolulu: University of Hawaii at Manoa.

Bateson, M.C. (1989). *Composing a life*. New York: Atlantic Monthly.

Beck, A. (1976). *Cognitive therapy and the emotional disorders*. New York: International Universities Press.

Belenky, M.F., Clinchy, B.M., Goldberger, N.R., & Matuck, J.M. (1976). *Women's ways of knowing: The development of self, voice, and mind*. New York: Basic Books.

Burke, K. (1967). *The philosophy of literary form* (2nd ed.). Baton Rouge: Louisiana State University.

Caywood, C.L., & Overing, G.R. (1987). Introduction. In C.L. Caywood & G.R. Overing (Eds.), *Teaching writing: Pedagogy, gender, and equity* (pp. xi-xvi). Albany: State University of New York Press.

Crystal, D. (1991). *A dictionary of linguistics and phonetics* (3rd ed.). Oxford: Basil Blackwell.

Ellis, A. (1971). *Growth through reason: Verbatim cases in rational-emotive therapy*. Palo Alto: Science and Behavior.

Firth, R (1964). *Symbols, private and public*. London: Athlone.
Fort, K. (1975). Form, authority, and the critical essay. In W.R Winterowd (Ed.), *Contemporary rhetoric* (pp. 171-183). New York: Harcourt.
Freedman, A., & Pringle, I., (1984). Why students can't write arguments. *English in Education*, 18(2), 73-84.
Frey, O. (1990). Beyond literary Darwinism: Women's voices and critical discourse. *College English*, 52, 507-526.
Holland, D., & Quinn, N. (1987). *Cultural models in language and thought*. New York Cambridge University Press.
hooks, b. (1989). Toward a revolutionary feminist pedagogy. In *Talking back. Thinking feminist, thinking black* (pp. 49-54). Boston: South End Press.
Hudson, R.A. (1980). *Sociolinguistics*. New York: Cambridge University Press.
Lakoff, G. (1984). Classifiers as re)flection of mind: A cognitive approach to prototype theory (Berkeley Cognitive Science Rep. No. 19). Berkeley: University of California Institute of Human Learning.
Lakoff, G., & Johnson, M. (1980). *Metaphors we live by*. Chicago: University of Chicago Press.
Lamb, C.E. (1991). Beyond argument in feminist composition. *College Composition and Communication*, 42(1), 11-24.
Lamiel, N. (1992). *Metaphors of teaching: The student connection*. Unpublished Senior Honors Thesis, Department of Anthropology., University of California, Davis.
Mandziuk, R.M. (1992). Feminist pedagogy: Report of the 1991 Conference on Research in Gender and Communication. *Women and Language*, 14(2), 26-29.
Mills, S. (1987). The male sentence. *Language and Communication*, 7(3), 189-198.
Ruby, L. (1954). *The art of making sense*. New York: J.B. Lippincott.
Ruddick, S. (1989). *Maternal thinking*. Boston: Beacon.
Smithson, I. (1990). Introduction: Investigating gender, power, and pedagogy. In S.L. Gabriel & I. Smithson (Eds.), *Gender in the classroom: Power and pedagogy* (pp. 1-27). Urbana: University of Illinois Press.
Ulichny, P., & Watson-Gegeo, K.A. (1989). Interactions and authority: The dominant interpretive framework in writing conferences. *Discourse Processes*, 12(3), 309-328.
Watson-Gegeo, K.A. (1986). The study of language use in Oceania. *Annual Review of Anthropology*, 15, 149-162.
Watson-Gegeo, K.A. (1992). 'Heavy words' and 'important silences': Cognitive apprenticeship in Kwara'ae (Solomon Islands). In A. Bayer & E. Brandt (Eds.), *Between minds: Apprenticeship in thinking*. Unpublished manuscript.

Watson-Gegeo, K.A., & Gegeo, D.W. (1986a). Calling-out and repeating routines in Kwara'ae children's language socialization. In B.B. Schieffelin & E. Ochs (Eds.), *Language socialization across cultures* (pp. 17-50). New York: Cambridge University Press.

Watson-Gegeo, K.A., & Gegeo, D.W. (1986b). The social world of Kwara'ae children: Acquisition of language and values. In J. Cook Gumperz, W. Corsaro, & J. Streeck (Eds.), *Children's worlds and children's language* (pp. 109-128). Berlin: Mouton de Gruyter.

Watson-Gegeo, K.A., & Gegeo, D.W. (1989). The role of sibling interaction in child socialization. In P.G. Zukow (Ed.), *Sibling interaction across cultures: Theoretical and methodological issues* (pp. 54-76). New York Springer-Verlag.

Watson-Gegeo, K.A, & Gegeo, D.W. (1990). Shaping the mind and straightening out conflicts: The discourse of Kwara'ae family counseling. In K.A. Watson-Gegeo & G.W. White (Eds.), *Disentangling Conflict discourse in pacific societies* (pp. 161-213). Stanford: Stanford University Press.

Watson-Gegeo, K.A., & Gegeo, D.W. (1992). Schooling, knowledge and power: Social transformation in the Solomon Islands. *Anthropology and Education Quarterly, 23*(1), 10-29.

White, G.M., & Watson-Gegeo, K.A. (1990). Disentangling discourse. In K.A. Watson-Gegeo & G.M. White (Eds.), *Disentangling: Conflict discourse in pacific societies* (pp. 3-49). Stanford: Stanford University Press.

CHAPTER 10

The Background to Argument in the Far East

Robert E. Carter

If an argument is a set of reasons or claims put forward in an attempt to convince others that a certain conclusion or claim is true or preferable, then it is important to be clear about just what it is that "counts" as a reason. This, in turn, is dependent on what sort of conclusion or claim is anticipated: one of certainty, one of approximation, one of suggestiveness, or one that is but a "pointer" to another claim which is itself intrinsically unarticulable. In other words, it may be that not all expectations concerning what arguments can achieve are alike from culture to culture. Again, it may be that a "suggestive" premise may be inadequate from one cultural perspective and convincing from another.

It does remain true that a good argument is a logical argument, and that what is logical in one cultural tradition is also logical in another. However "inscrutable" we in the West think the cultural traditions of the Far East to be, they do not have a "different" logic from ours. One need not become illogical or irrational to comprehend the East. Nevertheless, if, as Nishida (1987) observes, logic is "the form of our own thinking" (p. 126),[1] then logic is not simply completed by any one

---

[1]While the rule is not always followed, it is generally the case that in the Far East Surnames or last names aK listed first, followed by one's given name or names.

culture's formalizations, for the *context* of logical argument and its purposes must also be included. For example, it is at least a common perspective in the multistranded Western tradition that language is adequate to the task of capturing reality "objectively." This perspective is a semiotic one and assumes that signs (words, grammar, logic) are adequate to describe me world, certainly the world of experience if not reality itself. The multistranded traditions of the Far East have from the very beginning viewed this thesis as either inadequate, uninteresting, or both. In Chinese Taoism, the sage Lao Tzu warned that those who know do not speak and those who speak do not know. In the very first paragraph of the Tao Te Ching, we read:

> The way that can be spoken of
> Is not the constant way;
> The name that can be named
> Is not the constant name. (Lao Tzu, p. 57)[2]

The ultimate ground or origin of things is, necessarily, nameless and beyond words. Similarly, in Japan, as Moore observed, Zen Buddhism's "anti-intellectualism" is popular "because of its positive attitude toward living naturally rather than intellectualizing life, since such intellectualizing falsifies and distorts life " (p. 289) Yet this is not necessarily an anti-intellectual approach, or at least it need not be, but a

---

Occasionally, because of deference to Western custom, surnames are listed last. Thus, to speak of "Nishida" is akin to referring to me as "Carter." One would not refer to him as "Kitaro" any more than Kant as "Immanuel." Those wishing to read more about Nishida's philosophy might consult Carter (1989).

[2]This particular translation is by Lau (1963, p. 57), but another that focuses on the linguistic issues is translated by Bynner (Tzu, 1962, p. 25):
Existence is beyond the power of words

> To define:
> Terms may be used
> But are more than absolute.
> In the beginning of heaven and earth there were no words,
> Words came out of the womb of the matter;
> And whether a man dispassionately
> Sees to the core of life
> Or passionately
> Sees the surface,
> The core and the surface
> Are essentially the same,
> Words making them seem different
> Only to express appearance,
> If name be needed, wonder names them both:
> From wonder into wonder
> Existence opens.

reminder that the lived world of everyday experience is not to be confused with the significantly reduced and twice-removed generalizations or stereotypical expectations abstracted from experience. Thus, tonight's dinner is but one dinner among an indefinite number of similar dinners, and its nutritional requirements are strictly numerable. But it is also a dinner unlike any other, and it may even serve as an occasion for an experience of radical transformation, or for the renewing of a relationship, or simply for tasting as though for the first time. It is unique, as well as one of many: potentially transformative, or hum drum, unique or stereotypical.

The Japanese language itself is highly evocative in function and suggestive in structure: "The forms of expression of the Japanese language are more oriented to sensitive and emotive nuances than directed toward logical exactness" (Nakamura, 1964, p. 531). Nouns give no clear distinction between singular and plural uses; genders are not specified, articles are not used, and verbs do not distinguish person and number. Furthermore, as Kishimoto Hideo observes, "the Japanese language is . . . able to project . . . [a human being's] experience in its immediate and unanalyzable form " (Kishimoto, p. 110). He draws out the significance of this difference as follows: Although we can say things in abbreviated ways in Western languages,

> The syntax of Western languages requests, in their construction, more distinct and full indication of the subject-object relation than does the Japanese. So, a full statement of the subject-object relation is expected in English, while the Japanese language is more closely connected with . . . [a human being's] immediate experiences. (Kishimoto, 1967, p. 111)

Indeed, Kishimoto argues that the issue is not simply one of language alone, but also seems to be reflected in the way the Japanese people "think." It is not simply a linguistic or a logical issue, but an issue about how different people think differently as demonstrated by their use of logic and language.

English (and Indo-European languages generally) has been classified as having a *subject-predicate* structure, whereas Japanese has a *topic-comment* structure (Li & Thompson, 1976, pp. 457-489). English linguistic structure is not only subject-predicate structured, but the subject is given prominence. A topic-prominent language, by contrast, is a discourse-oriented language, rather than a sentence-oriented language, and the topic is always known between the interlocutors and when the topic is self-explanatory it can be omitted. The sentence fixation of English tends to focus attention on the internal structure of a single sentence and on the subject-verb agreement between sentences. The topic orientation of Japanese allows the topic as discourse notion to be independent of the sentence, and the linearity of an argument is maintained by the context as a whole. It is an open *field* of dialogue, rather than a closed system of sentence structures. What results from this is that in English the subject emphasis is on the individual subject, as expressed in the individual sentence, whereas in Japanese the emphasis is on the network of dialogical relationships that the context implies and continues to carry. Language does not determine our thought completely. Japanese speakers can think the idea of the individual and English speakers can think of the whole or the network of relations. Nevertheless, each language has a habitual way of saying things. English more or less emphasizes the idea of the individual and Japanese more or less emphasizes the relations.

The centrality of the self in Western cultures is certainly not present in Japanese culture—indeed, it is frowned on, for undue emphasis on self equals selfishness, and selfishness is the result of forgetting one's social interconnectedness, that is, one's contextual relationships. Indeed, the term for *self* in Japanese is *jibun* or *jiko*. Jibun means to be a self, but only in so far as one is aware of one's relationship to any group to which one belongs, to be aware of one's proper place in society, or in nature. Indeed, even when one speaks of oneself, the words used always already presuppose the other to whom one's words are addressed. The other is necessary and prior to the naming of self, for one names oneself for and to the other. It is "the assimilation of the self, who is the observer, with the other, who is observed, with no clear distinction made between the positions of the two" (Suzuki, 1978, p. 145). The use of personal pronouns is more often than not considered impolite except when absolutely necessary, for they place too much emphasis on the self or on the individual out of relationship with the group.

What can be concluded from this is that Japanese is less an instrument for conveying precise and necessarily formulated accounts of what was seen, but instead a contextual web of expressions of experiences, with little or no emphasis on the individual perceiver. There is less of a gap to be bridged between the utterances and the experiences that they seek to describe. The topic to be spoken is a "stream of experience," with scant attention paid to the experiencing subject. Language either describes the contextual experience that one has become, or one remains silent—the other approach in Eastern communication. And the gap between self and other is also already overcome, for the relationships between you and the other are already assumed and are present as the context and topic are shared. The sharing is a communal-oriented sharing, and what is shared is the immediate or "pure" experience or experiences that the *topic discussion* seeks to lay out by looking at the experiential whole from a variety of perspectives or by commenting on aspects of the topic, as with the blind men and the elephant. Each described an aspect of the elephant—leg, ear, trunk, tail except that because they were blind, they had no *context* in common, nor were they interrelationally sensitive enough to be open to the others for commentary or dialogue on the whole of the elephant. The commentary must be a shared exploration of the topic held in common, by more or less non-self-oriented inquirers.

Continuing the same topic in a different direction, the Japanese make a less than sharp distinction between subject and object. In more formal terms, the various strands of the East generally have been described regularly as nondualistic, or at least as less dualistic in their radical separation of subject from object. The Western traditions instinctively distinguish me, as subject, from the tree that I look at. And scientific objectivity has depended on being able to isolate those properties that belong to the object under investigation from those subjective properties of the investigator. By contrast, the Japanese emphasize immediate experience itself, even as (supposedly) prior to the subject-object distinction. More about this later. For now, and using Kishimoto's example, a Japanese walking in the woods may say, "lonesome." It is not said that she or he is lonely, or that one is lonely while walking in these woods, or that he or she is feeling lonely. It is neither an objective nor a subjective experience, but both, or perhaps something in between: It is at least a subjective/objective awareness, or even an awareness before the subject/object distinction has been made. Perhaps it is a more primal drinking in of the whole as one's entire world of the moment. Quoting Kishimoto once more:

> The Japanese people introspectively ponder and explore the domain of immediate experience. This is a very concrete domain for a Japanese. If conceptual speculation goes too far into abstract thinking a Japanese quickly loses interest. And he wants to be less abstract and more concrete and realistic. (Kishimoto, 1967, p. 112)

To add an example from Japanese religiosity, when one stops by a Shinto shrine after work and claps reverently to awaken the god therein, it is utterly unimportant which god it is that is supposed to be within the shrine, or by what name it is known. There is no creed, no scripture, no history that must be known. One stops by in order to feel awe and holiness directly within one's heart and soul. It is the immediate experience that is sought. It is this immediacy of directly felt experience that matters, not the abstract "information" and claims made on behalf of the resident god. This is knowledge, but it is not "objective" knowledge, nor is it encapsulated in a creed, for it is to be directly felt in the presence of divinity. Words, creeds, and scripture are all beside the point. They are not experiential matters, but abstract formulations of now long past and dead immediate experiences in the past.

It was James's (1948, 1955) account of *pure experience* that provided Nishida Kitaro with a bridge between Western and Eastern thinking. In James he found a Western philosopher who emphasized the importance of immediate experience. What Nishida sought to explain through James's term *pure experience* was the significance of the undifferentiated, the "empty," the nothingness underlying all particular things in the cosmos. Immediate or pure experience is undifferentiated, undichotomized, and prior to the subject/object distinction. James himself wrote:

> Out of this aboriginal sensible muchness attention carves out objects, which conception then names and identifies forever—in the sky "constellations," on the earth "beach," "sea," "cliff," "bushes," "grass." Out of time we cut "days" and "nights," "summers" and "winters." We say *what* each part of the sensible continuum is, and all these abstracted *whats* are concepts. (James, 1948, p. 50)

What was once a unified and undivided whole or flow of experience becomes separated into parts, concepts, relations, according to human needs and purposes. But pure experience is never so divided. It is always and everywhere "the instant field of the present" (James, 1955, p. 199). Immediate experience is reality as it presents itself to us directly, or as directly as is possible for us. By contrast, conception *halts* the flow of pure experience, isolates one or more aspects of it, abstracts these from the whole for practical purposes, and thereby harnesses reality for our conscious and deliberate use. All of this makes possible the manipulation of the world, but it does so by fixating on a few characteristics of what is experienced. But these selective abstractions are not anything like the full equivalent of reality, but are partial selections from the whole and static fixations of a reality that is always and everywhere a flux, a changing flow. It is not, of course, to be concluded that the Japanese are either uninterested in or incapable of precision in their thinking. Their recent engineering and technical design prowess makes abundantly clear that they are skillful analysts and dividers of the undistinguished tapestry of being. Yet, while seeing the part, they also maintain a hold on the seamless whole that somehow grounds the variety and distinctions. What arises from this tension between the pragmatically differentiated and the experiential flow is an identity of self-contradiction, as Nishida wrote, a seeing of the parts as parts of a distinctionless whole and the whole as manifest in the distinctiveness of the parts. In Buddhist terms, *Nirvana* (awareness of the whole as undifferentiated) is *Samsara* (the everyday world of distinctions and common sense), and Samsara is Nirvana. It is a sort of stereoscopic vision, an awareness of the *interconnectedness* of all things and of the multiplicity of differentiation.

Three aspects of this account need to be explored further (a) the precise meaning of the "self-contradictory" in the phrase "the identity of self-contradiction," (b) the notion of the indefinite as a suitable result of argument and thinking, and (c) the unusual emphasis on impermanence and change as a basic category of understanding in contrast with permanence and the fixity of being. If *being* is the fundamental category of Western philosophical and scientific understanding, *nothingness* is the Far Eastern foundational equivalent. But what role does *nothingness* play in Eastern thought?

THE IDENTITY OF SELF-CONTRADICTION

Toward the end of his life, Nishida wrote that "this world of historical reality, wherein we are born, act and die, must be, when logically seen, something like the contradictory self-identity of the many and the one. I have come to this point after many years of pondering" (Nishida, 1938, p. 290; see also Yusa, 1983, p. 223). The phrase used to translate what I am calling the identity of self-contradiction as "contradictory self-identity," but the point is the same either way: To stress the contradiction is to plunge into the world as many; to emphasize the matrix or ground is to plunge into the world as one. The world of experience can be viewed in two directions—a sort of double aperture of awareness, or stereoscopic vision—and its unity is not the unity of oneness without distinction, but the unity of self-contradiction. It is both one and many, changing and unchanging, past and future in the momentary present.

Nishida's dialectic has as its aim the preservation of its contradictory terms or moments. His is no Hegelian dialectic in which the opposing thesis and antithesis are both overcome and eradicated in a new synthesis. Of course, some would argue that Hegel, too, wished to preserve the earlier tension in the synthesis, but the point is that Nishida wished to retain the original tension, to preserve both thesis and antithesis as such. They are the *yin* and the *yang* of the equation. The unity is the circle drawn around the *yin/yang* polarity that makes plain that although they are complementary or polar opposites, they are not antagonistic, but parts of a unified whole. Notice the choice of words: "complementary," "polar opposites," rather than "opposites" or "logical opposites." In order to be able to identify black and white as opposites, they must already be the same: "to think of one thing is to distinguish it from the other. In order for the distinction to be possible, it must originally have something in common with the other" (Nishida, 1938, p. 73; see also Yusa, 1983, p. 223). Black and white are polar opposites, or extremes, of the otherwise undifferentiated continuum called *color* or *hue*.[3] So what they have in common is their membership in the whole of color. They are more alike than black is to sand, or to fudge, or to fox. Black and fox are not members of the same logical "club," but black and white are: They are members in good standing of the "color club." Nothing in the world is perfectly black, or perfectly white, and so it follows that everything that is black is also white to some degree, and vice versa.

That is why the *yin/yang* symbol is drawn with a small circle of the polar opposite within it. White/black are extremes on the same spectrum of possibility. Notice also that the *yin/yang* symbol has the two polar opposites snuggling up to one another. They are not enemies, but friends in difference. The resultant logical emphasis is not an *either/or* sort of logical stand, in which the world is precisely sliced into fragmentary opposites, but a *both/and* logic, which correctly observes that every thing that is in opposition is also in opposition from a common place, a common starting point, a common heritage, a common perspective, and has a complementary role to play within the identity of the whole of opposition/unity.

This identity of opposition works its way out in cultural history. The Japanese emphasis on consensus is a good example. Whereas we in the West tend to take our stand on "principle" or "law" or basic "rights," the Japanese assume that principles and laws and rights are also relative to some extent. Just as one can always think of examples that will call a principle or a right into question, so changing circumstances and the chemistry of the persons involved make it better to go into negotiation with a degree of flexibility. It is true that one side can always win. But in winning there is often the greatest loss as well. One can force a conclusion in court, and thereby destroy all possibility of future reconciliation. One can conquer another country, and thereby make a thousand times more difficult the creation of good relations. It is not that not being strong and forthright is the correct way either. One must feel one's way along in negotiation, with the willingness to give in a little if necessary.

In Japanese consensus "argument" and negotiation, what is sought is some *compromise* that is good enough for all to "win" in some significant sense, or for no one to be the clear "loser." No one will leave, in all likelihood, wish everything they had hoped for, but no one will leave the dear loser. Everyone leaves the discussion with something, and although the solution is no one's favorite, each negotiator can live with

---

[3]The terms polar complete and absolute fragmental, or my variations on his themes, are from Holbrook (1981).

the result and indeed affirm sincere loyalty to it. Everyone remains "on side." There is no *black and white*, but only various shades of *grey* from which a compromise must be crafted. The result is a *both/and* decision that is decidedly grey in color—neither extreme black, nor extreme white. What is lost are the various visions of the *ideal*, but they were many to begin with. If there was only one clear way ahead at the start, then negotiation would have been unnecessary. All "ideals" are, in deconstructive language, "temporary closures," and because they are temporary and not absolute, final, eternal and unchanging, they are easier to give up. One collectively crafts another "ideal" that will preserve the relations among the members in negotiation, give them all some "face" and dignity and chart the way ahead for success in business or government, or in interpersonal relationships, depending on the nature of the negotiation in the first place.

Applying the theory to another sphere that is an instantiation of the *both/and* logic of complementaries rather than that of the agony of radical opposition, I consider the Japanese attitudes toward religious difference. Using a personal instance, one of my students from Japan moved to our small Ontario town and asked me where the nearest Buddhist temple was to be found. I told him that Toronto was the closest city with an active Buddhist population. He was disappointed, but a week later came to my office to inform me that he had found a church that was close enough to the Buddhist tradition to please him. But not only did he decide to attend, but he was committed to becoming a Roman Catholic. I asked him whether he had thought carefully enough about abandoning his Buddhist faith, which, for one thing, is generally nontheistic, and he looked at me in surprise, saying: "I will be a Catholic only while here. When I return to Japan I will be a Buddhist again." It is not unusual to find a Buddhist, a Shinto, and a Christian shrine within a single Japanese home. Shinto shrines are even now to be found within Buddhist temple grounds. Nakamura Hajime wrote of Kegon Buddhism in Japan, and of a 12th- or 13th-century priest named Koben (1173-1232), who adopted the ways and practices of many religions. Nakamura asked:

> What was the reason for this? According to his own interpretation, "Each attains well-rounded enlightenment according to his customary practice. Since there is not just one customary practice (but many), well-rounded enlightenment also cannot be just one." He recognized the justification of multiple religious faiths. (Nakamura, 1964, pp. 387-388)

The Japanese emphasis on spiritual tolerance, and on the creation of *harmony* (wa),[4] can be found even in its earliest history, but not without the usual exceptions to be found in every cultural tradition in those times when tolerance is rejected for direct action against a perceived hostile threat. No culture ever lives up to its ideals, but what matters here, in this exploration, is the difference that is to be discerned within the *ideal*. And the ideal comprehends differences in belief and practice as nonthreatening insights into the immanent and transcendent dimensions of a reality that we never comprehend intellectually, but do apprehend to some extent experientially.

Self-contradictory identity, then, is composed of the complementarity of polar opposition (not an antagonistic struggle of logical opposites), but situated within a whole that preserves their difference while enveloping or embracing both in a greater whole of identity. All that exists is an expression of or a "self-unfolding of the eternal, formless nothingness; all finite forms are shadows of the formless" (Schinzinger, 1973, p. 37).

THE INDEFINITE

Nothingness, emptiness, the undifferentiated primal ground, the enveloper of all things, is the unifier of opposites, the identity of its own self-contradictory expressions. It is like the lining of a kimono or of a fine garment of any sort: It is unseen, but nevertheless manifests itself in the hang and shape of the garment. The formless is to be seen in the shape and hang of the formed: the voiceless in the sounds of the many voices in the world.

Japanese Zen Buddhists distinguish between rational, logical, discursive understanding (*vijnana*) and intuitive, immediate, or enlightened awareness (*prajna*).[5] The latter goes beyond the former. The former is dualistic "in the sense that there is one who sees and there is the other that is seen—the two standing in opposition" (Suzuki, 1967, p. 66). In the immediacy of *prajna*, this differentiation does not occur: "What is seen

---

[4]The Japanese word wa means harmony and includes the various submeanings of mutual tolerance, mutual respect, and the willingness to interact with others in a spirit of reconciliation.

[5]Loy (1988), in his groundbreaking work, presented the etymologies of vijnana and prajna: 'The vi-prefix of vijnana . . . signifies 'separation or differentiation.' Hence vijnana refers to knowing that functions by discriminating one thing from another. In contrast, the pra-prefix of prajna means being born or springing up'—presumably referring to a more spontaneous type of knowing in which the thought no longer seems to be the product of a subject but is experienced as arising from a deeper nondual source. In such knowing the thought and that which thinks the thought are not distinguishable" (pp. 136-137).

and the one who sees are identical; the seer is the seen and the seen is the seer" (p. 66). Division is the work of rational, logical awareness, whereas *prajna* takes the whole as it is, as an immediate experience. The one takes the whole as its focus, the other the parts. One integrates, the other analyzes. *Prajna* awareness is immediate and is typified by an "absence of deliberation, no allowance for an intervening proposition, no passing from premises to conclusion. *Prajna* is pure act, pure experience" (pp. 67-68). It is important to understand, however, that the nonduality of *prajna* awareness is awareness in which "consciousness does not disappear but becomes one with its 'object'" (Loy, 1988, p. 158). From Suzuki's (1967) perspective, which he takes to be the Zen perspective, and to that extent also foundationally Japanese, *prajna* or immediacy as identity underlies *vijnana* or the rational and logical separation into opposites and parts. It is worth quoting his conclusion at length:

> That *prajna* underlies *vijnana*, that it is what enables *vijnana* to function as the principle of differentiation, is not difficult to realize when we see that differentiation is impossible without something that works for integration or unification. The dichotomy of subject and object cannot obtain unless there is something that lies behind them, something that is neither subject nor object; this is a kind of field where they can operate, where subject can be separated from object, object from subject. If the two are not related in any way, we cannot even speak of their separation or antithesis. There must be something of subject in object and something of object in subject which make their separation as well as their relationship possible. And as this something cannot be made the theme of intellectualization, there must be another method of reaching this most fundamental principle. The fact that it is so utterly fundamental excludes the application of the bifurcating instrument. We must appeal to *prajna*-intuition. (Suzuki, 1967, p. 73)

What follows from *prajna* is a heightened awareness of the immediacy of the moment. Even a single blade of grass is pure magic, for it is now one's whole world, and one sees it in a way that one has never seen it before. Nishida wrote that it is through this kind of awareness that the Japanese culture attempts "to become things themselves" (Nishida, 1958, p. 362). One empties the self through *meditation*, by letting go of one's habitual distinction making, and plunges into the things themselves. One becomes "no-minded," that is, empty of concepts, empty of abstractions, empty of distinctions, devoid of logical analysis. One is immersed in things; one becomes one "in things and events. It is to become one at that primal point in which there is neither self nor others" (Kitano, p. 362).

One does not remain in this no-minded state, of course, for there are automobiles and stereos to build, meals to prepare, and children to care for. One moves from the quiet state of regeneration and unity to the willful state of distinction making and determined activity. Yet one never sees the world in quite the same way again, for now there is some thing less than final about the distinctions one makes, about the successes one has, about the "image" of self one presents at work and at home. One is now aware of being much more than this, as are all the parts and distinctions with which one works, and of all of the activities which one performs, for they all arise out of and are expressions of an indistinct, undifferentiated whole of potentiality that is forever taking on new forms, new ways, new discoveries, and new meaning. The world shifts and flows on, as should we.

IMPERMANENCE IS REALITY

We in the West, from the time of the ancient Greeks and Hebrews to the present day, have emphasized the eternal, unchanging, and immutable as the proper description of reality. We have called this *Being*, or *being* (or God). The Far East has emphasized *Nothingness*, or *nothing*, as their fundamental ground. Whether Buddhist, Shinto, or primitive animist, the Japanese have accepted that the reality of change and flux is everywhere apparent. Even the Buddha is impermanence, we read in place after place in Japanese Zen Buddhist writing: "For Dogen . . . the fluid aspect of impermanence is in itself the absolute state. The changeable character of the phenomenal world is of absolute significance. . . . Impermanence is the Buddhahood" (Nakamura, 1964, p. 352). His emphasis is on the dynamic, the mobile, for this is experience as it is given. We stop it, fixate on a part of it, label it here and there, cut it up for practical purposes. But everything is experienced as a flowing, a growing, and a decaying, as seasonal alteration. Therefore, if one does see the Buddha walking down the street, one should (metaphorically speaking) kill him. For this cannot be the real Buddha, but an idol, a hardened flow of Buddha expression, a glib answer to the questions about who he was and how we should be. There is no adequate image of the Buddha, nor can there ever be, for it is the flux itself that is the divine working out in cosmic history. All images are but pointers, fingers directing us to look at the "moon" of the direct experience of flow and readiness for change, of perpetually renewed experience in our own lives.

It is no surprise to learn that cherry blossoms (sakura) are a symbol of this alteration. Nothing in Japan rivals the short period of time when the blossoms come and the sidewalks and parks are crammed with people who celebrate this beauty in their lives. Hospital patients are, whenever possible, brought to a window or even wheeled outside the hospital confines to view the blossoms. school children are taken to famous blossom-viewing sites. Even at night the parks are filled with those who wish to experience the "night viewing" of cherry blossoms (*yosakura*). But one must see them now, take them into one's consciousness this very instant, for they are incredibly delicate and short-lived. A single storm and you will have missed them. As it is, under perfect conditions, they will be at their peak for but a handful of days. Symbolically, the cherry blossom is a Japanese reminder that one ought to live each day, each hour, and each second in a mindful way, for a moment like this very one will not occur ever again. Life is precious, nature is precious, blossoms are precious both because of the beauty inherent, as well as the obviously associated fragility. Live each moment to the fullest. Life is good although fragile and quick to turn to tragedy. We are good although vulnerable to so many fluctuations of existence. And the world of nature is good although it may bring a typhoon or an earthquake at any moment. One lives with one's eyes open, aware of the vicissitudes of life, and yet joyously aware of what is given in the immediate, in the now, in the momentary. What one cannot change; one must accept.

The emphasis on the goodness of nature, of life, and of ourselves is an assumed attitudinal stance throughout. Whatever one makes of the distinction between guilt and shame cultures, Japan and the Far East generally have been life affirming. The earliest known primer, which very young children used to learn to read and write Chinese, began with the statement, "the nature of man is originally good" (Fung Yu-Lan, 1948, p. 1). This first sentence of childhood is a far cry from "run Jane run" or "see Spot run." It is of particular interest to us because it highlights an abstract cultural attitudinal and valuational preference at this extraordinarily early point in a child's development. As well, it takes for granted that we are intrinsically good. We are not born in sin; we are not fallen creatures as the result of early disobedience in eating of the fruit of the tree of the knowledge of good and evil. Is this perhaps a "golden time" before the distinction between good and evil, as it might well have been for Adam and Eve? In a way, yes. We begin with a tendency toward the good, in a world that supports us and with which we identify. It is our home. It is a good world, a beautiful world, and it is our task to find our way in a hospitable world. Evil arises in the course of the living of our lives together. We do not begin living in sin, already corrupt, already immoral. Still, one can be led to despair and feel alienated and pessimistic. Yet, Japanese pessimism, Nakamura related, is not an existential weariness of the phenomenal world of nature or of our own corrupt nature. Rather, Japanese pessimism "means to be wearied only of complicated social fetters and restrictions from which they wish to be delivered" (Nakamura, 1964, p. 371).

One rejuvenates oneself in the presence of nature and through reminders of it. One listens to the water bubble in the iron kettle of the tea ceremony; one sits quietly in front of the single flower in the small alcove (*tokonoma*) in one's living room; one prunes the roots of one's *bonsai* tree; or one visits one of Japan's incredibly lush and magnificent public gardens. It is in the midst of such quiet contemplation that one becomes acquainted once more with the indistinct background out of which the particular flower arises and against which it stands out. The plain background of the alcove almost back lights the single iris; the grand sweep of the park is too much to take in all at once, yet it serves as the lush background to the several stones forming a path in the foreground; the rock garden has a background of sand or crushed rock, out of which arises a few large rocks or larger rocks ringed by moss; the moss garden is a green background of many mosses, against which the bamboo trees and shoots, themselves green, stand out in brilliant relief; the background of almost complete silence serves to heighten the sound of the bubbling kettle, which breaks the silence as though a great roar.

The identity of self-contradiction, that A is A and not A, and therefore is both, and yet from the perspective of unity is neither, or both and neither, points toward a standpoint or horizon on the world that is stereoscopically one and many, indistinct and distinct, whole and part. The complementarity of seeming opposites breeds a spirit of tolerance and openness to consensus. The impermanence of all that is reminds one of the artificiality of static conceptualization and of supposedly unchanging laws and principles, thereby opening us to continued reflection on what it is that we hold dear and to humility with respect to our seeming knowledge gains. Our world is one of flux, and wisdom is the taking of change as it comes, changing what is within our power and flowing with the rest. We must encourage flexibility in our life styles, in our thinking, and in our arrangements with others. The bamboo tree, another common symbol is as successful as it is not because of its rigidity and size, but because it can bend in even the strongest of winds. It can bend to the ground without breaking. What keeps it from toppling over under such extreme conditions is that it has as deep a root system as any tree. It runs deep, it has ample foundation, and it is remarkably flexible and unbreakable. Is this not, perhaps, a worthy attitudinal stance for fruitfully engaging in argumentation? Is this a possible way, perhaps even an enviable way, of describing a way of discussing, acting, and living with others? It is, of course, and it sets the arrangements for argumentation within a specific cultural tradition. Still, it is but one among many arrangements and cultures, and a flexible thinker will take what is useful and worthwhile from this account, and of course, from many others as well.

REFERENCES

Carter, R E. (1989). *The nothingness beyond God: An introduction to the philosophy of Nishida Kitaro.* New York: Paragon House.
Fung, Y. (1948). *A short history of Chinese philosophy.* (D. Bodde, Trans.).New York: The Free Press.
Holbrook, B. (1981). *The stone monkey: An alternative, Chinese-scientific,reality.* New York: Morrow.
James, W. (1948). *Some problems of philosophy.* London: Longmans, Green.
James, W. (1955). *Pragmatism, and four essays from the meaning of truth* (R.B. Perry, Ed.). New York: A Meridian Book, New American Library. (Original work published 1909)
Kishimoto, H. (1967). Some Japanese cultural traits and religions. In C.A. Moore (Ed.), *The Japanese mind: Essentials of Japanese philosophy and culture.* Honolulu: University of Hawaii Press.
Lao Tzu (1962). *Tao Te Ching* (W. Bynner, Trans.). New York: Capricorn Books.
Lao Tzu (1963). *Tao Te Ching* (D.C. Lau, Trans.). New York: Penguin.
Li, C.N., & Thompson, S.A. (1976). Subject and topic: A new typology of language. In C.N. Li (Ed.), *Subject and topic.* New York: Academic Press.
Loy, D. (1988). *Nonduality: A study in comparative philosophy.* New Haven, CT: Yale University Press.
Moore, C.A. (1967). Editor's supplement: The enigmatic Japanese mind. In C.A. Moore (Ed.), *The Japanese mind: Essentials of Japanese philosophy and culture.* Honolulu: The University of Hawaii Press.
Nakamura, H. (1964). *Ways of thinking of Eastern peoples: India, China, Tibet, Japan.* Honolulu: University of Hawaii Press.
Nishida, K. (1983). *Collected works Vol. XII* (M. Yusa, Trans.). Tokyo: Iwanami. (Original work published 1938)
Nishida, K. (1958). The problem of Japanese culture. In R. Tsunoda, W.T. Bary, & D. Keene (Eds.), *Sources of Japanese tradition* (Vol. II). New York: Columbia University Press.
Nishida, K. (1987). The logic of the place of nothingness and the religious worldview. In *Last writings: Nothingness and the religious worldview* (D. Dilworth, Trans.). Honolulu: University of Hawaii Press.
Schinzinger, R. (1973). Introduction. In *Intelligibility and the philosophy of nothingness.* Westport, CT: Greenwood Press.

Suzuki, D.T. (1967). Reason and intuition in Buddhist philosophy. In C.A. Moore (Ed.), *The Japanese mind: Essentials of Japanese philosophy and culture*. Honolulu: The University of Hawaii Press.
Suzuki, T. (1978). *Japanese and the Japanese* (works in culture). Tokyo: Kodansha International.
Yusa, M. (1983). *'Persona originalis': 'Jinkaku' and 'personne,' according to the philosophies of Nishida Kitaro and Jacques Maratain*. Unpublished doctoral dissertation, University of California at Santa Barbara.

CHAPTER 11

Rescuing the Failed, Filed Away, and Forgotten: African Americans and Eurocentricity in Academic Argument

Dorothy Perry Thompson

In *Black Communications, Breaking Down the Barriers* (1991), linguistics and reading specialist Dandy, like Smitherman, Folb, and various others before her, describes and analyzes features characteristic of African-American speech. Dandy includes a summary of origins in the African oral tradition (such as call and response), indigenous phonetic, structural, and vocabulary lists, and-explanations of verbal strategies such as "woofin'," "rappin'," and "playing the dozens." Gates has legitimized these strategies for the literary criticism academy by articulating a black aesthetic based on them and by posing a folk character associated with them, the Signifying Monkey, as metaphor for the complexities of the African-American communications system. Additionally, pioneer scholar Shaughnessy has looked at written features that distinguish African-American communication from that of the power class.

In spite of the scholarship, some of which enlightened composition teachers more than 15 years ago (see Smitherman, 1977), too many of us are still struggling in the dark with African Americans who are failing most of their college courses because they have not mastered "edited American English." Although composition teachers know about dialect influence, embrace multiculturalism, and celebrate diversity, they are still designing Eurocentric exams, rubrics, and assignments that help them to fail, file away, and forget African-American students.

It is time to look not only at how much we are penalizing students for zero copula, hypercorrection, and other surface features, but also how assumptions, priorities, and other deeper structures in the writing of African Americans result in teacher labels such as "incoherent," "rambling," "too predictable," and "vague." Such labels are often indicative of a clash of cultures in the classroom: Afrocentricity and Eurocentricity. World views that include approaches to tasks, valuing of "the word," and ideas of order must be considered as they manifest themselves in the writing of African-American students. It is time to look at how the hierarchical system of academic discourse, in its privileging of argument as its highest form, and at how the conventions within that form predispose some African-American writers to failure.

A first step in rescuing African Americans from the failed files is to recognize that some of them bring to their writing fixed priorities and paradigms of a cultural tradition different from the one that prevails in the classroom. this is not at variance with what happens to students from other cultures. Spanish and French students who transfer into my American university, for example, write in ways that show first language and first culture influence. However, the African-American student whose cultural background has been kept largely Afrocentric has the added complexity of having to operate in a system that devalues and is at war with his own.

What are the characteristics of these warring systems? African historian Cheik Anta Diop's world view differences (in Kambon, 1992) offer some insight (see Table 11.1).

Table 11.1. Diop's Two-Cradle Theory of African and European Wold View/Cultural Differences.

Basic Cultural Categories	Southern Cradle (African)	Northern Cradle (European)
Mode of Lifestyle	Agrarian/Sedentary	Nomadic
Descent	Matrineal	Patrineal
Gods/Deity	One Universal God	Familistia Gods
Social Philosophy	Collectivism and Xenophilia	Individualism and Xenophobic
Death Ritual	Burial	Cremation
Human/Anthropocentric Relations	Nonracial	Racial

Diop theorizes that the social philosophy of people originating from the southern (or African) cradle of the earth is characterized by xenophilia (love of strangers), whereas the philosophy of those originating from the northern (or European) cradle leans toward individualism and xenophobia (fear of strangers).

These theories coincide with psychologist Kambon's (1992) oppositional world-views schematic (see Table 11.2).

In Table 11.2, the African-American world view includes an ethos based on the survival of the group, inclusiveness, synthesis, cooperation, and collective responsibility, whereas the European-American ethos espouses survival of the fittest, exclusiveness, dichotomy, competition, and individual rights. In the category of values and customs, these oppositions are listed: African/African-American tendencies toward corporateness, interdependence, circularity, complementarity, and understanding; and European/European-American tendencies toward separateness, independence, ordinality, and intervention. The psychobehavioral modalities of the two groups show the same kind of dialectic pattern: groupness and sameness on the one hand, and uniqueness and difference on the

Table 11.2. Comparative Worldviews Schematic.

European/ European-American World View	African/ African-American World View
Control/Mastery over Nature	Oneness/Harmony with Nature
ETHOS	
Survival of the Fittest	Survival of the Group
Exclusiveness/Dichotomy	Inclusiveness/Synthesis
Competition-Individual Rights	Cooperation-Collective Responsibility
VALUES AND CUSTOMS	
Separateness-Independence	Corporateness-Interdependence
Materialism-Ordinality	Spiritualism-Circularity
Intervention-Oppression	Complementarity-Understanding
Individualism	
PSYCHO-BEHAVIORAL MODALITY	
Uniqueness-Differences	Sameness-Commonality
European/White Supremacy (Racism/Anti-African)	Humanism-Religious

other. Some of these philosophies, values, and customs (perhaps arguable, as they have been for years) do manifest themselves in the assignments we design for our students and in their responses to them.

In Eurocentric Academic Discourse (which I refer to hereafter as EAD), there is, in form and content, a move from the the abstract idea (thesis) through detailed examples back to the abstract idea. It is a discourse formula that prioritizes in this way: First, what is most important is the abstract idea. Second, concrete details are needed, but they are only incidentals used to support the abstract idea.

Finally, this abstract idea is so important that it is restated in the conclusion. One circles back to it (in the most elemental paradigm we offer students in our composition courses). This practice is evident in my university's Writing Proficiency Examination (see Appendix). Professional writer Amitai Etzioni, in the excerpt used in the test, states the abstract idea in the first paragraph: "Americans have been loathe to live up to their responsibilities in recent years." He develops the idea with these particulars:

1. A survey showed that few young Americans are willing to serve on a jury.
2. Another survey showed that Americans favor a flat tax only if their favorite loophole is not closed.
3. His (Etzioni's) class at George Washington University defined duty as something imposed, alien, authoritarian.
4. Another survey showed that about 80% of Americans subscribe to a philosophy of self-fulfillment.
5. Finally, the last paragraph restates the main idea.

An AWV operant (my term for the African American steeped in the traditions of the African world view) reads such a prompt and responds with great difficulty because it is a reversal of the value and order system he or she knows. The African concept of Nommo, a belief in the magic power of the word, is, in my opinion, the pervasive mindset at work in the responses of some African-American students who have to take such a prompt and invert its priorities so that it makes sense in their own value system. In the Nommo African belief system, the oral word is used to "give shape and coherence to human existence" (Smitherman, 1977, p. 77). Smitherman (1977) elaborates on the African concept:

> The preslavery background was one in which . . . Nommo was believed necessary to actualize life and give mastery over things. "All activities of men, and all the movements in nature rest in the word, on the productive power of the word, which is water and heat

and seed and Nommo, that is life force itself. . . . The force, responsibility, and commitment of the word, and the awareness that the word alone alters the world." No medicine, potion, or magic of any sort is considered effective without accompanying words. So strong is the African belief in the power and absolute necessity of Nommo that all craftsmanship must be accompanied by speech. (p. 78)

Explaining how African-Americans continue the tradition, Smitherman writes:

Both in slavery times and now, the black community places high value on the spoken word. In fact, the black oral tradition links Black American culture with that of other oral "preliterate" people—such as Native Americans—for whom the spoken word is supreme. The persistence of the black oral tradition is such that blacks tend to place only limited value on the written word, whereas verbal skills expressed orally rank in high esteem. This is not to say that Black Americans never read anything or that the total black community is functionally illiterate. However, it is to say that from a black perspective, written documents are limited in what they can teach about life and survival in the world. Furthermore, aside from athletes and entertainers, only those blacks who can perform stunning feats of oral gymnastics become culture heroes and leaders in the community. (p. 76)

Therefore, to imbue the word with its proper power, the AWV operant takes a text such as Etzioni's and looks for what I call its "life value." He or she asks, "What do these words have to do with people and the way they live in the world? What do they teach or tell about life?" In other words, following directive 2 of the essay examination prompt—Take a clear stand, arguing that the passage is either (a) substantially correct or (b) essentially misleading—becomes problematic for the AWV operant. First, the student's cultural tradition makes him or her understand that one does not argue for the sole purpose of proving that someone else's point of view is "substantially correct" or "essentially misleading." "The word" is more important than that. Its purpose, according to Nommo and African-American traditions, is to accompany, alter, and order acts of living. Second, writing, the act of committing one's thoughts to the page by-using conventional signs, is an act of secondary importance because it is merely a flat copy—minus the dimensions of sound, gestures, and so on—of the original speech. Therefore, one tries, in writing, to infuse the word as much as possible with some of the significance of the oral tradition. What that means, for one thing, in an African/African-American world view, is that "the word" should be used for complementarity and understanding (see Table 11.2). In commiting the act of writing, one must make it matter beyond the page. What that means, ultimately, is that one must make the written word relate to the utterances and lives of others in the community of human existence.

Jene, a 19-year-old male college student, responded to the Etzioni exam excerpt this way:

> I have a duty to act like a Black man. To me, duty to your race is more important than duty to your country. Why? Because if I act "white," then other Blacks would see me as a sell-out. If I don't sell out, then other Black people will look at me and say, "Now that's a Black man," and have pride in being Black themselves.

When I asked Jene why he decided to write this first in his essay instead of following the directions on the test by discussing examples in three of the seven designated areas, he answered thusly:

> It jumped out at me that responsibility to race was not on the test as one of the categories that could be discussed. Perhaps because of our different histories, whites don't consider that an important responsibility the way we do. But, I'm Black before business, politics, athletics, religion, interpersonal relationships, and citizenship [discussion areas designated on the test]. So, if I'm going to write a paper about duty, I have to write about the duty I have just being a Black male. I feel responsible for other, younger Black men.

Here, Jene voiced a priority that the test makers may not have considered. During our conference, he added the following:

> I argue to find out what's right, not who's right. When I argue on paper, I try to put the reader in the same frame of mind that I'm in so he can see where I'm coming from. It doesn't matter whether he agrees or not, as long as he *understands* [emphasis mine] and recognizes my point of view.

Clearly, this student's priorities are at variance with those evident in the test prompt; moreover, they echo some of the ideas in Diop's and Kambon's theories regarding world views.

Another student, Duchess, who took the Winthrop University Writing Proficiency Test (given to all incoming transfer students who wish to be given credit for composition courses taken at another school), read the Etzioni passage and decided that it was, to use her description, "not straightforward enough." She read it a second time, she reported, and decided that it must be about civil duty. Then she read it again and decided that it had something to do with "self," or people caught up in the concept of "me-ism." During my conference with Duchess, she identified factors that made her decide not to consider civil duty the central topic: First, it was not a topic that she and other college students thought about. Second, she could relate better to the me-ism concept. In other words, Duchess rearranged the priorities in the prompt to suit her own life and the lives of her fellow students. In her opinion, her essay would have been meaningless if she had tried to argue about civil duty. Her words, once transferred to the page, had to be there, not to respond to an abstract idea, but to say something about her own real life. This is how an AWV operant gives the sacred word its "propers"—its depth, power, and complexity as representative of reality—or adheres to the concept of Nommo. (Of course, it can be argued that any student not familiar with an assigned topic reshapes it to suit his or her own experiences, whether or not he or she is an AWV operant. However, the important difference here is this: All of the African-American students with whom I worked in this study reshaped in ways that give priority to the concrete "about real life" details in the text of the prompt. Picking up on these, they meandered into whatever areas the details led them.)

Duchess began her essay with these sentences: "Yes, I must confess I am in the self fulfillment category. I admit it, all I think about is me." Continuing, she tried to tie me-ism to civil duty by way of the definition for the word duty she found in the dictionary: "the act or course of action that one must do [sic?]." After quoting the definition, she explained in the first paragraph of her essay:

> Well, in all my twenty years, their [sic] really hasn't been any act or action that I have had to do. I agree with Etzioni's article, and with those students that "people ought to be free to do what they believe in."

From there, following the directions of the prompt, Duchess chose religion as one of the categories from which to draw supporting examples. However, in her own way of reshaping the test so that it relates, somewhat, to things that she knows about, she discusses the rights of her friend Scott, an atheist who does not feel that he has a religious duty to believe in God. [At this point, the two graders who read this essay were probably wondering how in the world this student got from the original topic, civil duty, to atheism.]

Another student whom I identified as an AWV operant also left her readers wondering how she got from topic A, civil duty, to topic Z, wayward husbands. In her body paragraph on interpersonal relationships (one of the discussion areas suggested on the test prompt), Quin began by stating that she agreed with the George Washington University students mentioned in the excerpt. She wrote:

> People should be free to do what they want, especially in America. The reason I say in America, is because this is a free country. For instance, you're married, and in your marriage sex is wanted or expected. If the wife in the marriage doesn't want sex, the husband will go elsewhere. The husband that's not getting any sex or shall I say loving, he will be expected to go outside the marriage. Now, in this situation its both the husband and wife duty to satisfy each other.

Quin conveniently discarded the first part of the phrase "civil duty" in favor of "sexual duty," a topic that, obviously, in her life is much more important in the ways that it is connected with human existence.

AWV responses to this particular test included other surprising elements. Both Quin and Duchess told me that they thought the word *pollster* used in the prompt was a part of the name of the person mentioned. ('The sentence read, "Pollster Daniel Yankelovich estimated that 17 percent of Americans were deeply committed to a philosophy of self-fulfillment and another 63 percent subscribed to it in varying degrees.") To these students, African Americans, Pollster, as a first name, is no more unusual than Yankelovich as a last name. Moreover, neither student had ever heard of pollster as an occupation identifier. (In their essays, both students had sentences that indicated this name or word confusion.) Also, Duchess said that she had tried to find the term flat tax (from the test) in the dictionary. It is a term she never heard. Unfortunately, she could not find it; therefore, Etzioni's example did not make any sense to her. These may seem small points. The overarching, bigger one is that our discourse will continue to baffle African-American students as long as it contains elements indigenous to a middle class, predominately white culture. The percentage of African-American students who are first-generation college students is much greater than the percentage of white students who are; moreover, many African-American students, especially in the South where I teach, come to college from communities that are still segregated. Therefore, the culture gap, especially its language component, is a bigger one for them. Consequently, they sometimes miscue in their struggles to bridge it or to make connections.

For example, in giving the word duty its propers, Quin connected it with a topic—sex in marriage—about which she could teach a lesson. As in the Nommo tradition, the word must be used to illuminate life. However, the way the test prompt offers light to go by for some AWV operants is not in the place that-EAD wants them to look (that is, thesis), but rather in the concrete details that can be pulled out and connected with their own experiences.

None of this is aimed at concluding that AWV's cannot understand abstract ideas; instead, it is meant to indicate that they do not expect the thesis to be the sole purpose of the words on the page. That purpose would be useless in that it would divorce the tradition of the word from its connection with real life. Some AWV operants do understand that there are other traditions that require a different approach to a writing task. Duchess, for example, came into the Writing Center (a help lab) two days after our conference about the Writing Proficiency Test to get some assistance with a paper on *Lysistrata*. She was trying to do a Marxist-feminist reading of the work for a literary criticism course and obviously was having no problems understanding the complicated abstracts involved. What was the difference? The situations were. One, the writing exam was an essay test on a current issue; the other was a paper on a work from the past, a work written by a dead writer. For Duchess, the critical analysis of *Lysistrata* did not warrant a concentration on concretes that could help shape current lives; it was a piece about the dead. Therefore, the approach to the task could be divorced from the concept of Nommo. She would be allowed to concentrate on abstracts. On the other hand, the exam prompt was set up as a piece by some individual (a contemporary writer) supposedly discussing current human existence.

Duchess's difference in approach to these two writing tasks illustrates perfectly what composition specialist Ball (1992) has pointed out: "Research on inter-ethnic discourse has confirmed that successful communication depends on participant expectations and inferential process by which participants judge the goals of the communicative task" (p. 523). In her AWV expectations, the student saw Etzioni's piece as one wherein the writer sets up his experiences as an index for others. As such, his voice should be clear and authorial, perhaps, like that of the African griot (tribal historian) or like that of the African-American master storyteller. For Duchess, Etzioni was neither clear nor "singular" enough. She complained: "Whose essay is this anyway? Etzioni's? Well, too many other opinions are brought in."

When the griot speaks the history of his people, or when the storyteller narrates, no one is allowed to interrupt. In the case of the African griot, no other voice has been trained to do the telling, as it is the sacred duty of the chosen person to function as the keeper of the village's history. However, within the context of the griot's narration, all listeners have a place. In other words, the purpose of the telling is to show others where and how they belong to the village or tribe. (Alex Haley, for example, after finally finding the griot of the Kinte clan, his African family, was not allowed to interrupt the hundreds of years of history the teller had to recount before he got to Kunte, Haley's much celebrated ancestor in the Roots saga.) In the African tradition, it is the listener's duty to recognize his or her own connection with the history or to infer a message, if, for example, it is a morality tale that is being told.

In the African-American tradition, storytelling carries the same rules. Whoever has the floor must show singular authority with the material. That person has the right, although the listeners may know the tale well, to improvise as he or she sees fit, in order to show his or her own expertise as teller, as a part of his or her purpose is to entertain. The job of the audience is to listen, especially for the innovations, nuances, or meanderings that may bring special surprises and delights within the context of an old tale. Gates (1988) has likened this oral tradition to another African-American one: the playing of jazz. He can find no better summary (as metaphor) than this passage from novelist Ralph Ellison:

> There is a cruel contradiction implicit in the art form itself. For true jazz is an art of individual assertion within and against the group. Each true jazz moment (as distinct from the uninspired commercial performance) springs from a contest in which each artist challenges all the rest, each solo flight, or improvisation, represents (like the successive canvases of a painter) a definition of his identity: as individual, as member of the collectivity and as link in the chain of tradition. Thus, because jazz finds its very life in an endless improvisation upon traditional materials, the jazzman must lose his identity even as he finds it. (p. vii)

Unfortunately, the AWV would-be "jazzmen" in the college composition classroom are riffing from a score whose melody is not familiar to most of us composition instructors.

Quin, whose writing shows that she was even less acquainted with EAD than some of the other AWV operants with whom I worked, produced an essay exam response that was assessed as unsatisfactory not only because of the seeming irrelevance of the details she included, but also because of the meandering pattern in which she offered them. Her first body paragraph alludes to Desert Storm, and is her attempt to show that, contrary to what Etzioni stated, some Americans are patriotic.

However, the example is vague. When I asked her why she included it, she explained that her brother was involved in Desert Storm. When I asked her why she did not write in more detail about her brother, her response was not surprising to me. As an African American (and, in my opinion, an AWV operant) coming in to take a test for transfer credit at a predominately white institution, Quin's inclination was toward generalities that might fit whatever the test makers expected. The vagueness is a safe way to try to key into whatever the mysteries of EAD are. Spouting personal details (expected in the vernacular tradition) might get one into trouble, especially if the test maker's world (culture) is assumed to be vastly different from the test taker's.

From Desert Storm, Quin jumped to sex in marriage. When the word *duty* occurred in the body paragraph about wayward husbands, it reminded her, again, of military duty; thus, she returned to that topic and explained that because society had changed, "people think only of themselves instead of doing duty for the military." She ended her essay: "Now is the time to do duty for yourself and your family. The only other duty that really should be done is military. Before you enlist . . . you should think about the different types of duty you'll have to take on. Duty is a hard task in today's society." Characteristically, for the AWV operant, the word, ultimately, is used to teach a lesson about life. Quin ended with both an instruction for the reader and a warning.

In an essay on the differing narrative styles of African-American and white children, Michaels explains that African-American children tell topic-associating stories, whereas white children tell topic-centered ones. A topic-associating story associates a series of segments through implicit links to a particular topical event or theme and relies heavily on shared knowledge. A topic-centered one is tightly structured around a single topic, has thematic coherence, clear thematic progression, and is short and concise (quoted in Gee, 1986, p. 727). Smitherman (1977) also discusses the "episodic journeys and tributary routes" characteristic of the African-American oral narrative (p. 148). She comments that although such meandering may be highly applauded by African Americans, it is a linguistic style exasperating to whites who wish the speaker would be direct and hurry and get to the point. Additionally, researcher Ball (1992) identifies three patterns in the language of African-American adolescents: circumlocution, narrative interspersion, and recursion. She explains:

> 1. The circumlocution pattern is characterized by a series of implicitly associated topics with shifts that are lexically marked only by the use of *and*. Thematic development [is] typically accomplished through anecdotal association.
> 2. Narrative interspersion is a pattern, or a subpattern embedded within other patterns in which the speaker or writer intersperses a narrative within expository text.
> 3. The recursion pattern is one in which the speaker discusses a topic then restates it using different words or images. (pp. 509-511)

Ball uses Dr. Martin Luther King's "How Long? Not Long" speech to show how African Americans use the recursive pattern in persuasion. She writes:

> King uses a recursive pattern to drive his point home and to give special emphasis to his message. He states the basic idea that he

wants to emphasize, that 'no wave of racism can stop us.' He then repeats that same message five times using different specific images ['and the burning of our churches will not deter us, and the bombing of our homes will not dissuade us, and the beating and killing of our clergymen and young people will not divert us. The wanton release of their known murderers will not discourage us. We're on the move now!] The repeated syntactic structure and the parallel reinforcing images characterize the pattern. The technique is commonly used in the tradition of Christian biblical texts. (pp. 511-513)

Quin's essay meanders in the tradition of African-American orality. Also, as is evident, at times, in the tradition, it uses a voice that creates a distance between the words and the speaker's own private life. One of the most difficult tasks instructors may have with AWV students is convincing them that the details of their lives can be used in their writing. Although they are quick to dismiss abstracts in favor of concretes that deal more directly with their day-to-day lives, they are very reluctant to make these topics private. (Quin, who is married, wrote, for example, "The husband . . . will be expected to go outside the marriage," not, "My husband," and so on.) The purpose of the word is to communicate group values and lessons for the well-being of the community. However, the method, in the tradition of African-American narrative, is to choose an example or spokesperson outside of one's self: The slaves, for fear of punishment from the master, chose rebellious animals; the preacher, entities from the Bible. This is similar to African folklore wherein the storytellers pose Esu-Elegbara (grandmaster trickster and communicator, brother of Legba in the hoo doo culture of the United States). The African American also uses Big John or the Signifying Monkey.

The Monkey's reputation as master arguer is legend in the African-American community. Gates (1988) explains, in his seminal work, that this important figure is a cousin of Esu-Elegbara, the central figure of the African Ifa system of interpretation, and that, as such, the Monkey stands as the rhetorical principle in African-American vernacular discourse (p. 44). His (the Monkey's) forte is indirect argument. He persuades through the language of implication—begging, goading, or boasting with characteristic puns, metaphors, and so on. Gates concluded: "The Monkey's antics unfold in a signifying system wherein there is free play of language itself; things turn upon the displacement of meanings" (p. 53). Therefore, it is not surprising that an AWV operant who knows the Monkey, who knows the beauty of his linguistic play and understands his system of narration with "no holds barred," might think it a wonderful phonetic and narrative trick to swap the "s" sound in "civil duty' for the same sound in another topic, "sexual duty." The tactic is reminiscent of a well-known African-American comic's joke about a black man's retort to an Oriental gentleman with whom he was arguing. The black man responded, "No, I don't know karate, but I know some ka-razor." In Quin's switch, I hear the appropriation of the Monkeys voice and a knowledge of the rules of the black vernacular.

In the context of the argumentative essay, when that "other" voice or character will not work, the AWV operant will write above the minute details of his or her own life and make vague allusions, much like some signification and call and response, which, in the tradition, rely on shared knowledge between speaker and listener for understood, unvoiced specifics. Also, I think these specifics are not shared by the AWV operant as a result of his attempt to move toward groupness and sameness (a la the Diopian description). For example, one student, Phyllis, who was writing an essay on religion for her freshman composition course, came into the lab for help. Her professor had labeled her draft "vague." She asked me why the professor did not consider her mention of Jim and Tammy Bakker specific enough. I asked her why she had not written about her own minister. She responded, "Well, I was trying to come up with something that everybody could relate to. Everybody has read about the Bakker scandal; besides so much has gone on in my church lately. No one wants to hear about that. It's been awful." From there, she proceeded to tell me, in wonderful, imagaic specifics, the history of her church's 2-year struggle to find a decent minister. I suggested that she put the details in her essay, even such phrases as "Reverend Goodwin could really pack 'em in on Sunday's," referring to that trial pastor's oratory skills that brought many people back to the church.

The omission of details and/or failure to move beneath vague allusions is costly for the AWV operant. As the Winthrop University sample freshman composition exam (a departmental test that counts as 15% of the student's grade) and the accompanying rubric show (see Appendix), details are a top priority in EAD. The second sentence of direction 2 in the prompt reads "Be sure to use specific examples." The rubric shows the gradual decrease or increase in points awarded, largely dependent on the nature of the student's examples and/or details. Since the beginning of the Fall 1993 term to the present (Spring, 1994), test results show a 51% failure rate for African-American students. Only 14% of non-African Americans who took the test failed, and 55% of those were internationals whose first language is not English.

Of course these statistics indicate an immediate need for ways of rescuing our African-American students from the failure files. Our solution strategies, I believe, on the university campus, could begin with acculturating ourselves to the world views of these students and the encompassed values, ideas of order (priorities and paradigms), and general traditions related to their ways of communicating. We need to be aware of how these elements intersect with the inherent cultural components of composition assignments we design for AWV operants. Also, AWV operants need more help bridging the wide gap between what they know and Eurocentic Academic Discourse—its vocabulary, tone, purpose, and so on. Features identified as cultural variables in our composition assignments and tests should be discussed openly with them. In my conferences with Duchess, Phyllis, Quin, and other students, I recognized some features as cultural variables only after the students identified them as trouble spots, things they did not understand. (Although I am, too, an African-American and an AWV operant, I am also a college professor used to more than two decades of EAD.) Duchess and Phyllis were quick to explain how these elements compare with what they know from their own lives. Phyllis was amazed when I suggested that the detailed, concrete examples she gave me during our lab session were appropriate for her essay. She saw them as too different from those in the prompt. The test examples, she said, were more "intellectual." AWV operants need lots of feedback from their teachers especially when teachers can articulate how the AWV's writing habits and ideas intersect with EAD, or what is considered academic or "intellectual."

Finally, we need to conquer the monster: thesis. Many African American students that I have worked with in more than 20 years of teaching have trouble as soon as they hear the word. Two students in my Writing 101 class offer good examples of how they see the beast and can, perhaps, give us some clue as to how we can calm its growling in their heads. (I use the heavy-handed metaphor to dramatize the seriousness of the problem.)

Chandra, on rough draft days, likes to be last in sharing her main idea and development strategies with the class. She listens to the others and asks questions about what they claim as the thesis. When it is her turn, we can usually see that she prioritizes whatever her best "story" example is. She is still having trouble distinguishing valid thesis from simple fact. I constantly remind her of the McDonalds and birds' nests "distinctions":

- "McDonalds is a fast food restaurant" is not a good thesis sentence.
- "McDonald's is the best fast food restaurant in the city" is. This statement calls for argument or development.
- "Birds make nests" is a simple fact—no room for development.
- "Birds' nests are intricately made" begs for support or discussion.

Another student, Kimbrelli, has the same problem that Chandra has. Kimbrelli usually ignores my call for thesis and jumps immediately into whatever her "story" is. For example, about her paper on domestic violence (a topic she chose), she said on rough draft day, "Well, I discuss Darryl, a construction worker who is worried about his job. Then his wife Brenda and how he abuses her." (It had taken a while before I convinced her to move from generalities to Darryl and Brenda.) With some prodding from me and the class, she began to understand that a simple statement summarizing the cause/effect relationship she insinuated would be a valid thesis. In her view, typical of AWV operants, the tale had become most important; the underlying, abstract idea was not. This prioritizing becomes more understandable to teachers if we see it in the context of Nommo and the African-American oral tradition. About the latter tradition and its connection with writing, Ball (1992) explains that African-American students rely on narrative (the story) to carry the main point of an essay or fail to distinguish the narrative used as example or evidence from the main point itself.

To help African-American students move from failure to success in composition, we must begin to understand these connections. We must begin to rethink and restructure the tasks we set before them. Our assignments and exams should not alienate AWV operants who come to writing with their own world views and communicative systems, views and systems different from those of EAD.

REFERENCES

Ball, A. (1992). Culture preference and the expository writing of African American adolescents. *Written Communication*, 9(4), 501-532.

Dandy, E.B. (1991). *Black communications: Breaking down the barriers*. Chicago: African-American Images.

Gates, H.L. (1988). *The signifying(g) monkey: A theory of Afro-American literary criticism*. New York Oxford University Press.

Gee, J.P. (1986). Orality and literacy: From the savage mind to ways with words. *TESOL Quarterly*, 20(4), 719-746.

Kambon, K.K.K. (1992). *The African Personality in America: An African Centered framework*. Tallahassee: Nubian Nations Publications.

Smitherman, G. (1977). *Talkin' and testifyin': The language of Black America*. Boston: Houghton Mifflin.

Shaughnessy, M. (1977). *Errors and expectations: A guide for the teacher of basic writing*. New York: Oxford University Press.

APPENDIX
WRITING PROFICIENCY EXAMINATION
20 NOVEMBER 1993

Your task is to write a well-organized, coherent, and concretely developed essay of 400-600 words in response to the excerpt below form Amitai Etzioni's article "Duty: The Forgotten Virtue. In your essay, you should do the following:

1. Briefly summarize (not paraphrase) Etzioni's main points about American attitudes toward duty. Make sure that you use any summaries, paraphrases, or quotations in such a way as to avoid plagiarism.
2. Take a clear stand, arguing either that the passage is a) substantially correct or b) essentially misleading. Do not assume that you are expected to agree with the passage; a good essay could be written from several points of view. You could, for example, agree with some of Etzioni's ideas and reject others. You can, of course, accept or reject the whole argument. (If you are a foreign student, you may discuss Etzioni's ideas about duty in terms of your own culture.)
3. Support your position with discussion and examples drawn from at least three of the following categories: a) education and academic life; b) business; c) politics; d) athletics; e) religion; f) interpersonal relationships such as friendships, sexual relationships, family; g) personal responsibilities of citizenship.
4. Be sure that what you produce is a single, coherent essay and that you follow the conventions of standard English spelling, usage, grammar, and punctuation.

There is some evidence to suggest that Americans—always ambivalent about their duties—have been particularly loath to live up to their responsibilities in recent years.

A survey of young Americans found that most rank trial by jury high among their rights. However, few indicated willingness to serve a jury.

Patriotism is reported to be in vogue; however, Americans would rather pay volunteers to serve in the military than support a draft in which all would share the burden.

A survey conducted by H&R Block shows that Americans favor a flat tax. However, that support is offered on one troubling condition: that the respondent's favorite loophole not be closed.

These observations led me to ask my class at the George Washington University what the term "duty" brought to their minds. They responded uneasily. They felt that people ought to be free to do what they believe in. Duties are imposed, alien, authoritarian—what the principal, the curriculum committee, the society, "they" want you to do. . . . Okay, they said, maybe there was room for duty, but compliance ought to be voluntary, they insisted. . . .

Pollster Daniel Yankelovich estimated that 17 percent of American were deeply committed to the philosophy of self-fulfillment and another 63 percent subscribed to it in varying degrees. These people said they "spend a great deal of time thinking about myself" and "satisfactions come from shaping oneself rather than from home and family life." Today, Americans do not subscribe to a social philosophy which endorses commitment. Instead, we celebrate a generation rich in Meism. Duty stands in the way of self-fulfillment.

RUBRIC FOR THE WRITING PROFICIENCY EXAM

Primary Traits of a Satisfactory Paper ("S"):

1. Demonstrates some understanding of the reading passage and the ability to respond to directions. A competent paper, however, may take an original approach which ignores some of the directions.
2. Shows an ability to develop both abstract ideas and concrete examples that are specific and relevant to the student's topic.
3. Is coherently organized.
4. Shows proficiency at the sentence level in the use of grammar, punctuation, sentence structure, diction. The presence of a few problems in these areas should not prevent an otherwise competent paper from receiving an "S."

All other papers should receive a grade of "U."

SAMPLE WRITING 101 EXAMINATION

Your task is to write a well-organized, coherent, and concretely developed essay of 400-600 words in response to the excerpt below from an interview with Willard Gaylin on the PBS program *A World of Ideas*. In your essay, you should do the following:

1. Briefly summarize (not paraphrase) Gaylin's main point about the loss of commitment to community and service.
2. Discuss Gaylin's observation in terms of your own experience, the experience of others, and your understanding of American society. Be sure to use specific examples from such categories as school experience, civic experience, religious experience, family experience, or observations from movies, television, radio, or reading. (Provide at least three examples to support your ideas.)
3. In your response, properly use at least one quotation from Gaylin's interview. Be sure that you handle all quotations, summaries, and paraphrased material in such a way as to avoid plagiarism, to distinguish clearly between borrowed material and your own words and ideas.
4. Be sure that what you produce is a single, coherent essay and that you follow the conventions of standard English spelling, usage, grammar, and punctuation.

"The most important thing we face is a rediscovery of community. We're a very individually oriented country, and I love that. But somewhere along the line we've gotten a peculiar idea of what an individual is, what individual pleasure is, what individual purpose is. We see everything in terms of personal autonomy—in terms not only of my rights under law, but also in terms of pleasure in terms of privilege. I think we have trained a whole generation of people to think in terms of an isolated 'I.' Somehow or other we've developed a concept of *personal* pleasure, of *personal* fulfillment. . . . The concept of attachment, the concept of service, the concept that somehow pleasure can involve pain or sacrifice those ideas have simply been dissipated in our culture.

"One of the most incredible things to me really is to see the typical middle class Kid who's given everything he wants except the privilege of service, the privilege of self-sacrifice, and the joy of being a giver. We've become a passive society that sees everything in terms of our open mouth—fill it with something! The idea that we can actually do things for something broader—a community—is lost."

SAMPLE WRIT 101 EXAM RUBRIC

6-point essay:
- gives a valid interpretation of the passage which implies a more mature, complex definition of community
- develops all elements of the prompt (summarizes Gaylin, discusses the concept of community using at least three examples from personal experience and/or from the experience of others [may be individuals, groups, literary works, etc.], uses a quotation from the passage)
- has well-developed supporting examples and/or details which reflect more sophisticated thought
- has a clearly expressed or implied central idea, appropriate paragraphing and transitions, and an effective concluding paragraph
- shows maturity (variety) in diction and/or sentence structure
- may have a few grammatical errors but they do not detract from the content

5-point essay:
gives a valid interpretation of the passage which implies a more mature, complex definition of community
- develops all elements of the prompt
- has examples that are well-developed but less consistently so and with somewhat less unity and originality than in a 6-point essay
- has identifiable central idea and appropriate paragraphing
- may have some grammatical errors but they do not detract from the content

4-point essay:
gives a consistent interpretation of the passage (but may demonstrate an egocentric or trivialized view of an community)
- uses examples which may be predictable but are developed
- may incorrectly handle or omit quotation
- is coherent and unified but may have paragraphing errors
- does not contain so many grammatical errors as to interfere with the essays readability

3-point essay:
- gives a superficial interpretation of the passage has predictable (and/or generalized) examples which may be trite, bland, or lifeless

- is reasonably coherent and unified if the reader makes inferences and interpolations
- may have significant problems with grammar, usage, or syntax
- may incorrectly handle quotation

2-point essay: is a legitimate attempt to deal with the assignment but has at least two of the following problems:
- has significant problems with summarizing Gaylin's ideas (summary may be hazy, or writer may rely on a patchwork of quotations)
- has few details and examples and those supplied may be vague or only loosely connected to the student's ideas
- is only minimally organized and coherent
- has significant problems with grammar, usage, or syntax

1-point-essay: will show at least two of the following:
- omits summary or show misunderstanding of the passage or the question
- shows almost no evidence of organization or development
- has serious and persistent problems with grammar, syntax, or usage
- may exhibit such a variety of problems (such as lack of focus, purpose, organization development, language skills) as to suggest little familiarity with or experience in the composing process

*Essays may be awarded one bonus point for particularly mature or impressive writing.
**Essays that are 100 or more words short of the assigned 400 word length should receive a grade no higher man 3.
***If the student has obviously failed to finish copying his or her draft into the bluebook, you should make a U under the grade.

CHAPTER 12

Opening the Composition Classroom to Storytelling: Respecting Native American Students' Use of Rhetorical Strategies

Karen A. Redfield

> An ultimate value of oral tradition was to create a situation for someone who had not lived through it so that the listener could benefit directly from the narrator's experience. . . . The persistence of stories and storytelling suggests that oral narrative is central to an indigenous intellectual tradition and provides the core of an educational model. (Cruikshank, with Sidney, Smith, & Ned, 1990, p. 340)
>
> The problem of cognitive competence—the ability to recognize and use higher order thinking—may be more in the eye or ear and brain of the interpreter than in the mouth and brain of the speaker of a culturally nonstandard way of speaking. This is a problem of ethnocentric bias in the study of relations between language and thought, a problem of which much educational research on students' reasoning seems to be unaware. (Erickson, 1988, p. 213)

About midway through the spring semester of 1993, a courageous and articulate Native American student confronted me about my demands and her frustrations in our Composition I course. I, too, was frustrated: All my detailed comments on the deficiencies in her essays were having little effect except on surface grammatical errors. The gulf between the student's rhetorical form and the acceptable college essay I was so sincerely trying to teach was widening. After much intense discussion—I am paraphrasing what I remember as faithfully as possible—the student said: "I don't understand what you want. I told the story in my own way and you say this is not how they write in college. I've been writing stories for a long time. This is my way of using language. How can I write for white people who won't understand me anyway?"

I had no answer for her. Indeed, it took me a while to truly understand her question. Having taught English as a second language both here and abroad, I was accustomed to looking for the problems arising from first language transfer errors and culturally based rhetorical differences in my students' essays. What I had clearly not considered in my Native American student's essay, however, was that similar principles were at work. I had been reading her writing from the perspective of a deficit model, seeing only what it lacked when compared to a "standard" form. To draw on Catherine Lamb's (chap. 13, this volume) use of Kenneth Burke's parlour metaphor, I was assuming that once I gave the student the proper academic forms, she would be able to speak—and others would listen and understand. What I found out was that I had not been listening at all.

WHY A CHAPTER ON STORYTELLING IS NOT OUT OF PLACE IN A BOOK ON ARGUMENT

As the argument is believed to reflect cognitive and rhetorical competence in Western intellectual tradition, storytelling reflects similar qualities in Native American intellectual tradition (Cruikshank, et al., 1990, p. 340). The story form is historically significant, rhetorically complex, sociologically powerful, and educationally effective, teaching everything from community moral standards to mathematical principles (Hankes, personal communication, June 1, 1994). This use of stories is not uncommon; stories are also symbolically important teaching events among Pacific Islanders, as Watson-Gegeo shows (chap. 9, this volume).

Although the argument per se does not seem to exist as a separate Native American rhetorical genre, listeners are expected to learn something useful from a story (Cruikshank et al., 1990, p. 340). Bartelt (1982) noted that redundancy of lexical items is often used by Navajo and Apache politicians: "When trying to persuade community members to support a particular policy. This feature of rhetorical redundancy for persuasion is, of course, also a likely part of the discourse resources available to most Navajo and Western Apache speakers" (p. 167).

Although exploring the possible existence of argument as a traditional Native American rhetorical form would be fascinating, my intentions here are slightly different. Through a review of current research and a close reading of two Native American students' essays, I hope to prove at least that a culturally based structure underlies my students' work. Both pieces—which I called essays and they called stories—have a main point that is supported through thoughtful, logically organized detail. As Berrill suggested in her introduction to this volume, we do need "a different word for reasoning processes which are 'logical' in non-hierarchical ways." Such new terminology would free Native American student writers from the burden of being labeled *basic* or *deficient* writers. Such labels combine with a lack of clarity about writing competencies to produce sad results for students.

As Farr noted (1993, pp. 6-7): "To render essayist literacy problematic, we must first make explicit the style of discourse that now underlies most expository writing instruction. Currently this is a poorly understood but nevertheless real construct (Walters, in press)." Coming up against this very real construct, students often lose.

Writing about the University of New Mexico, which has the highest Native American population of any 4-year institution in the United States, Gregory (1989) stated that the attrition rate is 77%—the highest of any group on campus. She theorized that "the inability to produce acceptable academic writing serves as one of the major stumbling blocks for academic success among Native Americans" (p. 1). McLaughlin (1988) painted a similarly dismal picture; based on his research, the dropout rate for Native American students is from 3 to 10 times the national average. Informal interviews I conducted in Madison, WI, tend to support such figures, although it should be stressed that this is not true for all Native American students. For Native American students in general, though, writing college assignments is an especially trying task.

USING CONTRASTIVE ANALYSIS IN THE CLASSROOM

What choices do students make when faced with such a daunting task? A logical assumption is that they use forms that are already familiar. Such culturally influenced rhetorical forms may not be conscious, so it is difficult for the students to explain their explicit, surface features. As I suggest at the end of this chapter, the work of contrastive analysis can and should become a partnership between the teacher and students from different cultures—extending to other students in the classroom.

I began my search for culturally distinctive Native American rhetorical forms in my students' writing—as I had begun research into ESL students' writing previously (Redfield, 1987)—with the hypothesis of Kaplan (1966, p. 2). "Logic (in the popular, rather than the logician's sense of the word) which is the basis for rhetoric, is evolved out of a culture; it is not universal. Rhetoric, then, is not universal either, but varies from culture to culture."

To support his hypothesis, Kaplan used the essays of his English as a second language college students from various cultural and linguistic backgrounds. These students had done well in mastering the syntactic and lexical forms of English, but their writing still suffered from a lack of focus. The main and supporting points were arranged differently than "the expected sequence of thought in English . . . essentially a Platonic-Aristotelian sequence" (p. 3). Although Kaplan stressed the need for more research and more accurate descriptions, he offered the following diagrams of the paragraph movement in various language groups (see Figure 12.1).

In general, English essays are arranged in a linear pattern; Semitic language essays are constructed along parallel lines of themes or images; Oriental language essays begin in a more global sphere and wind down into the particular; and Romance and Russian language essays tend to contain what an English reader would deem digressions to the main point.

Assuming that an underlying logical pattern exists, I approached my students' writing with the intention of making this pattern more visible to non-Native American readers like myself. By contrasting actual student writing with an expected Western cultural model, I was employing the "weak" version of contrastive analysis, a theory that seeks to explain similarities and differences between language systems (Wardhaugh, 1983). Because Native American culture is not monolithic, it would be inappropriate to apply the strong version of contrastive analysis that would attempt to predict patterns in a given student's writing based on the discovered patterns in another student's work.

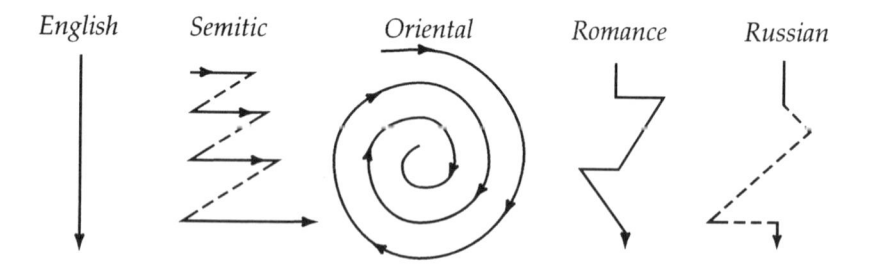

From "Cultural Thought Patterns in Inter-Cultural Education," by R.B. Kaplan, Language Learning, 1966, Vol. 16, Nos. 1 and 2, p. 15. Reprinted by permission.

Figure 12.1 Contrasting rhetorical patterns

However, the knowledge that certain patterns might exist gives me a framework from which to work. Using this hypothesis of weak contrastive analysis, I must always begin with evidence "provided by linguistic interference," as Wardhaugh noted (1970, p. 10). Such evidence can then be used:

> To explain the similarities and differences between the systems . . . systems are important because . . . the approach does [not] result in merely classifying errors in any way that occurs to the investigator. . . . The starting point in the contrast is provided by actual evidence . . . and the reference is made to the two systems only in order to explain actually observed interference phenomena. (1983, p. 10)

The implications of such hypotheses on Native American writing have recently been explored by several researchers such as Bartelt (1982), Basso (1979), Bataille and Mullen Sands (1984), and Ghezzi (1993). Before looking at broader implications, however, I turn to Sarah and Cheryl's stories.

Sarah's Story

Sarah entered a general equivalency diploma (GED) course of study through Madison Area Technical College's Homeless Basic Skills Program in 1989. The essay that follows was written in response to my directions to "write something of interest, perhaps a story about your life." Our goal was to work toward the GED essay requirement eventually; Sarah moved on before we came to that stage.

Sarah's story follows:

> This is a story about my Mom and Dad and my Grandma who lived on the Chippewa Reservation.
>
> The Chippewa Reservation was up in Red Lake Minnesota.
>
> I was very little at the time when I was there.
>
> My Dad used to get up real early and go out hunting for deer or whatever he could get for my Mom and Grandma to fix for dinner.
>
> He would leave way before anyone in the house awoke.
>
> When my Mom awoke she would fix a hot breakfast made from corn meal and fried bread.
>
> She would boil the corn meal and pour it in a cup and we would drink it from the cup.
>
> After breakfast and dishes were done we would go outside and enjoy the warm sunshine.

Now my Grandma she would sit and work on her Indian beads or whatever she was working on.

I would sit and watch her.

She would always tell me stories about herself when she was a little girl while she was sitting and working.

In the winter she made Indian blankets to keep us warm and they were made from deer or bear fur.

They would keep us warm in the winter.

My Dad he would go out and bring plenty bear meat, deer meat, fish and hang them on a tree where the wolves couldn't get ahold of them.

Then he would take the meat and put the meat in a hot little house and keep it warm and dry for the winter.

My Dad was a hard working man.

My Grandma kept busy making warm clothes for us.

My Mom she did what she could to take care of all of us.

When school started we went to school and learned to do Indian dances and talk in our own language.

The school was very different then the schools we have now.

The school was 5 miles out of the reservation.

Mom got up and got us dressed warm and had us off every morning at 6:00 AM unless it was really snowing hard and it was really cold then she had our deer coats and the boots my Grandma made to keep my feet warm.

Early day like that we started off at 5:00 in the morning and be to school at 8:00.

Late in the afternoon my Dad met me at the end of the road leaving from the school to walk home.

It would be just getting dark when we reached home.

But supper was waiting all nice and warm.

But after a long while we had to move.

Now where our home used to be is all flat land and farmers have their crops there.

How I miss my people.

The Chippewas remain together and are all settled here in Wisconsin.

There are over 400 Chippewas here in Wisconsin.

We may be apart but we are all family brothers and sisters in spirit.

We never forget our old ways we used to live.

The new ways are very different for us but we will get used to them.

> We were used to living on the reservation just all Indians but to some of us it is very strange and different to live in a mixed world.
> The clothes are different and shoes and boots are different but we are used to them.
> Even the schools are different we are also used to them.
> I like living this way but I miss the old way I used to live among my Indian brothers and sisters.
> One day I hope we will all get together again and live like we used to.

I was moved by Sarah's story on a first reading; however, I was also concerned about the long road it seemed we would have to travel from this story to an acceptable GED essay. Viewed in this way, the essay lacked several "standard" features such as paragraph structure, a thesis statement, supporting points, and a conclusion. It was not even clear "whose" story this was—Sarah's or her family's. What I was missing—along with the rhetorical strategies inherent in supporting Sarah's main point—was that her sense of self within a community was the main point.

In writing of the Dune-za/Cree people of British Columbia, Canada, Ridington (1990) foregrounded the connection between storytelling and a person's place in the community:

> You are a character in every other person's story. You know the stories of every person's life. You retain an image or model of the entire system of which you are a part. Each person is responsible for acting autonomously and with intelligence in relation to that knowledge of the whole. Each person knows how to place his or her experience within the model's meaningful pattern. Each person knows the stories that connect a single life to every other life. People experience the stories of their lives as small wholes, not as small parts of the whole. (p. 192)

Both the student essays included in this chapter clearly demonstrate this. Although one writer is Chippewa and one Menominee, and although the topics are as seemingly disconnected as a family history and a women's softball league, the main themes are community: how a "single life" is connected "to every other life," in Ridington's words.

Sarah began by saying that the story was about her parents and grandmother; it was equally about herself. She did not make herself part of the introduction, though; instead she wove her own reflections and memories into the story. The story of Sarah's family was also woven into the larger story of the Chippewa family in Red Lake and the sadness

Sarah felt at being separated from those "brothers and sisters." The main point of Sarah's essay, embedded two-thirds of the way into her piece, and shortened for dramatic effect was, "How I miss my people." Her conclusion echoed the sentiment, and the hope that she would one day be able to live with her people again.

Community as a central focus in a broader world view is also found, as Dorothy Perry Thompson noted (Chapter 11, this volume) in African-American storytelling. Values such as interdependence, groupness, and communality are reflected in much the same way as they are in Native American stories. In Sarah's story, such "groupness" had been rent by outside forces. The site of her community had been appropriated: "Now where our home used to be is all flat land and farmers have their crops there."

This line signals a shift in theme and tone; it functions as an "argument," if you will, that life on the reservation was much preferable to life off the reservation, in which a sense of real community did not exist.

Reading backward from the second half of Sarah's main point—"How I miss my people"—and then forward, a rhetorical method of support becomes clear: repetition. Sarah used 10 repetitions of the words *warm* or *hot* throughout the first half of her story. No references to warmth were made in the second half of the story.

As noted earlier in this chapter, Bartelt (1982, p. 171) explained that redundancy may be used for persuasion. Deliberate emphasis in a first tribal language appears as redundancy in oral or written English:

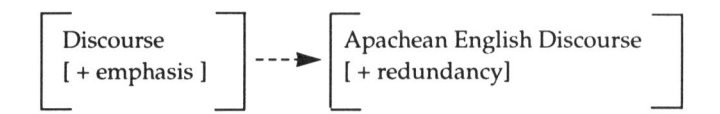

$$\begin{bmatrix} \text{Discourse} \\ [+ \text{emphasis}] \end{bmatrix} \dashrightarrow \begin{bmatrix} \text{Apachean English Discourse} \\ [+ \text{redundancy}] \end{bmatrix}$$

Ghezzi (1993) also examined the traditional uses of rhetorical devices such as repetition, markers such as "now presently" and "and then," and "truncated, staccato-like" lines for emphasis in her article "Tradition and Innovation in Ojibwe Storytelling: Mrs. Marie Syrette's 'The Orphans and Mashos'." All of these devices appear in Sarah's story, pointing to a living consistency in contemporary Chippewa/ Ojibwe storytelling.

Sarah's story is most compelling when read aloud as I did at a recent conference. When I reached Sarah's main point—"How I miss my people"—an audible sigh arose from the audience. The images of a happy childhood inside of a warm family and community circle did not seem to lead to such a statement. Through her impressive use of traditional storytelling forms, Sarah was able to make the audience feel the sadness of one woman and her community. And yet, such clear rhetorical competence would likely receive a low grade for "deficiencies" such as paragraph structure.

Cheryl's Story

It was Cheryl's question—paraphrased at the beginning of this chapter—that guided my research.
    The following essay was written in response to an assignment to write a cause-and-effect essay in a university transfer Composition I class at Madison Area Technical College. Though it did not seem to reflect the traditional cause and effect rhetorical form, it did answer the title question and gave, I realized upon subsequent readings, causes for why Cheryl enjoys softball. My comments after a first reading, however, caused Cheryl's frustration with a deficit-model grading scale to become articulate. After my discussions of this piece, I suggest possible grading strategies.

    Why I like to play softball? Cheryl Dodge (Menominee):

1. Playing softball every summer for 10 weeks is very invigorating and exciting.
2a. Every year, around the middle of February when the snow is knee deep and the temps are still quite cold, the Madison Recreation Dept. sends out to all softball managers, the "blue cards" to be filled out and returned usually by the end of February.
2b. It is still difficult during this time of the year to get people thinking of "softball" but in order to have a team you need to turn in the amount of 12 "blue cards".
3. So as one or two people run around getting players out of "hibernation", the excitement grows and one can start visualizing the softball diamonds in their natural state instead of covered with "snow".
4. Playing on a all women's slow pitch softball team is fun as well as competitive, considering our team is in the 7th league and we do quite well every summer.
5. I personally like the "high" I get from playing 3rd base, because playing that particular position one has to be quick and have a strong throwing arm. I like the fact that when the ball is hit, whether it be on the ground or a line drive in the air, it is coming at you full speed.
6. I also enjoy playing this sport because it is an all "women's" team and that is how we play. There is no "classroom" study to go through, no having to be a "Mom", just simply playing softball.

7   The "fans" are another reason I like to play, they are very supportive and fun. It's exciting to stand out there, on that diamond, under the lights and perform in front of about thirty people.

8   Hitting a "home run", with the bases loaded, has to be one of the most "happy" "exciting" feelings one can experience while playing a game.

9   There are many "good" reasons why I like to play this sport but mainly it is just "simply fun" and relaxing and I get to be a "hero" every now and then, it also brings together about fifteen "women of color" the only "minority" women's team registered with the rec. dept. in the city of Madison.

10 So for one whole "hour", once a week, I get to leave the student/Mom world and be in the best fantasy I can think of and just what I love doing and that is "play softball"!

Cheryl began with a question—"Why I like to play softball?"—that was "answered" throughout her essay with elements and themes also evident in Sarah's writing: repetition and the theme of community. The implicit tone here was to justify rather than simply state that Cheryl had "good" reasons to enjoy this sport. By the end of the essay the reader was in a sense persuaded to see the positive aspects of Cheryl's participation in the sport, as if the reader might feel that a "student/Mom" should not have time to play.

Leaving the episodic structure aside for the moment, I focus on Cheryl's sense of self within a group. The "I" of the title question did not reenter the story until section 5: "I personally like the 'high' I get from playing third base." Until this point there was no clear sense of agency; many sentences were in the passive voice. Cards were sent out and received, but Cheryl did not clarify if she was one of the team's managers receiving the blue registration cards. What was very clear, however, was the importance of the team. "Team" was used repeatedly, as were "people," "women of color," and "fans"—10 plural nouns or noun phrases referring to a community punctuated the essay. Being an actively contributing member of this community—a quick third base player with a strong throwing arm—was one half of the main point of the essay. The personal enjoyment and sense of satisfaction of being on this team was the second half: Playing on an all-women "minority" softball team was exciting and fun.

The softball team was Cheryl's community here, as Sarah's Chippewa family was hers. This theme is not uncommon for a broader context. Ghezzi (1993) reminded us that, although "There are differences in the narrative traditions between tribes [and] . . . differences between the creative acts of individuals within a tribal group" (p. 47), community acts as a major theme and as a rhetorically shaping force in much Native

American writing. In a discussion on Louise Erdrich's novel *Love Medicine* (1993) the following semester, Cheryl said that she saw similarities in theme and style between her writing and that of Erdrich. This connection allowed Cheryl to take pride in her own writing—a bonus of dong such contrastive analysis in class. This issue will be discussed further at the end of this chapter.

Also, like Sarah, Cheryl employed the rhetorical strategy of contrast. Cheryl also used cold and warmth. Although she could speak only of summer games, she began with winter and images of "hibernation," a time when people do not often form groups. The softball diamonds themselves seemed unhappy, covered in snow, rather than being in "their natural state."

McLaughlin and Leap (1991) pointed out similar use of contrast as a common Native American rhetorical strategy in their Navajo students' writing. They also commented on the coherence of the episodic format, once it was perceived to support a main point. They began to see "much more coherence in the construction of this text and in its presentation of message.... Seemingly random comments ... turned out to be elements within a tightly connected, closely ordered statement" (p. 9).

This was also the case with Cheryl's essay on softball. She framed her essay as an answer to a reader's or listener's (in this case the teacher's) question, using rhetorical devices of contrast and repetition as strategies. The emphasis on herself as part of a community of softball players is both a common theme in Native American writing—both published and private—and an element in standard essayist literacy, which presents "a rationalization of one's own position and a consideration of alternative positions while arguing one's own" (Farr, 1993, p. 10). Any reader should be convinced of the importance of playing on an all woman-of-color softball team by the end of Cheryl's essay, regardless of whether or not the reader is a woman of color, a regular player, or a watcher of softball.

Once I was able to see the rhetorical strategies underlying Cheryl's work, I was able to explain the expected academic forms of future assignments more clearly. I adopted a more flexible portfolio method of grading, using progress as my measure rather than grades on individual assignments. Cheryl has been successful in writing assignments for subsequent college transfer courses. She has also written new stories in the context of a Native American literature class, suggesting that she now has mastery over two distinct forms of writing.

THE VALUE OF CLASSROOM-BASED CONTRASTIVE ANALYSIS

This brief analysis of two students' essays cannot hope to delineate the complex, varied, or historical storytelling strategies of Native American writers. I sincerely hope, however, that I have been able to persuade you that both Sarah and Cheryl are exhibiting cognitive competence and culturally based rhetorical forms in their writing. Clearly more work is needed on our part. As Farr (1993) stressed:

> To understand and, one would hope, to teach students more effectively, researcher and educators must identify and describe the range of discourse styles they bring to the classroom ant to treat this range of styles as contrastive models to essayist literacy. (p. 13)

This perspective should apply to all students, as Dorothy Perry Thompson (Chapter 11) demonstrated with African-American students in this volume. That students speak English as a first language does not—and really has never meant—that students naturally write Western academic discourse. Much work that has been done in applied linguistics can be adapted for use with Native American students, such as Sarah and Cheryl, if we broaden our definition of *target language* to include mainstream academic discourse as well as English as a second language. As Houghton and Hoey (1982) pointed out, factors of linguistic and cultural relativity are at work within a framework of contrastive rhetoric (see Figure 12.2).

Doing this kind of contrastive rhetoric research should provide fascinating relative implications in the field of discourse analysis. More classroom-based contrastive analysis will also yield several benefits for the student writers, the class as a whole, and the field of composition theory. Such research foregrounds students' individual forms of communicative competence and allows students to explain their forms to other students and the teacher. Such explanations fit naturally into the well- established peer review format and its reliance on concrete points in the genuine, insightful, and constructive exchange of comments between students. Contrastive analysis will also force us to clarify all implicit and often personal expectations of "good writing" as we expand our notions of essayist literacy and the boundaries of argument to fit the demands made on education in the late 20th century. Farr (1993) advocates a debate on what traditional characteristics of essayist literacy should continue to be taught—a debate supported by this volume.

To engage in an honest and truly lively debate, we have to allow our students to debate in their own voices. In *Literacy: Reading the Word and the World* (1987), Freire and Macedo remind us of the importance of the student voice:

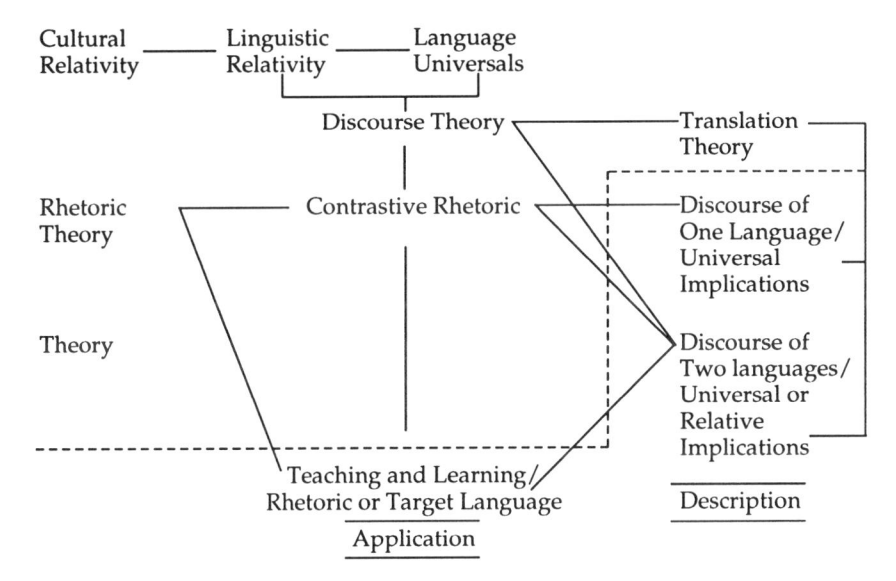

```
Cultural _____ Linguistic _____ Language
Relativity     Relativity        Universals
                       └────┬────┘
                    Discourse Theory ──────── Translation
                            │                 Theory
Rhetoric  ─────── Contrastive Rhetoric ────── Discourse of
Theory                      │                 One Language/
                            │                 Universal
                            │                 Implications
Theory                      │                 Discourse of
                            │                 Two languages/
                            │                 Universal or
                            │                 Relative
------------------------------------------    Implications
         Teaching and Learning
         Rhetoric or Target Language          Description
              Application
```

From Linguistic and Written Discourse: Contrastive Rhetorics, by Diane B. Houghton and Michael M. Hoey, *Annual Review of Applied Linguistics*, 1982. Reprinted with permission.

Figure 12.2. Linguistic and cultural factors in rhetorical forms

> As Giroux elegantly states, the students' voice 'is the discursive means to make themselves 'heard' and to define themselves as active authors of their world.' The authorship of one's own world, which would also imply one's own language, means what Mikail Bakhtin defines as 'retelling a story in one's own words.' . . . The students' voice should never be sacrificed, since it is the only means through which they make sense of their own experiences in the world. (p. 151)

Ridington (1990) also reminds us that culture—of which writing is a part—is never fixed or static. Reflecting Bakhtin and Giroux's feelings on the importance of all voices, Ridington wrote:

> Discourse is only a problem when we talk past each other or worse use talk to suppress another person's ability to express him—or herself freely. Discourse is as old as language. It is as fundamental to human experience as culture. It is also as new and as fragile as each new breath of life. We create our culture in the act of speech and the intersubjectivity of discourse. (p. 190)

Finally, this debate is also heralded by Hill (1990), in her book *Writing from the Margins*. Coming out from behind old definitions and old barriers between standard forms and new possibilities puts teachers on "the margin between self and other, old ideas and new" (pp. vii-viii). It is, she feels, an invigorating place to be:

> There one can read things better, see how lines get drawn, tell new stories, create different kinds of spaces, live at the risky critical edges between one's own values and those of others, have a say perhaps in generating changes in people's minds.
> Such a job. But such an exciting idea of writing to give our students. (pp. vii-viii)

CONCLUSION

Assuming an underlying cognitive competence and culturally based rhetorical form whenever I come to a student paper has not only opened me to expanded notions of essayist literacy and the boundaries of argument, it has also made reading compositions a good deal more enjoyable. Being able to first share a genuine sense of the strengths in a piece of student writing with the writer makes it easier and more effective to then discuss other form and style options. Respecting a Native American student's knowledge first also allows the student to be more open to what I need to teach—and together we can start building a bridge between Native American culture and the halls of Western academic discourse.

This bridge, once built, may enable Native American students to more easily cross over to academic success without feeling that their cognitive competences have been totally left on the other side. We, as educators, have an exciting chance to learn new ways of reasoning and to rethink what we now so rigidly define as logic and argument.

In conclusion, I invite you to reread your own Native American student essays from this "bridge." Where you once saw no thesis statement, there may be an embedded but clear main point. Where you once saw unclear pronoun references, there may be a writer who is framing his or her sense of self within a larger sense of community. You may see supporting points where you first saw disjointed ramblings. Overall, you may see culturally influenced rhetorical devices where you once saw only a deficient college essay.

Our views may not be dramatically different, but even small differences in our perspectives will make a difference to the writers. We need to engage our colleagues in discussions on how logic, reasoning, and argument may be reflected in the writing of all of our students. Then we can discuss how our own teaching and writing can reflect what we have learned.

REFERENCES

Bartelt, H.G. (1982). Rhetorical redundancy in Apachean English interlanguage. In H. Bartelt, S.P. Jasper, & B.L. Hoffer (eds.), *Essays in Native American English* (pp. 157-172). San Antonio: Trinity University Press.

Basso, K.H. (1979). *Portraits of the Whiteman: Linguistic play and cultural symbols among the Western Apache.* Cambridge, UK: Cambridge University Press.

Bataille, G.M., & Sands, K.M. (1984). *American Indian women: Telling their lives.* Lincoln: University of Nebraska Press.

Cruikshank, J. with Sidney, A., Smith, K., & Ned, A. (1990). *Life lived like a story: Life stories of three Yukon native elders.* Lincoln: University of Nebraska Press.

Dodge, C. (1993). *Louise Erdrich's Love Medicine: A Native American student's reading.* Unpublished paper, Madison Area Technical College.

Erdrich, L. (1993). *Love medicine* (New, expanded ed.). New York: Harper Perennial.

Erickson, F. (1988). School literacy, reasoning, and civility: An anthropologist's perspective. In E.R. Kintgen, B.M. Kroll, & M. Rose (Eds.), *Perspective on literacy* (pp. 205-226). Carbondale: Southern Illinois University Press.

Farr, M. (1993). Essayist literacy and other verbal performances. *Written Communication, 10*(1), 4-38.

Freire, P., & Macedo, D. (1987). *Literacy: Reading the word and the world.* New York Bergin and Garvey, Critical Studies in Education Series.

Ghezzi, R.W. (1993). Tradition and innovation in Ojibwe storytelling: Mrs. Marie Syrette's 'The Orphans and Mashos'. In A. Krupat (Ed.), *New voices in Native American literary criticism* (pp. 37-76). Washington and London: Smithsonian Institution Press.

Gregory, G.A. (1989). Composing processes of Native Americans: Six case studies of Navajo Speakers. *Journal of American Indian Education, 28*(2), 1-6.

Hankes, J. Personal interview. June 1, 1994.

Hill, C.E. (1990). *Writing from the margins: Power and pedagogy for teachers and composition.* New York: Oxford University Press.

Houghton, D., & Hoey, M. (1982). Linguistics and written discourse: Contrastive rhetorics. *Annual Review of Applied Linguistics, 3,* 23-37.

Kaplan, R.B. (1966). Cultural thought patterns in inter-cultural education. *Language Learning, 16*(1 and 2),1-20.

McLaughlin, D. (1988, April). Curriculum for cultural politics: *Lessons from literacy program development in a Navajo school setting.* Paper presented at the Conference of the American Educational Research Association, New Orleans.

McLaughlin, D., & Leap, W.L. (1991, April). *What Navajo students know about written English.* Paper presented at the Conference of the American Educational Research Association, Chicago.

Redfield, K.A. (1987, April). *The need for a contrastively based theory of rhetoric.* WITESOL Conference (Wisconsin Teachers of English to Speakers of Other Languages), University of Wisconsin-Madison.

Ridington, R. (1990). *Little bit know something: Stories in language of anthropology.* Iowa City: University of Iowa Press.

Walters, K. (1993). Writing and its uses. In H. Gunter & O. Ludwig (Eds.), *Schrift und schriftlicheit* [Writing and its uses].

Wardhaugh, R. (1983). The contrastive analysis hypothesis. In B.W. Robinette, B. Wallace, & J. Schacter (Eds.), *Second language learning: Contrastive analysis, error analysis, and related aspects* (pp. 3-14). Ann Arbor: University of Michigan Press.

CHAPTER 13

Other Voices, Different Parties: Feminist Responses to Argument

Catherine E. Lamb

> Imagine that you enter a parlour. You come late. When you arrive, others have long preceded you, and they are engaged in a heated discussion, a discussion too heated for them to pause and tell you exactly what it is about. In fact, the discussion had already begun long before any of them got there, so that no one present is qualified to retrace for you all the steps that had gone before. You listen for awhile, until you decide that you have caught the tenor of the argument; then you put in your oar. Someone answers; you answer him; another comes to your defense; another aligns himself against you, to either the embarrassment or gratification of your opponent, depending upon the quality of your ally's assistance. However, the discussion is interminable. The hour grows late, you must depart. And you do depart, with the discussion still vigorously in progress.
> —Kenneth Burke (1967, pp. 110-111)

I thank Patricia Bizzell, Gesa Kirsch, and Jody Norton for their thoughtful comments on this essay.

Kenneth Burke's description of the "unending conversation" of humankind probably appeals to most practitioners and scholars of composition, whether feminist or not. We want to see ourselves and our students as part of something valuable that is larger than any of us and that will continue indefinitely. When I read this passage as a feminist, however, I ask questions that make me less comfortable about it. The "you" in it takes it for granted that he is invited and can enter the parlour; he also seems to have no doubts about being able to speak, using the proper forms, and being listened to once he speaks. His challenges are only those of timing and strategy. I, on the other hand, ask who has been invited and who has been left out. Why should only these forms be used and not others? Must we assume an antagonistic relationship between participants? What other parties can we imagine that might continue the conversation?

Feminist composition—approaches to the teaching and practice of writing that draw on women's experience and theorizing about it for goals, pedagogy, and forms of discourse—offers new ways to answer these questions. For most of the past 20 years of this field's history, the emphasis has been on developing the personal voice. Argument, techniques of persuasion for gaining acceptance of one's point of view, if it was dealt with, was seen usually in pejorative terms, as an expression of patriarchy. Although the confrontation implicit in such a view does not reflect the attitudes of some of the most influential 20th-century rhetorical theorists, including Kenneth Burke (in the essay from which I quoted earlier, he spoke, for example, of the value of "cooperative competition"), it remains popular both for our students and, judging from the orientation of most composition textbooks, for many teachers of composition. For practitioners of feminist composition, however, there are now suggestions that other alternatives are possible.

With recent changes in the place of argument in feminist composition, we have alternatives to argument that can enlarge our vision of possible responses to conflict. The goals are arrived at through theory and practice that return to women's experience in spite of the pitfalls of idealizing or overgeneralizing that experience. We have not had and do not wish to have the luxury of remaining in theory; because we cannot assume we will be heard, we have had to articulate concrete ways to respond when there appears to be little, if any, common ground from which to negotiate a relationship. Burke's image of the parlour suggests a spatial relationship between the participants—in this case, the writer and reader. Our concern as teachers and practitioners of feminist composition is how to enter that space and keep it open, developing a sense of spaciousness in the resolution of the conflict. As actors in that space, we exercise power in defining the nature of the space. We also enable others to do the same. Both actions change the texture and shape of the space.

CONFLICT AND THE PLACE OF PERSONAL VOICE IN FEMINIST COMPOSITION

Feminist composition has always been concerned with creating and maintaining a space from which women can speak and be heard. In 1971, *College English* published Howe's "Identity and Expression: A Writing Course for Women," which was her response to the feelings of inferiority she saw in women students and in their attitudes toward women writers. Or one could go back to Emig's article, "The Origins of Rhetoric: A Developmental View," which first appeared in 1969, in which she examined the mother's role in language learning as the first "co- speaker/co-writer" who "expands" on what the child says. Essays written in the intervening 20 years have continued the emphasis on developing women's voices, usually without considering the effects of race, class, or sexual orientation on the "difference" to which they are giving expression, although varieties of expression are valued (see, for example, Caywood & Overing's, 1987; see also Annas, 1985; Flynn, 1988; Osborn, 1991). It seems reasonable to assume that the emphasis on women's personal voices reflects a continuing need to develop them—a need that I welcome and trust will continue.

Although the expressionist orientation in feminist composition need not have meant necessarily that responses to conflict would be avoided, that is what has happened. Feminist composition was developing at a time also of great idealism in the women's movement. In their commentary on their collection of essays, *Conflicts in Feminism*, Hirsch and Keller (1990) noted that the "'dream of a common language'"—the title of a collection of Adrienne Rich's poetry published in 1978—was sustained "by the illusion of a domain internally free of conflict. For the most part, feminists of the seventies wrote, and tried to think, of conflict as operating between feminism and its alternatives" (p. 379). The title of Morgan's anthology, *Sisterhood Is Global* (1984), reflects a similar orientation. We should not be surprised that the variables of race, class, and sexual orientation were not a concern.

Another reason for the absence of a response to conflict is that the expressionist pedagogy accompanying an emphasis on developing a personal voice means there is no need to consider conflict; it may even be discouraged. As Jarratt demonstrates in "Feminism and Composition: The Case for Conflict," even though the teacher's authority is displaced, the emphasis on uncritically accepting what another has written means that real differences, whatever their source, are elided (pp. 108-111). The relationship to readers is also seen as unproblematic. Audiences, when considered, are usually thought of as sympathetic (see, again, Caywood & Overing, 1987; Farrell, 1979; Flynn, 1988; Howe, 1971), or they are ignored, as in Juncker's discussion of how one can bring the spirit of French feminists, especially Helene Cixous, into the classroom. At some point, voice is taken over by egocentrism. Nothing beyond self-expression seems to matter; readers may or may not be confused, angry, or delighted. Once again, the personal voice will always have a place in feminist composition. But any attempt to respond to conflict must also include with it a recognition of how one is to relate to an audience with whom one disagrees. Doing so is likely to call on the confidence engendered by attention to the personal voice and may test that confidence by requiring that the voice be modified.

If feminist composition has not typically developed responses to conflict, its practitioners and other feminists have been vocal in criticizing the "male mode" as the usual way we have been taught to respond to conflict—persuading someone else to one's way of thinking by making a claim and then supporting it. Many of the criticisms may best be called problem definitions, which actively invite alternatives. Shotter and Logan (1988) called for a new rhetoric in the social sciences that reflects feminist ways of knowing. Gearhart (1979), in speech communication, said simply, "Any intent to persuade is an act of violence" (p. 195). Moulton (1983), a philosopher, noted the prevalence of the "adversary method" in philosophical reasoning and the limitations it puts on thinking. And Frey (1990) demonstrated how widespread such an approach is in contemporary literary critical writing.

FEMINIST RESPONSES TO ARGUMENT

With our history of either ignoring conflict or criticizing others' attempts to respond to it, and our use of women's experience as a source for theorizing, we have not talked much about how it can be feminist to both at times be confrontational and at other times advocate approaches that minimize confrontation. It has been far easier for me to begin at the latter point, in which I assume I have a voice that will be heard; the question becomes how to reconcile it with an opposing voice. How one can speak and be heard where the spaciousness required for conflict resolution does not yet or may never exist is at least as complicated a question. I have avoided it because any response has appeared to require a use of force I found as unacceptable as the antagonism in argument.

In this discussion of feminist responses to argument, I begin with what has been easier for me, situations for conflict resolution in which one strives for an outcome that is acceptable to both parties. To return to Burke's metaphor, a person in such a situation assumes she is invited and can speak in the party in the parlour. She also believes she may be listened to: She is bold enough to want to change the rules by which the discussion is held. In "Beyond Argument in Feminist Composition" (Lamb, 1991), I advocated mediation and negotiation as alternatives to argument as it is often taught and practiced, in which the goal is to win, making confrontation virtually inevitable. Making this switch requires a contrasting view of power—that it is not something one can possess and therefore use on others in the manner that one applies force; rather, following Arendt in *The Human Condition* (1958) and more recent contemporary feminist theorists, power is present when a group comes together for a particular purpose. It can energize and enable, thus increasing competence and reducing hierarchy. (One implication of the line of thinking I am developing in this chapter is that the opposition between the two views of power I have just summarized is overdrawn—even though it is certainly convenient. Here, I am continuing to explore more aspects of Foucault's [1978] definition of power in *The History of Sexuality*: "Power is not something that is acquired, seized, or shared, something that one holds on to or allows to slip away; power is exercised from innumerable points, in the interplay of non-egalitarian and mobile relations" [p. 94]. A major difference, however, is Foucault's interest in analyzing power as it has been exercised historically or in existing societies and institutions and not in imagining new, positive ways in which it might be used, as I do here.)

In "Beyond Argument" I showed how an egalitarian orientation toward power can be exercised in an enabling way between writer and reader or, in collaborative work, between the writers who produce the writing and who are also its primary audience. To imagine how such a relationship would work, I began with Ruddick's (1988) notion of "maternal thinking" discussed in her book of the same name. Maternal thinking is thought and practice derived from reflecting on mother-child relationships, although Ruddick was careful to say that one need not be a biological parent or a woman in order to engage in it. A central notion is that of "attentive love or loving attention": "Loving attention is much like empathy, the ability to think and feel as the other. In connecting with the other, it is critical that one already has and retains a sense of one's self" (Lamb, 1991, p. 16). A writer-reader relationship characterized by loving attention reduces the inequality between writer and reader, inviting the reader into the act of making meaning. When writer and reader are in conflict, it can still permit them to remain connected "while also going through the giving and receiving necessary if they are to resolve their conflict" (p. 17). Techniques of mediation and negotiation provide concrete ways to resolve conflict when the goal is no longer winning but finding a solution in a fair way that is acceptable to both sides. Argument as it is usually taught has its place at the beginning of the process, not the end, where one usually finds it. Participants use it to be clear about their own positions before the negotiating or mediating begins. They also employ its tools—for example, identifying fallacies, evaluating the strength of the link between premises and conclusion in an inductive argument—in preparing the writing, which is the final outcome of the process. In the case of mediation, it is an agreement arrived at by the disputants and the mediator, stating what each party is willing to do to resolve the conflict. In negotiation, the outcome is a paper written by the disputants that records the process by which the two of them reached an agreement (Lamb, 1991, pp. 17-22).

Mediation and negotiation as I have described them and use them with my students are examples of what I think Dietrich would have us do if we take seriously the assumption that argument, like knowledge more generally, is socially constructed. First, the win-lose orientation of agonistic argument is quickly exposed as inadequate. In a positive way, we would look at the process of argumentation as problem solving rather than a contest; we would require students to seek out and understand perspectives other than their own; we would encourage students to acknowledge the place of emotions and personal experience in decision making; we would require that any solution advocated be seen as fair by all those with legitimate interests in solving the problem; and we would make the process of defining and developing the line of argument itself a social process, open to assessment and reformulation (Dietrich, 1992). We are thus acknowledging that writing is never "socially neutral" (Flynn, 1988, pp. 148-149), the same point made by a feminist critique of the conversation in Burke's parlour. Who can write, and why, using what forms, are always questions to ask.

The potential for nonadversarial approaches to conflict resolution in writing classes is great. And yet, if we think only in those terms, rich as they are, when we consider the place of argument in feminist composition, we are not exploring the full range of a healthy use of power in writer-reader relationships. Neither do we have a way to account for the variety of practices engaged in by feminists writing in response to situations of conflict. Advocating mediation or negotiation may also be seen as an emphasis on coming to closure. Although anyone who has mediated or negotiated knows the process can easily break down, the restrictions of using these techniques in the classroom can mean an artificial emphasis on finding a solution at the expense of really exploring the nature of the conflicts involved. Karis (1989) made the same point in discussing the place of conflict in collaboration from a Burkean perspective: "This *predisposition* for finding manageable solutions of the 'truth' in some middle ground before fully exploring the problem through dialectic can become a restrictive element in the collaborative process" (p. 113). As Karis stated later, it is possible to move too soon to identification, the point at which the parties in the conflict agree their interests are the same.

That my classroom uses of mediation and negotiation might be encouraging such an orientation was not something I gave much thought to until this past semester when, for the first time in the five years since I first began my experimenting along these lines, a mediation group (composed of the mediator and two disputants) informed me that they were unable to come up with an agreement. Their case was based on an actual disagreement with a member of the Student Life staff at Albion over what was to be done with unused college furniture in the suites of a fraternity house. The students describing the situation insisted that this staff person was rarely willing to negotiate on any issue. The student playing his role simply chose to stay in character. Two other groups were using the same scenario and did arrive at agreements, which they regarded as unrealistic because of their experience with this staff person.

If feminist responses to argument are to be viable, they must include in them a broader range of possibilities in their responses to conflict. Is it possible that power exercised can eventually be enabling? Surely there is a place for focusing on practices of writing or speaking that might end as well as begin in the giving and receiving of maternal thinking; resolution may or may not be possible or even desirable. Such an approach can be enabling if one is clear about one's goals and intentions. The goal is still for writer and reader to establish and maintain a subject-subject relationship, clearly the assumption if one is applying maternal thinking. The main feature of the relationship, however, may be needing to honor the present tension, staying in the moment of the disagreement, recognizing that resolution may never occur but that continuing the conversation is still a legitimate way of maintaining a relationship. The other party remains a subject, I think, if her or his views are still taken seriously, even if there appears to be no movement in the dialogue. Continuing to talk or to write may seem a small goal. But consider what too often happens when faculty (at least at Albion) have deep disagreements over matters of ideology—they just stop talking, and any possibility for movement and cooperation, let alone the new knowledge they might generate, is foreclosed. I believe the Palestinians and Israelis now participating in peace talks would say that talking at all is a miracle.

In expanding the space of feminist argument—the possibilities for how a practitioner of feminist composition can be in conflict—I am drawing on examples of recent discourse, not all of it specifically feminist, but feminist at least in spirit. There is first of all the question of how one even enters a tradition of discourse if the terms under which that discourse is conducted are antithetical to the assumptions under which one is operating, that is, if the system is closed and its adherents show no interest in an opening. We might, as with Cixous (1968) in "A Woman Mistress," not be particularly bothered if we gain a place in that space by simply playing the rules of the game as they have already been defined:

> I distrust the identification of a subject with a single discourse. First, there is the discourse that suits the occasion. I use rhetorical discourse, the discourse of mastery, orally, for example, with my students, and obviously I do it on purpose; it is a refusal on my part to leave organized discourse entirely in men's hands. I never fell for that sort of bait. (p.136)

Or we might, as Frey (1990) did in "Beyond Literary Darwinism," use the adversarial method, exercise our power in this way, because we believe we have no other choice if we are going to be heard. Her hope is that the adversarial method is useful in her essay "if only as a means to its own destruction" (p. 524). Or we might, like hooks (1989), feel no necessity for justifying our use of it, but still take great care in how it is exercised. In her essay "Toward a Revolutionary Feminist Pedagogy," hooks talked about the place of confrontation in her classes in which her goal, as an African American modeling her pedagogy on African-American teachers she had as a child, "is to enable all students, not just an assertive few, to feel empowered in a rigorous, critical discussion" (p. 53). My guess is hooks's classroom style is like her writing and her public appearances: When she criticizes, she is extremely focused, a practitioner of verbal laser surgery. Although her comments are intense, they are not personal, possessing a degree of lightness that makes it clear they apply only to the matter at hand.

hooks is doing what Nye (1990) in *Words of Power* called "responding"; both are instances of maternal thinking. *Words of Power*, as the book's subtitle indicates, is a "feminist reading of the history of logic" Noting that all the logicians of history have been men, who have tried to show how Truth can be arrived at, regardless of who speaks it or under what conditions, she wished instead to illuminate the social and historical conditions in which logic has been developed. Doing so requires, as she said, committing fallacies: the genetic fallacy, in which one claims that the source of an idea is relevant to whether or not it is true; or the ad hominem fallacy, in which one might claim that it is relevant to know who said something and why. A basic assumption for Nye is that "all human communication, including logic, is motivated" (p. 175). The answer to masculinist logic is not some new feminist version or a new women's language. Nye's answer—responding—is disarmingly simple, and yet, as her book demonstrates with eloquence, very powerful:

But if a refutation can always be refuted, a response cuts deeper. A response might refashion the words of those in power into a serpent whose bite is exposure, the exposure that pricks inflated vanity, the exposure that weakens the resolve to continue on in ridiculous, imperious blindness to reality, the exposure that makes it impossible to continue to deny one's vulnerability and the limits of any human power, the exposure that shows all men to be mother's sons dependent on others. (p. 176)

The type of response that Nye advocates is one that cultivates the skills of reading, one that sounds much like the practice of maternal thinking: "attention, listening, understanding, responding" (p. 83). In the response that is her book, Nye is creating a new space or at least putting a new overlay on the old one. The principles of logic do not allow for mediation: A syllogism is or is not valid. (Hirsch & Keller [1990] made a similar point when they assessed the tactics used by the writers in their volume, *Conflicts in Feminism*: The writers "begin with an attempt to displace 'opposing views' by disputing their very delineations, and accordingly, to shift, or even refuse, the original ground of the discussion" [p 372].) Nye is taking the power she has as a writer to name something new in which we as readers have the choice of participating, thus setting in motion a new circulation of power.

When I thought about how I could use negotiation and mediation in a writing class, the primary task I faced was how to adapt oral forms of discourse that depended for their success on the give and take of conversation. In the case of negotiation, I wanted a type of writing that reflected the process through which the two parties had gone. I was willing to sacrifice the forward momentum of a well-structured argument moving to its conclusion to get this sense of process. For mediation, the outcome—a mediation agreement—was definitely writing as product, but arrived at in a collaborative way. Having new forms of writing to which I can point makes it easier to say that here really are alternatives to argument as we have taught and practiced it

If I am "responding," in Nye's sense of the word, what I or my students might be doing is less clear. My task as a teacher in this context is not to provide the clarity and security of a prescribed form. I believe it is to create the kind of atmosphere in which students can think honestly and openly about their position on an issue about which they care and then can reflect on the most generous response of which they are capable. In my upper-level expository writing course this semester, students will again be working in pairs as they do if the assignment is based on negotiation. The partners will agree on the topic on which they are writing (preferably something in which both of them have some emotional investment) and will each take contrasting positions. The first paper they will write individually; it could be recognized as traditional argument. Its function, however, will be primarily to enable them to be as clear as possible about their positions. The second paper can be written either together or separately. When I ask them for their most generous response to the conflict, they may feel they can negotiate; perhaps the most they will be capable of is a paper in which they respond to their partner's first paper, indicating what they think has been overlooked or misrepresented. One can see the conversation continuing from there.

Or they might choose to step back, as did the abbot of St. Gregory's Abbey, an Episcopal Benedictine abbey near Three Rivers, MI, in a recent article on gays and lesbians in the church, particularly on the question of whether homosexuals in a committed relationship should be ordained. Readers unfamiliar with current controversies in the Episcopal Church should know this question is as inflammatory as any it has faced in recent years. The governing body of the Church did not take any decisive action at its triennial meeting in July 1991; in the meantime, some bishops, applauded by some and attacked by others, have continued to ordain out homosexuals. I provide this background for some indication of the depth of feeling on both sides. It is also an issue on which I cannot see any compromise: Homosexuals in a committed relationship either can or cannot be ordained. (Most people I know in the Episcopal Church will agree that throughout its history it has been ordaining gay men. In theory at least, they have been celibate.) So it is in this atmosphere, and in the middle of a $5,000,000 capital campaign for substantial new construction at the Abbey, that Abbot Andrew chose to write on homosexuality for the Fall 1991 issue of the *Abbey Letter* (Marr, 1991).

After some general comments on inclusiveness in the Episcopal Church, the abbot proceeded to consider Christian perspectives on homosexuality, noting it is "a mystery which does not lend itself to an easy explanation," and that our task is to learn to live with such mysteries constructively rather than fearfully. He noted the passages in Leviticus and Romans often used to attack homosexuality; without denying what they say, he also provided us with broader contexts in which to interpret them, thus showing that the primary issues may not be homosexuality. There is then the question of what is acceptable sexual behavior in the church. Abbot Andrew refused to rule out the possibility of a legitimate permanent union between homosexuals within a Christian context; he also noted, however, that we tend to believe too easily that "sexual contact is the only way to deepen a relationship" and to forget that "many caring relationships develop with the greatest depth when there is no physical sexual involvement." Later, he noted that we are to empty "ourselves of all that makes us want to push others away just because they are different.... If our identity is threatened by the difference of another that is a signal of our own need to empty ourselves of that identity, in the faith that we will discover ourselves more deeply in the other person and in God." I hope these selections suggest the balance and evenness of tone that run throughout the article. The abbot never took an explicit position; the emphasis instead was on broadening the context in which the discussion takes place, creating openings for anyone except possibly the most diehard on either side. From what I know, the abbot was successful. In a later letter to people associated with the abbey, he said he had never had so much correspondence on an article; most of the responses on both sides had been "constructive and rational," in spite of how "explosive" the subject has been in the church.

I want to be clear about how difficult it can be to respond, as I have been using the term. What is one to do with one's anger or, more generally, with the strong commitment felt toward an issue, and whatever emotion accompanies the commitment? Certainly the commitment must be there, or the response will sooner or later be exposed as a manipulative exercise. In the case of the abbot, he communicated his commitment by deciding to write and by using his authority as an abbot to gain an audience. His own position on the issue is less important than that the conversation continue. Responding is also not likely to be the only way anyone is or should be in conflict. Anger probably will come first, but with time and awareness, one can create a space in which it is possible to move toward the other. (A single writing assignment will not permit this evolution.) Is such an act persuasion and therefore violent, as Gearhart claims? Persuasion in the broadest sense, yes, as in this chapter, and not to be apologized for as long as we live in community. Violent? Only if any invitation to redefine oneself is seen as invasive. A person responding is thus claiming a legitimate authority, one to be exercised with openness, humility, even lightheartedness.

Mediation, negotiation, responding—all suggestions for what might characterize a feminist "unending conversation." It probably would not happen in a parlour; that way more people could come more easily. The people there would be able to tell from observing that they could speak, if they wished, from difference. There would be more silence because people would be listening more. Groups would be fluid, forming and dissolving around issues. This image is not impossibly idealistic: Each encounter would require that one again chooses with whom and how to speak, and toward what ends.

REFERENCES

Annas, P.J. (1958). Style as politics: A feminist approach to the teaching of writing. *College English, 47,* 360-371.
Arendt, H. (1958). *The human condition.* Chicago: University of Chicago Press.
Burke, K. (1967). *The philosophy of literary form* (2nd ed.). Baton Rouge: Louisiana State University Press.
Caywood, C.L., & Overing, G.R. (Eds.). (1987). *Teaching writing: Pedagogy, gender, and equity.* Albany: State University of New York Press.
Cixous, H. (1986). A woman mistress. In H. Cixous & C. Clement (Eds.), *The newly born woman* (B. Wing, Trans., Vol. 24, pp. 136-146). Minneapolis: University of Minnesota Press.
Dietrich, J. (1992). *Toward a social argumentation.* Unpublished paper.
Emig, J. (1983). The origins of rhetoric: A developmental view. In D. Goswami & M. Butler (Eds.), *The web of meaning* (pp. 55-59). Upper Montclair, NJ: Boynton/Cook. (Reprinted from School Review, September 1969)
Farrell, T.J. (1979). The female and male modes of rhetoric. *College English, 40,* 922-927.
Flynn, E.A. (1988). Composing as a woman. *College Composition and Communication, 39,* 423-435.
Foucault, M. (1978). *The history of sexuality, Vol. 1: An introduction.* (R. Hurley, Trans.). New York: Pantheon.
Frey, O. (1990). Beyond literary Darwinism: Women's voices and critical discourse. *College English, 52,* 507-526.
Gearhart, S.M. (1979). The womanization of rhetoric. *Women's Studies International Quarterly, 2,* 195-201.
Hirsch, M., & Keller, E.F. (1990). Conclusion: Practising conflict in feminist theory. In M. Hirsch & E.F. Keller (Eds.), *Conflicts in feminism* (pp. 370-385). New York: Routledge.
hooks, b. (1989). Toward a revolutionary feminist pedagogy. In *Talking back: Thinking feminist, thinking black* (pp. 49-54). Boston: South End.
Howe, F. (1971). Identity and expression: A writing course for women. *College English, 32,* 863-871.
Jarratt, S.A. (1991). Feminism and composition: The case for conflict. In P. Harkin & J. Schilb (Eds.), *Contending with words* (pp. 105-123). New York: Modern Language Association.
Karis, B. (1989). Conflict in collaboration: A Burkean perspective. *Rhetoric Review, 8,* 113-126.
Lamb, C.E. (1991). Beyond argument in feminist composition. *College Composition and Communication, 42,* 11-24.

Marr, A., O.S.B. (1991). Letter to Confraters. On being an inclusive church. *Abbey Letter*, No.167, n.p.

Morgan, R. (1984). *Sisterhood is global: The international women's movement anthology.* New York: Anchor Press/Doubleday.

Moulton, J. (1983). A paradigm of philosophy: The adversary method. In S. Harding & M.B. Hintikka (Eds.), *Discovering reality: Feminist perspectives on epistemology, metaphysics, methodology, and philosophy of science* (pp. 149-164). Boston: D. Riedel.

Nye, A. (1990). *Words of power.* New York: Routledge.

Osborn, S. (1991). Revision/re-vision: A feminist writing class. *Rhetoric Review, 9*, 258 273.

Rich, A. (1978). *The dream of a common language.* New York: Norton.

Ruddick, S. (1988). *Maternal thinking.* Boston: Beacon.

Shotter, J., & Logan, J. (1988). The pervasiveness of patriarchy: On finding a different voice. In M.M. Gergen (Ed.), *Feminist thought and the structure of knowledge* (pp. 69-86). New York: New York University Press.

Author Index

A

Adler, P., 198, *202*
Andrasick, K., 140, *166*
Annas, P.J., 259, *268*
Anson, C.M., 140, 141, 144, 148, 151, *166*, *167*
Applebee, A.N., 66, 70, 142, *166*, 175, 176, *186*
Arendt, J., 261, *268*
Arnold, C.C., 51, *53*
Atwell, N., 48, 49, *53*, 140, *166*
Ayim, M., 84, *89*

B

Bakhtin, M.M., 5, *15*, 95, 111, *119*
Balagangadhura, S.N., 85, *89*
Ball, A., 229, 231, 235, *235*
Barnes, D., 176, *186*
Barnes, D., 176, *186*
Barnsely, G., 27, 30, *33*, 66, 72
Barritt, L.S., 36, *53*
Bartelt, H.G., 245, 248, *255*
Bartholomae, D., 123, *136*
Barton, G., 18, *32*
Basseches, M., 174, *184*
Bataille, G.M., 245, *255*
Bateson, M.C., 190, *202*
Batson, T., 151, *167*
Bazerman, C., 122, *136*

Beach, R., 141, 151, *167*
Beck, A., 198, *202*
Becker, A.L., 4, *15*
Becker, J., 4, *15*
Belcher, G.L., 135, *137*
Belenky, M.F., 150, 165, *167*, 190, 200, 202, *202*
Bereiter, C., 47, *54*, 64, *70*, 175, *186*
Berrill, D.P., 24, 26, *32*, *33*, 141, *167*, 173, 177, 178, *186*
Bitzer, L., 93, *119*
Bizzell, P., 134, *136*
Bjorklund, D.F., 36, *53*
Bram, W., 18, *32*
Brand, N., 102, *119*
Brandt, D., 139, *167*
British Columbia Ministry of Education, 60, *70*
Britton, J.N., 150, *167*
Brooke, R.E., 47, 48, 49, 50, *53*
Brooks, C., 58, 63, 65, 66, *71*, 92, *119*, 175, *186*
Brown, P., 150, 152, *167*
Bruner, J., 17, *32*, 91, *119*, 175, *186*
Burke, K., 93, *119*, 195, *202*, 257, *268*

C

Campbell, K.K., 93, *119*

Carey, J., 97, *119*
Carter, R.E., 206, *219*
Caywood, C.L., 190, 200, 202, 259, *268*
Chang, G.L., 26, *32*
Chickera, E. de, 17, *32*
Christie, F., 95, 96, *102*
Cixous, H., 264, *268*
Clinchy, B.M., 190, 200, 202, *202*
Coe, R., 106, *119*
Conry, R., 58, 66, *70*, 175, *186*
Cooper, M., 111, *119*
Crowhurst, M., 58, 59, 64, 65, 68, 69, *71*, 175, *186*
Cruikshank, J., 241, 242, *255*
Crusius, T., 149, 163, *167*
Crystal, D., 196, *203*

D

Dandy, E.B., 221, *235*
Dasenbrock, R.W., 145, 151, *167*
Davidson-Mosenthal, R., 166, *168*
Davies, A., 24, 26, *33*
Davis, F.A., 140, *167*
de la Luz Reyes, M., 150, *167*
DeFoe, D., 31, *32*
Degenhart, R.E., 66, *72*
Devitt, A.J., 95, *119*
Dietrich, J., 262, *268*
Dixon, J., 66, *71*, 111, *119*, 177, 184, *186*

E

Ellis, A., 198, *202*
Emig, J., 68, *71*
Enright, D.J., 17, *32*
Erdrich, L., 251, *255*
Erickson, F., 241, *255*

F

Faigley, L., 122, 123, 134, *136*
Farr, M., 243, 251, 252, *255*
Farrell, T.J., 259, *268*
Firth, R., 196, *203*

Flower, L., 36, 37, *53*, *54*
Flynn, E.A., 259, 262, *268*
Fort, K., 192, *203*
Foucault, M., 261, *268*
Fox, C., 25, 32, 141, *167*
Freedman, A., 27, *32*, 58, 64, 66, 72, 94, 97, 107, 112, *119*, 122, 123, 133, 134, *136*, 175, 178, *186*, 192, *203*
Freedman, S.W., 38, *54*
Freire, P., 252, *255*
Frey, O., 192, 200, *203*, 260, 264, *268*
Fung, Y-., 217, *219*

G

Gadamer, H., 148, *167*
Gannett, C., 146, *167*
Gates, H.L., 230, 232, *235*
Gaustad, M.G., 140, *167*
Gearhart, S.M., 260, *268*
Gee, J.P., 231, *235*
Gegeo, D.W., 197, 198, *203*, *204*
Geisler, C., 151, *167*
Gere, A.R., 47, 48, *54*
Ghezzi, R.W., 245, 250, *256*
Gilligan, C., 182, *186*
Givens, S., 122, *136*
Goldberger, N.R., 190, 200, 202, *202*
Goodwin, C., 147, *167*
Goodwin, M.H., 147, *167*
Gorman, T.P., 58, 63, 65, 66, *71*, 175, *186*
Govier, T., 74, 75, 76, 82, *89*
Graves, D., 21, *32*
Gregory, G.A., 243, *255*
Grice, H.P., 144, *167*
Griffin, C.W., 38, *54*
Grootendorst, R., 83, *89*
Gunderson, L., 63, *71*

H

Hairston, M., 173, *186*

Halliday, M.A.K., 144, *168*
Halpern, S., 122, *136*
Hanna, P., 27, 30, *33*, 66, 72
Hansen, K., 122, 123, 134, *136*
Hardy, B., 7, *15*, 18, *32*
Harris, J., 163, *168*
Haswell, R., 148, 149, *168*
Hawisher, G.E., 151, *168*
Hayes, J.R., 37, *54*
Hearn, G.W., 135, *137*
Herrington, A.J., 96, 109, *120* 122, 124, 134, *136*
Hill, C.E., 253, *255*
Hill, J.H., 4, 14, 15
Hillocks, G., Jr., 38, *54*
Himley, M., 106, *120*
Hirsch, M., 259, 265, *268*
Hoey, M., 252, *255*
Holbrook, B., 212, *219*
Holland, D., 192, *203*
hooks, b., 200, *203*, 264, *268*
Hoover, J.H., 140, *168*
Houghton, D., 252, *255*
Hourd, M., 20, *32*
Howe, F., 259, *268*
Hudson, R.A., 193, *203*
Hughes, M., 23, *32*
Hunt, R., 144, *169*
Hymes, D.H., 5, *15*

J

Jacob, S.G., 36, *54*
James, W., 210, *219*
Jamieson, K.H., 93, *119*
Janik, A., 96, 101, 104, *120*, 123, 125, 126, 135, *137*
Jewett, J., 144, *169*
Johns, A.M., 122, 135, *137*
Johnson, M., 84, *89*, 171, 172, *186*, 192, *203*
Johnson, S.E., 140, *168*

K

Kambon, K.K.K., 222, 223, 235

Kaplan, R.B., 244, *255*
Karis, B., 262, *268*
Kegan, R., 149, *168*
Kell, J., 27, *32*
Keller, E.F., 259, 265, *268*
Kelley, A.B., 140, *168*
Keynes, G., 22, *32*
Kinneavy, J.L., 100, *120*
Kishimoto, H., 207, 209, *219*
Kispal, A., 58, 63, 65, 66, *71*, 175, *186*
Kluwin, T.N., 140, *168*
Knudson, R.E., 47, *54*, 143, *168*
Kreeft, J., 150, *168*
Kress, G., 31, *32*, 57, *71*, 95, 96, 104, *120*
Krieger, V., 166, *168*
Kroll, B.M., 36, *53*, 149, *168*

L

Lakoff, G., 84, *89*, 171, 172, *186*, 192, *203*
Lamb, C.E., 173, 181, 184, 185, *186*, 189, 190, 198, *203*, 261, 262, *268*
Lamiel, N., 200, *203*
Langer, J.A., 58, 59, 66, *70*, *71*, 142, 166, 175, *186*
Lao Tzu, 206, *219*
Lave, J., 92, *120*
Leap, W.L., 251, *256*
Lehmann, R., 66, *72*
Levinson, S., 150, 152, *167*
Li, C.N., 207, *219*
Lindemann, E., 38, 39, *54*
Logan, J., 260, *269*
Lovaas, K., 198, *202*
Loy, D., 214, 215, *219*
Luke, A., 113, *120*
Lunsford, A., 36, *54*, 148, *168*

M

Mabrito, M., 145, *168*
Macedo, D., 252, *255*
MacLure, M., 58, 63, 65, 66, *71*, 175, *186*

Maimon, E.P., 122, 134, 135, *137*
Mandziuk, R.M., 190, *203*
Marr, O.S.B., 266, *269*
Martin, J.R., 57, 66, *71*, 95, 96, *120*
Matuck, J.M., 190, 200, 202, *202*
McCann, T.M., 143, *168*
McLaughlin, D., 243, 251, *255*, *256*
Meek, M., 18, *32*
Messenheimer-Young, T., 140, *167*
Meyer, B.J.F., 131, *137*, 151, *169*
Midgley, M., 79, *89*
Miller, A., 97, *119*
Miller, C., 106, *120*
Miller, C.A., 139, 140, 151, *169*
Miller, J.L., 164, *168*
Mills, S., 200, *203*
Milner, M., 198, *202*
Moffett, J., 21, *32*, 66, *71*
Morgan, R., 259, *269*
Mosenthal, P., 166, *168*
Moulton, J., 84, *89*, 260, *269*
Mulac, A., 146, *168*
Mulkay, M., 152, *169*
Mullis, I.V.S., 66, *70*, 142, *166*, 175, *186*

N

Nakamura, H., 207, 213, 216, 218, *219*
Ned, A., 241, 242, *255*
Nelms, B., 35, *54*
Newkirk, T., 66, 68, *71*, *72*
Nishida, K., 205, 211, 212, 215, *219*
Nodine, B.G., 135, *137*
Nye, A., 264, *269*

O

O'Conner, F.W., 135, *137*
Olbrechts-Tyteca, L., 7, *15*, 39, 50, 53, *54*, 82, *89*
Osborn, S., 259, *269*
Overing, G.R., 190, 200, *202*, 259, *268*

P

Peel, E.A., 175, *186*
Perelman, C., 7, *15*, 39, 41, 50, 51, 53, *54*, 82, *89*
Perry, W.G., Jr., 148, *169*
Peyton, J.K., 150, *169*
Pinxten, R., 85, *89*
Pringle, I., 27, *32*, 58, 64, 66, 72, 112, *119*, 175, 178, *186*, 192, *203*
Purves, A.C., 66, 72

Q

Quinn, N., 192, *203*

R

Redfield, K.A., 243, *256*
Reed, L., 140, 150, *169*
Reither, J., 144, *169*
Ridington, R., 247, 253, *256*
Rieke, R., 96, 101, 104, *120*, 123, 125, 126, 135, *137*
Ritchie, J.S., 48, 49, 52, *54*, 176, 177, 178, 179, *187*
Rodgers, D., 58, 66, *70*, 175, *186*
Rose, M., 122, 134, *137*
Rothery, J., 57, 66, *71*, 95, 96, *120*
Rothery, Y.,
Ruby, L., 173, *187*, 191, *203*
Ruddell, M.R., 150, *169*
Ruddick, S., 181, *187*, 190, 200, *203*, 261, *269*

S

Sands, K.M., 245, *255*
Scardamalia, M., 47, *54*, 64, 66, *70*, 175, *186*
Schatzberg-Smith, K., 150, *169*
Schiffrin, D., 145, 151, *169*
Schinzinger, R., 214, *219*
Schwegler, R.A., 165, *169*
Schwiebert, J.E., 140, *166*
Selfe, C.L., 151, *168*
Seyoum, M., 150, *169*
Shamoon, L.K., 165, *169*

Author Index

Shaugnessy, M., 45, *54*, 122, 123, 130, 134, *137*
Shotter, J., 260, *269*
Shuy, R.W., 144, 150, *169*
Sidney, A., 241, 242, *255*
Smith, K., 241, 242, *255*
Smitherman, G., 221, 224, *235*
Smithson, I., 194, *203*
Sommers, N., 38, *54*
Sperling, M., 38, *55*
Spreitzer, 122, *136*
Staton, J., 140, 150, *169*
Stein, N.L., 139, 140, 151, *169*
Stratta, L., 66, 71, 177, 184, *186*
Suzuki, D.T., 208, 214, 215, *220*
Swales, J.M., 96, *120*, 122, *137*
Swan, M., 27, 30, *33*, 66, 72

T

Teale, W.H., 68, 72
Thomas, S.N., 75, *89*
Thompson, D., 20, *32*
Thompson, S.A., 207, *219*
Tizzard, B., 23, *32*
Toulmin, S., 96, 101, 104, *120*, 123, 125, 126, 135, *137*

U

Ulichny, P., 192, *203*

V

Van Emeren, F.H., 83, *89*
Vipond, D., 144, *169*
Vygotsky, L.S., 35, 53, *55*, 149, *169*

W

Wardhaugh, R., 244, 245, *256*
Wardlow, A., 18, *32*
Warren, A., 92, *120*
Warren, R.P., 92, *119*
Watson-Gegeo, K.A., 184, *187*, 189, 190, 192, 193, 195, 197, 198, *203*, *204*
Wellek, R., 92, *120*
Wells, G., 23, 26, *32*
Wells, J., 26, *32*
Wenger, E., 92, *120*
Wertsch, J.V., 5, *15*
White, G.M., 189, *204*
White, J., 57, 58, 63, 65, 66, *71*, 72
White, J.O., 102, *119*, 175, *186*
Wilcox, L.E., 144, *166*
Wilkinson, A.M., 17, 24, 25, 26, 27, 30, *33*, 66, 72, 141, *169*, 175, *187*
Willard, C.A., 106, *120*
Williamson, M.M., 140, *166*

Y

Yusa, M., 211, 212, *220*

Z

Zamel, V., 38, *55*

Subject Index

A

adversarial, 23, 84-86, 139, 156, 157, 158, 191, 260, 262, 264
African American, 4, 10, 14, 221-240, 264
alienation, 149, 151, 154-155, 161, 235
ambiguity, 8, 10
appropriate, 5, 149, 155, 233, 248
association, 19, 31, 36, 193, 230-231
assumptions, 8, 9, 141, 148, 159-161, 177, 190, 193, 197, 200, 217, 226, 230, 242, 262
audience, 3, 37, 40, 81-82, 96, 102, 124, 143, 159, 191, 259, 260, 261, 267
authority, 142, 159, 176, 200, 229-230, 267

B

Bakhtin, 5, 6, 13, 93, 94-95, 141, 174, 253
Burke, K., 257-258, 260-262

C

ceremony, 94
chronology, 19, 28, 31, 66
circular reasoning, 24, 223
classification, 19

collaboration, 109, 155, 166, 190, 200, 261-263, 265
combative, 10, 161, 171-185, 191-196, 257-267
commitment, 48, 145, 148
communally sanctioned, 96
community, 3, 5, 10, 11, 12, 13, 92-93, 104-105, 108-110, 121, 130, 133, 136, 189-202, 226, 232, 238-239, 247-254, 267
complementarity, 11, 218, 223
concrete, 224, 227, 229-234
conflict, 9, 13, 84-86, 121, 149, 164, 180, 184, 189-204
conflict resolution, 10, 180, 258-267
confrontation, 10, 84, 154, 260-267
connectedness, 11, 13, 166, 190, 197, 200, 229, 247-254, 261
context, 8, 9, 13, 206, 208-209
consensus, 86, 88, 155, 212, 218
contrastive analysis, 243-251, 252-254
cooperation, 86
culture and argument, 121-137, 177-185, 189-202, 205-219, 221-235, 241-254
cyclicity, 4, 14, 244

D

dialectic, 2, 9, 87, 105-106, 148, 149, 159, 161-163, 173-175, 177, 191, 211, 223, 262-263
dialogic, 2, 9, 83-84, 94, 148, 151, 163, 166, 173-175, 178, 182, 191, 208
dialogue, 5, 7, 9, 36, 46, 63, 83, 139-170, 176, 185, 195, 208, 263
difference, 76-77, 85, 89, 177-185
discourse community, 8, 12, 96-97, 108-109
dissociation, 40-44

E

egocentricity, 36, 239, 260
episodic, 250, 251
epistemology, 3, 5, 8, 205-219
epistemic, 8, 78, 92, 106, 108, 110
ethnocentric, 87-88
Eurocentric, 4, 10, 221-240
evidence, 6, 7, 12, 18, 74, 85, 88, 96, 194, 202
evidenced thinking, 26, 173, 121-136
explicitness, 8, 12, 76, 98, 101, 103, 122, 139, 147, 180, 181, 182, 185, 193, 195, 243, 267

F

feminist approaches, 3, 5, 10-11, 85-87, 190, 257-269

G

gender, 9, 160, 185, 200-201, 257-267
genre, 31, 66, 91-120, 141-162, 242
grounded, 77

H

Halliday, M.A.K., 93, 95, 144
heuristic, 177-184
hierarchical, 4, 6, 10, 14, 93, 105, 172-185, 189-202, 205-219, 221-235, 241-254

I

identity, 51, 185, 230, 266-267
implicitness, 84, 147, 252, 258
immediacy, 206-207, 209-210, 215
inclusiveness, 76, 172-185, 205-219, 221-235, 241-254, 257-267
initiation, 11, 109
interconnectedness, 210-211
interdependency, 11, 223, 248, 265
invite, 77, 260, 267

J

Johnson, M., 9, 171-172

K

Kress, G., 96, 104

L

Lakoff, G., 9, 171-172
legitimacy, 3
linear, 4, 10, 14, 192, 194, 208, 244-251

M

maintaining difference, 13, 263-267
mediation, 85, 181, 190, 195, 197, 199, 261-263, 265
metaphors of argument, 2, 9, 171-175, 192-196, 257-258, 267
Miller, C.A., 93, 140, 151, 164
monolithic, 134, 195, 244
monologic, 173-175, 176, 178, 185, 190, 191, 193, 196, 197

N

Native American, 10, 14, 225, 241-256
narrative, 2, 6, 7, 17-33, 61-62, 65-66, 140, 147, 190, 194, 231, 241-256
negotiation, 51, 85, 111, 112, 140, 185, 190, 191, 212, 258, 261-263, 265
Nommo, 224-240

Subject Index

O

Olbrecht-Tyteca, L., 7, 39-53, 82
opposition, 85-86, 157

P

Perelman, C., 7, 39-53, 82
perspective, 39
power, 261, 263, 264
premises, 73-75
privilege, 39, 257-267

R

race, 9, 221-235
readers, 79-84
reader-response, 8
reciprocity, 39, 144, 147, 150, 161, 166
reconstruction, 8
recursion, 231, 242
relationship maintenance, 151-154, 182, 189-202, 263
repetition, 248, 250
resistance, 4, 5
responding, 264-267

S

self, 207-208
self-contradiction, 211-216, 218
semiotics, 5, 206
signification, 221, 225, 232-233, 242
silence, 199, 208, 267
silencing, 2, 5, 9, 11, 146, 161, 174, 180, 185, 190, 253, 258,
social action, 12, 13, 91-120
social construction, 1, 91

social relationship 12, 150-158, 160, 195, 197, 199
social purpose, 91-113, 140, 189-202
social transformation, 9, 13, 189-202
sociocultural, 4, 5
sound reasoning, 121-138
speech-act theory, 93, 94
subjectivity, 207, 209
Swales, J.M., 96-97, 108, 122

T

tacit, 3, 8, 194
tension, 12, 163, 165, 210, 263
thesis, 178-184, 221-240, 247, 254
tools, 5, 89
Toulmin, S., 8, 93, 96, 101, 104, 125-133, 135
transformation, 148-149, 185, 189-202
truth, 14, 19, 78, 89
typification, 93

V

validate, 31
validity, 4, 5
voice, 253, 258-259
Vygotsky, L.S., 5, 35, 36, 53, 91, 149

W

war, 51, 84-86, 171-188, 195-196
Wertsch, J.V., 5
world view, 4, 196, 205-219, 221-240, 241-254, 257-26